INSTRUCTED SECOND LANGUAGE ACQUISITION

Applied Language Studies
Edited by David Crystal and Keith Johnson

This new series aims to deal with key topics within the main branches of applied language studies – initially in the fields of foreign language teaching and learning, child language acquisition and clinical or remedial language studies. The series will provide students with a research perspective in a particular topic, at the same time containing an original slant which will make each volume a genuine contribution to the development of ideas in the subject.

Series List

INSTRUCTED SECOND LANGUAGE ACQUISITION

Learning in the Classroom

Rod Ellis

Basil Blackwell

Copyright Rod Ellis 1990

First published 1990

Reprinted 1991, 1992

Blackwell Publishers
108 Cowley Road, Oxford, OX4 1JF, UK

238 Main Street, Suite 501
Cambridge, Massachusetts 02142, USA

British Library Cataloguing in Publication Data

A CIP catalogue record for this book is available from the British Library.

Library of Congress Cataloging in Publication Data

Ellis, Rod.
    Instructed second language acquisition: learning in the classroom/Rod Ellis.
        p.   cm. − (Applied language studies)
    Includes bibliographical references (p.   ).
    ISBN 0−631−16201−1   − ISBN 0−631−16202−X
    1. Language and languages − Study and teaching.   2. Second language
acquisition.   I. Title.   II. Series.
P51.E47   1990
418'.007 − dc20   89-49728
                                                                   CIP

Typeset in 10 on 12 pt Ehrhardt
by Setrite Typesetters Ltd
Printed in Great Britain by T.J. Press Ltd, Padstow, Cornwall

Contents

For Lwindi and Emma

Preface

I have been interested for a long time now in how an understanding of second language acquisition can contribute to language pedagogy. In an earlier book, *Understanding Second Language Acquisition*, I tried to provide an overview of the whole field. But Second Language Acquisition (SLA); as a field of enquiry, has grown enormously over the past few years. It has spawned countless empirical studies and is in danger of splintering into relatively isolated subfields. It has become almost impossible for one person to keep abreast of publications in all areas of SLA. I have chosen, therefore, to adopt a more focused approach in this book, by concentrating on the research that has addressed how **classroom** second language acquisition takes place.

This book is aimed at teachers and applied linguists who wish to develop their theoretical understanding of how learners learn a second language (L2) through instruction and to inform themselves about the research that has contributed to this understanding.

The book has the following aims:

1 To provide a historical context for the empirical study of classroom language acquisition by examining early attempts to formulate a theory through extrapolation from general learning theory and from the study of naturalistic language acquisition.
2 To review a wide range of research which has investigated classroom language acquisition.
3 To develop a theory of instructed second language acquisition which is compatible with the results of this research.

In my earlier book, I argued that teachers would benefit from trying to make their own theories of how acquisition takes place explicit. This is a view I still hold. By focusing specifically on classroom language acquisition I have tried to make my current position clear, so that readers can subject it to critical scrutiny and, by so doing, make explicit their own position.

I am very aware that there are many perspectives on how learners learn a second language in a classroom. A full understanding will need to make use of insights provided by sociological, sociolinguistic and educational enquiry. In choosing to operate from a relatively narrow base — the issues that preoccupy L2 acquisition researchers — I do not intend to suggest that this is the only or the most profitable line of enquiry. It is simply one possible way of obtaining insights into the processes that contribute to language learning. Other commentators will doubtlessly follow other routes. We need to guard against dogmatists who try to argue that one approach — whether linguistic, psycholinguistic, sociolinguistic or educational — provides us with a better view of the truth than another. I believe that we build up our understanding of the complex nature of classroom language learning bit by bit, drawing on different approaches and the insights they afford. The picture this book affords is a partial one. It will need to be filled out with the help of other types of enquiry.

I am indebted to a number of people who have assisted me in one way or another to write this book. I am grateful to Keith Johnson for helping me refine my own thinking without ever imposing his own. Ros Mitchell's comments on the first draft were also very valuable. I am also grateful to fellow lecturers and students at Ealing College of Higher Education who have responded to the ideas expressed in this book and helped me to refine them.

A Note on Pronouns

In this book I have used 'she' and 'her' to refer generically to learners, teachers, researchers etc. This is a departure from my previous practice, but I have come to realize that the choice of pronouns is an important issue to many women and that, overall, less offence is likely to be caused by the choice of the female gender.

Abbreviations

ESL	English as a Second Language
FL	Foreign Language
IRF	Initiate — Respond — Feedback
LAD	Language-Acquisition Device
L1	First Language (i.e. mother tongue)
L2	Second Language
MLU	Mean Length of Utterance
NNS	Non-native Speaker
NS	Native Speaker
SLA	Second Language Acquisition
TESOL	Teaching English as a Second or Other Language

1 Investigating Classroom Language Learning

Introduction

The question which this book tries to answer is 'How does second language (L2) learning take place in a classroom?' The primary aim of the book is to explore learning rather than teaching. It is concerned with how classroom learners construct the mental grammar that underlies their use of an L2, not with how teachers teach. This focus on learning has been motivated by the belief that it is necessary to understand as fully as possible the processes by which learners internalize a knowledge of a L2. Such an understanding will contribute to L2 acquisition research and will also serve as a basis for pedagogic recommendations. The focus on learning is additionally motivated by the conviction that a theory of classroom learning needs to be *explicitly* formulated so that statements about how learners learn and how teachers ought to teach can be subjected to critical scrutiny.

Of course, a book which sets out to examine how classroom L2 learning takes place cannot ignore teaching – for the obvious reason that what distinguishes the classroom from a naturalistic setting is the attempt to teach the L2. It is this which makes the study of classroom L2 learning such a fascinating subject of enquiry.

Classroom Language Learning

A good starting point, then, is to try to define 'classroom language learning'. The term exists in opposition to 'naturalistic language learning'. The difference between the two types of learning can be examined from a sociolinguistic, a pyscholinguistic and an educational viewpoint.

Sociolinguistically, the distinction between **classroom** and **naturalistic** L2 learning can be viewed as one of **domain** (Fishman, 1964). Domains are constellations of factors that affect the way language is used. The domains of classroom and naturalistic learning can be distinguished with reference to such factors as location, participants, topics and purposes. The differences on each of these dimensions is fairly self-evident and needs little comment. In general, the domain of classroom language learning is circumscribed in comparison to that of naturalistic language learning. The latter is likely to be characterized by a greater range of settings, participants, topics and purposes, although it is possible to envisage exceptional cases of each type of learning where the reverse applies – the classroom can provide the richer, more diverse learning experiences.

Psycholinguistically, the key distinction is between **formal** and **informal** language learning (Krashen and Seliger, 1976; d'Anglejan, 1978). Formal learning involves some kind of studial activity on the part of the learner – for example an attempt to learn *about* the language by obtaining information about explicit rules of grammar. Informal learning takes place through observation and direct participation in communication – learning is a process of discovery which takes place spontaneously and automatically providing certain conditions have been met. It would be a mistake to equate classroom and formal learning on the one hand and naturalistic and informal learning on the other. The fact is that classroom learning can and does involve informal learning – for instance when learners have the opportunity to engage in meaning-focused communication. Advocates of the communicative method (e.g. Brumfit, 1984) emphasize the importance of teaching activities designed to encourage informal learning. Similarly, naturalistic learning can involve formal learning, for example when a learner asks a question about a linguistic form in the middle of a conversation. However, it is probably true to say that the classroom setting affords more opportunities for formal learning and naturalistic settings more opportunities for informal learning. The psycholinguistic difference between classroom and naturalistic learning may not be absolute but it is nevertheless significant.

Educationalists often distinguish the idea of formal training and apprenticeship.[1] Formal training typically occurs in classrooms. It involves some deliberate attempt to shape the learning experiences in the belief that by so doing the learner will be able to acquire knowledge more efficiently. Thus Stern (1983:19) defines classroom language learning as 'learning which has been induced or influenced by some form of deliberately planned social intervention'.[2] The intervention need not be designed to cater for formal language learning. Instruction that seeks to provide opportunities for learning through natural communication is also an attempt at social intervention. After all, it is the teacher who supplies the materials for an information-gap activity and who instructs the learners to get into groups. Apprenticeship involves learning by doing. No deliberate attempt is made to shape the learning environment by devising a syllabus or providing special activities. The learner-apprentice works side by side with the master-craftsman and 'picks-up' skills through observation and practice. It should be noted, however, that the learning environment provided by apprenticeship is possible in the classroom, and formal training can occur in a naturalistic setting. But classrooms are ideally suited to formal training, while naturalistic settings tend to give rise to apprenticeship.

In many respects the distinction between classroom and naturalistic language learning is a crude one. It presupposes that it is possible to generalize about the characteristics of each domain and the types of learning and teaching that take place. In reality, there are many different types of classrooms and natural settings are multifarious. Nevertheless, providing that the inherent variety of both settings is borne in mind, the distinction is an important one. In studying classroom language learning, we are trying to discover how a typical constellation of social factors leads to attempts on the part of the teacher to control the environment in order to provide opportunities for language learning. The central questions are 'Does intervention promote L2 learning?' and 'What kind of intervention is most effective?' These are important question to ask both for theory building in L2 acquisition research and for language pedagogy.

Building a Theory of Classroom Language Learning: Three Approaches

How can we develop our understanding of classroom language learning? How can we build a theory of the way in which classroom learners acquire an L2? There are three basic approaches that have been used.

One way is to assume that classroom language learning is just like any other kind of learning and can be explained with reference to a general theory of learning. According to this view it is not necessary to build a separate theory of classroom language learning. All that is required is to demonstrate the applicability of a general theory to instructed L2 learning and to show how the hypotheses that comprise the theory can be applied to it. Such an approach has proved popular in the past and continues to do so today. It is, however, contentious, for not everyone agrees that language learning is the same as other kinds of learning. Chomsky (1965; 1986), for instance, has argued strongly that language constitutes a separate mental faculty and is not acquired in the same way as other knowledge systems.[3] Irrespective of whether Chomsky is right or wrong, it can be argued that extrapolating from a general theory is a hazardous undertaking on the grounds that important facts relating to both the nature of language and the classroom setting can be overlooked. It is significant that those applied linguists who have turned to a general theory of learning to explain classroom learning have rarely bothered to collect data from inside the classroom to test the claims of the theory. The process is one-way only; extrapolation occurs, but there is no attempt at falsification.[4]

A second way of building a theory of classroom language learning is to assume that instructed L2 learning proceeds in the same way as naturalistic language learning. This approach has also proved popular. It takes two forms, depending on whether the starting point is child L1 acquisition or naturalistic L2 acquisition. Clearly the degree of extrapolation to the classroom setting is greater in the case of the former than the latter. The claim that classroom language learning is identical (or similar) to L1 acquisition involves an acceptance of the L2 = L1 hypothesis. It also implies a belief that adults can acquire an L2 in the same way as children. It is possible to question both assumptions (cf. Bley-Vroman, 1988 and Long, 1988a) and very difficult to prove either. The claim that naturalistic L2 learning and classroom language learning have many features in common is a much safer one. It is also a claim that can be subjected more readily to empirical enquiry.

Neither of the first two approaches involves going inside the classroom to try to discover what actually happens when teachers 'intervene' in the learning process. This is one reason why they have proved popular. It is much easier to draw on the work of other researchers who have investigated the nature of learning in general or who have studied naturalistic acquisition than to enter the 'black box' and begin the messy business of trying to find out how learners learn a language there. The reluctance to engage in classroom research can be explained by the natural inclination not to undertake unnecessary work. Why study the classroom if it can be argued that classroom language learning is like other kinds of learning or like naturalistic language learning?

One reason why it proved necessary to research the language classroom was precisely because there was radical disagreement about the theories of classroom language learning which were derived respectively from a general learning theory and from comparisons with naturalistic language learning. This research − like all research − has been of two broad kinds: (1) exploratory−interpretative research and (2) hypothesis-testing research. The former makes use of a non-experimental design, collects qualitative data and provides an interpretative analysis (Grotjahn, 1987). The latter makes use of an experimental or quasi-experimental design, employs quantitative data and offers statistical analysis. There are also various mixed forms of research.

There tends to be a certain tension between the advocates of the two research paradigms. A number of researchers (e.g. Mitchell, 1988a; Van Lier, 1988) argue that an exploratory−interpretative approach is required in order to unravel the complexities of behaviour in the language classroom. They argue that in order to understand these behaviours it is necessary to study them in depth and in context. They emphasize the social nature of classroom activity and see the study of the interactions that occur between the classroom participants as the principal object of enquiry. Such an approach, they suggest, also has the advantage that it presents results in a form that makes them easily understood by teachers. They are advocates of a 'research-then-theory' approach (Reynolds, 1971). That is, although they are interested in theory-building, they do not feel the need to base their research on a strong and explicit theory. Rather they feel that the theory will evolve as understanding becomes more complete. The principal tool of this branch of research is ethnography. The emphasis is on describing and understanding classroom processes rather than on testing what has been learnt.

Other researchers (e.g. Long, 1985a; 1988b) have argued in favour of a 'theory-then-research' approach. That is, they believe that 'true experiments' should be designed to test hypotheses based on a well-grounded theory.

Hypothesis-testing research, it is claimed, is the principal way of understanding cause−effect relationships. Thus experimental research is necessary to investigate whether instruction actually results in learning. Long (1985a: 391) writes: 'The theory-then-research strategy and the related causal-process form of theory allow for more efficient research. This is because the theory governing the research at any point in time tells the researcher which the relevant data are, which is the crucial experiment to run.' Researchers like Long talk frequently about **explanation**. They point out that the qualitative study of classroom processes may help us to understand how events take place and what motivates them but they are unable to explain how the events contribute to language learning. To do this it is necessary to set up a controlled experiment.

The debate over the two research paradigms is an age-old one. It is also a sterile one. For a start much of the research that has taken place is of a mixed form. An experimental design does not preclude the collection of qualitative data and interpretative analysis. Ethnographic research can be combined with attempts to manipulate the learning environment in specific ways in order to observe what happens. Second, given the complexity of the task facing the researcher it would seem wise to employ as many and as varied strategies of research as are available. Third, it would seem to me that the real issue is not so much how the research is carried out as what is done with the results of the research. The danger of much classroom research is to try to apply the results directly to teaching by advocating specific methods or techniques. This danger exists quite independently of whether the research is ethnographic or scientific. Classroom research should be directed at building a theory of language learning − a goal which both types of research can help to meet. The theory can then serve as a basis for pedagogical advice. The piecemeal application of the results of classroom research should be avoided.

Figure 1.1 shows the three ways of building a theory of classroom L2 learning which have now been discussed in broad outline. Two points are

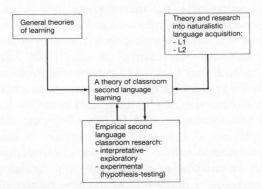

Figure 1.1   Three approaches for developing a theory of classroom second language learning

worth emphasizing. The first is that a general distinction can be drawn between theory-building that proceeds without direct reference to classroom behaviour — as occurs when extrapolation from a general learning theory or from naturalistic language learning occurs — and theory-building that results from attempts to research classroom activities. The second point is that the theories that have resulted from the different approaches have not always been coherent or even fully explicit. This is because the teaching—learning relationship has been viewed predominantly from the perspective of how to teach rather than from how learning takes place. One of the aims of this book is to remedy this by adopting a learning perspective.

Extrapolating from General Learning Theory

Now that the three ways of building a theory of classroom language learning have been outlined, we can begin to examine each one in a little more detail. We start with the attempts that have been made to extrapolate from general learning theory. This makes a convenient starting point as this was the initial approach adopted.[5]

In the fifties and sixties there was no field of enquiry that could be labelled 'second language acquisition'. In order to determine the views about classroom language learning which prevailed during that period it is necessary to examine what language teaching methodologists had to say. There was no attempt to develop an explicit theory of classroom language learning; rather views of learning were invoked to lend support to a set of claims regarding how language teaching should take place.

Ideas about language teaching during this period were derived in part from linguistic theory and in part from a general theory of learning. The linguistic theory was that propounded by structuralist linguists. A language was seen as a set of formal patterns that could be described rigorously without reference to meaning. The learning theory was that propounded by behaviourist psychologists. Learning was treated as a process of habit-formation that could be described in a terms of stimulus-response associations, often linked together in complex chains. Methodologists such as Brooks (1960) and Lado (1964) drew extensively on both structuralist and behaviourist theories in developing an approach to language teaching that became known as audiolingualism.

According to audiolingual principles the goal of classroom learning was the acquisition of the habits that comprised the target language. A habit consisted of the ability to perform a particular linguistic feature (a sound, a word, a grammatical pattern) automatically, i.e. without having to pay conscious attention to it. This ability entailed being able to link a particular response to a particular stimulus. It was acquired through massive practice of a mechanical nature. The teacher supplied the stimulus, the learner supplied the response. The teacher then reinforced correct responses or corrected erroneous responses. Ideally, errors were to be avoided because they were believed to have a negative effect on learning. A major source of errors was the learner's first language (L1). This interfered with the acquisition of the L2 because the learner tended to transfer the habits of her native language into the target language. These views on classroom language learning − derived entirely from a theory of general learning − were articulated with conviction and came to be accepted as received opinion by a large number of teachers.

It is easy to overemphasize the role played by behaviourist learning theory in audiolingualism. As Howatt (1984) points out, the progenitors of the method − Fries and Bloomfield − made little mention of behaviourist psychology but drew instead on structuralist descriptions of language as a basis for pattern-practice. However, there can be little doubt that behaviourist theories were used to underpin recommended instructional techniques. There was, for instance, a clear link between Skinner's theory of operant conditioning, which described how complex behaviours can be systematically shaped, and programmed language learning.

It is important to understand audiolingual learning theory and to subject its assumptions to careful scrutiny. There are two good reasons why. First, the theory addressed some key issues − issues which need to be addressed in any theory of classroom language learning. It dealt with the difference between explicit knowledge of a L2 (i.e. **knowledge about** the L2) and implicit knowledge (i.e. the knowledge that underlies the **ability to use** the L2) and made statements about which kind of knowledge should be the goal of learning. It considered the cause of learner errors and the role they play in learning. It articulated in some detail the kind of classroom behaviours which were needed to ensure successful L2 learning. Second, the theory has had a tremendous impact on teachers' popular conceptions about how L2 learning takes place in a classroom. This impact is still evident today, many years after the theory has been rejected as an adequate account of classroom language learning. One reason for this, perhaps, is that in audiolingual learning theory L2 learning is treated like any other learning and, therefore, the task of teaching a L2 can be seen as essentially the same as that of teaching any other school subject.

Audiolingual learning theory is not the only classroom language learning theory to have been based on a general theory of learning − although it has, perhaps, been the most influential. Currently considerable attention is being paid to cognitive theory (J. Anderson, 1980; McLaughlin, 1978b and 1987).[6] This exists in direct opposition to behaviourist learning theory as it emphasizes the role of internal mental processing rather than external behaviour. Cognitive theory seeks to explain three main aspects of learning: (1) how knowledge is established, (2) how knowledge becomes automatic and (3) how new knowledge is integrated into the learner's existing cognitive system. It draws extensively on research into information processing. A key distinction is that between **declarative** and **procedural knowledge**. Applied to language learning, the theory claims that the process by which new linguistic knowledge is internalized is different from the process by which control over this knowledge is achieved. New knowledge is 'declarative' (i.e. it involves 'knowing that'). Automated knowledge is 'procedural' (i.e. it involves 'knowing how'). Learners typically progress from declarative to procedural knowledge as they develop control. Many of the errors that learners produce are not the result of a lack of declarative knowledge but rather of procedural knowledge. The solution is to provide conditions of learning that enable them to practise using their knowledge in authentic communicative situations (Johnson, 1988).

Cognitive learning theory provides a much more convincing account of classroom language learning than audiolingual learning theory. This is because it does not seek to explain L2 learning solely in terms of observable behaviours but gives full recognition to the contribution of the learner's internal mental processing. The theory is particularly helpful in enabling us to understand what learners need to do in order to obtain full control over L2 knowledge. But, as we shall see, it is unable to account satisfactorily for a number of aspects of classroom language learning – in particular for the fact that there are remarkable regularities in the sequence in which L2 knowledge is acquired.

Extrapolation from general theories of learning is inevitable and desirable. Learning an L2 in the classroom must share a number of characteristics with the learning of other kinds of knowledge. After all, the conditions that prevail in a language lesson are not so very different from those that prevail in the history or science lesson. The fact that an L2 is acquirable in a classroom context suggests that at least some of the processes involved must be the same as in other kinds of learning. But there are dangers in extrapolating from a general theory. It is one thing to claim that classroom language learning is *like* other forms of learning, entirely another to assume that it is the *same*. There is now ample evidence to suggest that in some respects at least classroom language learning is special. Extrapolators are not likely to bother to go inside the classroom to test their hypotheses and, sadly, they are likely to ignore the evidence of those researchers that have done so.

Extrapolation from behaviourist learning theory is considered in chapter 2. Cognitive learning theory is examined in chapter 7.

Extrapolating from Naturalistic Language Learning

In the sixties behaviourist theories of learning began to buckle under the weight of Chomsky's (1959) attack on the general principles of associationist psychology. Mentalist theories of language learning began to assume ascendancy. These emphasized the importance of innate knowledge and the learner's contribution to the process of language learning. The learner was credited with a mental grammar that comprised her competence and which underlay her actual language behaviour. At the same time a number of important studies of L1 acquisition were undertaken (e.g. Bloom, 1970; Brown, 1973).

The rejection of behaviourism on theoretical grounds and on the basis of empirical studies had a considerable impact on applied linguists interested in language teaching. Articles applying the results of L1 acquisition research and theory to the classroom began to appear (e.g. Corder, 1967; Cook, 1969).

In the late sixties teachers-turned-researchers began to take an interest in L2 learning. This period saw the beginnings of Second Language Acquisition (SLA) as an area of empirical enquiry. There was sudden burst of research. Many of the early studies employed the methodology of error analysis (e.g. George, 1972); that is, corpora of learner utterances were inspected and deviations from target language norms identified, described and explanations for them sought. Other studies made use of performance analysis (e.g. Dulay and Burt, 1973); that is, the degree of correct usage of a number of different grammatical features was compared in order to establish an order of accuracy. There were also a number of longitudinal case studies of individual L2 learners (e.g. Ravem, 1968; Huang and Hatch, 978) which examined how grammatical sub-systems such as negatives and interrogatives were acquired.

There were two significant findings of this research. It was shown that many of the errors produced by learners were **developmental** in nature. That is, learners appeared to construct their own rules, which were independent of both their native language and the target language. This finding was used as evidence against the claim of audiolingual learning theory that the major source of learner error was L1 interference. The second finding was that there appeared to be a **natural sequence of acquisition** for many grammatical features. Learners from different language backgrounds displayed remarkable regularity in the rank ordering of grammatical morphemes or in the stages of development of negatives and interrogatives. It was argued that L2 acquisition was a process of creative construction not dissimilar to that found in L1 acquisition.[7]

All this provided a basis for some very different views of classroom language learning from that advanced by audiolingual learning theory. These views were cognitivist in nature. **Cognitive code learning theory** (Chastain, 1971) drew heavily on the learning theory that underpinned the study of generative grammar. One of its central tenets was that the perception and awareness of L2 rules preceded the actual use of these rules (i.e. competence preceded performance). Considerable importance, therefore, was attached to metalingual knowledge − knowledge *about* language. The cognitive code learning theory was directly opposed to **audiolingual learning theory** in this respect. Also opposed were the views of classroom language learning propagated by Newmark and Reibel (1968). These emphasized the classroom learner's innate capacity for language learning. It was argued that classroom language learning − like naturalistic language learning − would take place effortlessly and automatically providing there was sufficient exposure to the target language and the learner was sufficiently motivated. Errors were a natural concomitant of learning and were to be tolerated rather than corrected. Learning could best be fostered if there is no attempt to 'interfere' with it. Very similar views were propagated by applied linguists who drew on the early research into L2 acquisition (e.g. Corder, 1975).

A familiar feature of articles that appeared in journals such as *Language Learning*, *TESOL Quarterly* and the *International Review of Applied Linguistics* was a final section in which theoretical claims or the findings of empirical research were 'applied' to the classroom. This approach found its arch-disciple in Stephen Krashen, whose Monitor Model, developed in the middle seventies and popularized in the late seventies and early eighties, was specially devised to take account of classroom language learning. The Model itself, however, was based almost entirely on studies of naturalistic acquisition – L1 and L2. It represented the most complete attempt yet at extrapolation.[8]

Extrapolation from naturalistic L1 and L2 acquisition research is discussed in chapter 3.

Researching Classroom Language Learning

Although it is not entirely true to say that there was no classroom L2 research before the seventies, it is certainly true that the decade saw a remarkable growth of such studies. The research conducted in the sixties and earlier was typically experimental in nature and did not involve the observation of actual classroom behaviour. Scherer and Wertheimer (1964), for instance, sought to compare the efficacy of two different approaches to language teaching (grammar–translation vs. audiolingualism) and did so by measuring classroom learners' L2 proficiency by means of pre- and post-tests. The 'treatment' consisted of instruction based on the two approaches, but no attempt was made to investigate what actually happened when it took place. Another frequently cited comparative method study of the sixties was the Pennsylvania Project (Smith, 1970). This investigated the relative efficacy of three different methods: (1) traditional (grammar–translation), (2) inductive (the audiolingual method) and (3) deductive (the cognitive code method). It employed a similar pre/post-test design to the Scherer and Wertheimer study.

As Clark (1969) pointed out, there are inherent problems in studies that try to treat the real-life classroom situation as if it were a psychologist's laboratory. One of the main problems is that there can be no certainty that the instructions given to teachers are actually carried out by them. In other words there is no guarantee that the 'treatments' really are different. Methods that are distinct on paper may not be so in practice. Some effort was made in the Pennsylvania Project to carry out classroom observation in order to establish whether there were real differences in instruction, but this was of limited validity as the observation schedules employed were flawed in a number of respects.

Neither the Scherer and Wertheimer not the Smith study was able to demonstrate that one teaching method was significantly more effective in promoting L2 learning than another. One of the effects of these disappointing results was that researchers began to question whether large-scale comparative method studies were the right way to go about investigating teaching—learning. Allwright (1988a: ch. 1) describes in detail how the rejection of 'method' as an appropriate goal of enquiry set the scene for the detailed, small-scale observational studies of classroom behaviour that began to appear in the seventies.

The empirical studies of L2 classrooms which have taken place in the seventies and eighties and which provide a basis for building a theory of classroom L2 learning can be grouped under two headings: (1) classroom process research, (2) the study of formal instruction and L2 acquisition. A brief account of each category follows.

Classroom Process Research

Classroom process research has consisted typically of small-scale studies aimed at documenting the events that take place in L2 classrooms. A variety of methods have been employed — the use of observational schedules for interaction analysis, educational ethnography, the analysis of classroom discourse, case studies, interviews, action research (i.e. attempts to investigate teaching—learning while carrying out normal teaching) and introspection (e.g. asking learners to comment on how they set about performing different classroom tasks). Van Lier (1988: ch. 3) provides a useful survey of these methods. The general aim of classroom process research is to **describe** classroom behaviour in detail in order to build up an accurate record of what actually happens. Careful description serves as a basis for understanding and explaining what happens:

> What we are doing when we examine an utterance in context is basically of course *explaining* the occurrence of that utterance as the same time as *describing*. We therefore engage in explanation, and in that sense a distinction between descriptive and explanatory research is simplistic; it is not possible to do one without the other. (Van Lier, 1988: 10—11)

As this quotation makes clear, classroom process research is usually (although not exclusively) **sociological** in orientation. The 'explanation' it provides is of a social nature. That is, it does not provide an explanation of how L2 learning takes place in the mind of the learner, although it can provide some helpful clues about this.

Classroom process research has examined a number of different aspects of the teacher's and the learner's language, as well as exploring the nature of interaction between the participants. Some of the issues dealt with are:

1 Error treatment, i.e. how the teacher deals with learner errors.
2 Teacher talk, i.e. the formal and functional characteristics of the ways in which teachers talk to L2 learners.

3 Learners' language, e.g. the communication strategies which learners use to overcome communication problems in the classroom and the use of code-switching.
4 The differences between pedagogic and natural discourse.
5 The different types of classroom discourse.

These issues are considered in some depth in chapter 4.

The Study of Classroom Interaction and L2 Acquisition

Classroom process research has helped us to understand what happens in teaching—learning. It provides us with a clearer picture about the way in which teachers and learners go about their business. It has also afforded a number of insights about the relationship between overt classroom behaviours and language learning and produced some valuable speculation on this relationship. The research has tended to be piecemeal, however, and has not been informed by an explicit theory of classroom L2 learning. This comment is not intended as a criticism of classroom process research. Indeed, the strength of this kind of research rests in the detailed attention paid to specific aspects of classroom activity. There is danger, however, that investigators working in this tradition will be seduced by the attractiveness of manageable research questions that can be answered by means of easily collected classroom data but which add little to our understanding of how learning takes place. As a complement to classroom process research, therefore, there is a need for theory-led research, which addresses more directly the nature of the relationship between classroom interaction and L2 learning.

A number of applied linguists have argued for viewing teaching—learning as 'interaction'. Allwright (1984a: 157), for instance, argues that interaction should be viewed not just as an aspect of communicative language teaching but as '*the* fundamental fact of classroom pedagogy'. According to Allwright it is through the joint management of interaction by the teacher and the learners that learning takes place. 'Interaction' in this sense refers not just to those exchanges involving authentic communication but to every oral exchange that occurs in the classroom, including those that arise in the course of formal drilling.

A number of different hypotheses about the relationship between interaction and learning have attracted researchers' attention. One that has motivated a number of recent studies is the interactional hypothesis. This states that L2 acquisition occurs most efficiently when learners have plentiful opportunities to negotiate meaning whenever there is some kind of communication difficulty. Such negotiation, it is claimed, brings learners into contact with L2 data which they are likely to attend to and so incorporate into their L2 mental grammars. There are, however, considerable problems involved in testing this hypothesis empirically, not least that of determining what is actually learnt as a result of engaging in an interactional exchange where there is opportunity to negotiate meaning. The causal relationship between meaning-negotiation and acquisition has not been conclusively demonstrated.[9] However, the theory has served as a basis for conducting a number of classroom studies aimed at answering such questions as 'What kinds of pedagogic task provide the best opportunities for negotiation?' and 'Does small-group work provide greater opportunity for the negotiation of meaning than teacher–class interaction? These studies are, of course, only as good as the theory that motivates them.

It is probably true to say that we still know very little about the relationship between interaction and learning. Chapter 5 reviews a number of hypotheses (including the interactional hypothesis) which address the relationship, but the evidence to support each is often indirect and meagre.

The Study of Formal Instruction and L2 Acquisition

A different branch of classroom research has examined the effect that formal instruction has on L2 acquisition. 'Formal instruction' refers to the attempt to teach some specific feature of the L2 code – usually a grammatical feature – in one way or another. The studies belonging to this type of research fall into two categories, depending on whether they examine the effect of formal instruction on the rate/success of L2 learning or on the sequence/process of acquisition.

Recent surveys of research which fall into the first category (Long, 1983b, 1988a; Ellis, 1985a) indicate that learners who receive formal instruction generally outperform those who do not. The methodological basis of this research is a comparison between classroom and naturalistic learners. The assumption is made that if it can be shown that classroom learners learn more rapidly and/or achieve higher levels of ultimate success than naturalistic learners, then this must be the result of the essential difference in the two learning environments – the focus on form that occurs in the classroom.

Studies which have investigated the effect of formal instruction on the sequence/process of L2 acquisition have produced mixed results. Some researchers have compared the acquisitional sequences of classroom learners with those of naturalistic learners (e.g. Lightbown, 1983; Pica, 1983; Ellis, 1984a). In general the sequences appear to be very similar, but some interesting differences have also been observed. Other researchers have examined the effect of formal instruction more directly by carrying out classroom experiments (e.g. Pienemann, 1984; Eckman et al., 1988). That is, attempts are made to control the learning of specific grammatical features through formal instruction. The results show that some grammatical structures do not appear to be teachable unless the learner is developmentally 'ready'. Other grammatical structures, however, appear more amenable to instruction. There is also some evidence to suggest that formal instruction directed at one linguistic feature can not only result in the learning of that structure but also trigger the acquisition of other 'implicated' structures.

Much of this research has been motivated by theoretical questions concerning

SLA in general. The classroom serves as a convenient arena in which to carry out controlled experiments. Nevertheless, the research has helped us to form a clearer idea about the constraints that govern the acquisition of new linguistic forms and whether formal language teaching enables the learner to 'beat' the natural sequence. One of the strengths of this branch of classroom research is that it has been able to examine the relationship between teaching and learning directly because it utilizes measures of both.[10] It is examined in detail in chapter 6.

Summary

The empirical study of L2 classrooms came about largely as a result of dissatisfaction with global method comparisons. The different categories of research are summarized in table 1.1. It is not the purpose of this book to advance the claims of one approach over the others. No one approach is capable of providing the data needed to build a complete theory of L2 learning. The three approaches together, however, provide a picture of how learning takes place in the classroom.

Theoretical Issues

In this section we will consider a central distinction that any theory of class-room L2 learning will need to address: the role of form-focused and meaning-focused instruction. A number of questions will be raised but no attempt will be made to answer them at this juncture − that must wait until chapter 7.

The Role of Form-focused Instruction

We have already seen that classroom language learning can be distinguished from naturalistic language learning on the grounds that it involves planned attempts to intervene in the learning process. One of the key questions, therefore, is what form this planning should take. Broadly speaking, there are three options. The intervention can involve the provision of form-focused instruction where the learners are encouraged to focus their attention on specific properties of the linguistic code. Alternatively, intervention can take the form of specially contrived meaning-focused activities designed to promote authentic communication in the classroom. The third option consists of some kind of combination of form and meaning-focused instruction.

The choice of the form-focused option involves an acceptance of one of two assumptions. The strong assumption is that attention to the code is necessary for L2 learning in a classroom context. The weaker assumption is that it is not necessary but is desirable as an aid to learning. We will examine both assumptions in the following chapters.

Table 1.1   Empirical research of L2 classrooms

Category	Goal	Principal research methods
1 Classroom process research	The understanding of how the 'social events' of the language classroom are enacted	The detailed, ethnographic observation of classroom behaviours
2 The study of classroom interaction and L2 acquisition	To test a number of hypotheses relating to how interacting in the classroom contributes to L2 acquisition and to explore which types of interaction best facilitate acquisition	Controlled experimental studies; ethnographic studies of interaction
3 The study of instruction and L2 acquisition	To discover whether formal instruction results in the acquisition of new L2 knowledge and the constraints that govern whether formal instruction is successful	Linguistic comparisons of L2 acquisition by classroom and naturalistic learners; experimental studies of the effects of formal instruction

Both the strong and the weaker assumption imply that it is possible to influence the speed and/or course of L2 learning by directing the learner's attention to the formal properties of the code. In other words, it is accepted that learners are able to learn what they are taught. It is precisely this acceptance which has been challenged in recent years, notably in the publications of Stephen Krashen (1981; 1982; 1985). Krashen has argued that grammar-teaching is powerless to alter the natural route of L2 acquisition and that learners should be left to follow their own internal syllabus. This view has been strongly criticized by a number of applied linguists (McLaughlin, 1978b; Sharwood-Smith, 1981; Ellis, 1984a).

If it is accepted that attention to the code contributes to L2 acquisition, a further question arises. How should attention to the code be organized? The answer to this question depends on whether it is believed that L2 learning involves the incremental mastery of discrete items. Rutherford (1987) refers to this as the 'accumulated entities' view of language learning. Such a view underpins both audiolingual and cognitive code learning theories. Imparting the necessary information about the items that comprise the code can be attempted inductively (as in audiolingualism) or deductively (as in the cognitive code method). That is, the instruction may simply provide the learners with plentiful opportunities to produce utterances containing the target item or it can provide explicit information about the properties of the item. An alternative to the 'accumulated entities' view of learning is **consciousness-raising**. This differs from traditional grammar-teaching in that it sees form-focused instruction as a means to the attainment of grammatical competence not as an attempt to instil it. Consciousness-raising aims to facilitate acquisition, not to bring it about directly. It recognizes that the learner will contribute to and shape the process of acquisition herself.

Form-focused instruction can be considered from the point of view of how the input to the learner is planned (i.e. syllabus-design and lesson-planning) and also from the point of view of the processes that occur in the course of teaching (i.e. classroom methodology). The choice of syllabus type is based on a particular view of classroom language learning – be this overt or covert. Methodological choices are similarly based. For instance, the teacher who believes that it is necessary to correct learners' errors does so because she believes that this will contribute, in one way or another, to learning. The construction of a theory of language learning that addresses the role of formal instruction is, therefore, of importance not just for curriculum planning but also for curriculum implementation.

The Role of Meaning-focused Instruction

Meaning-focused instruction consists of the provision of classroom activities that encourage learners to communicate using whatever resources, linguistic and non-linguistic, they have at their disposal. Two pedagogical arguments have been advanced in its favour (Ellis, 1986). The first is that learners need the opportunity to communicate in order to develop fluency. Through trying to communicate they develop the strategic competence they need to deal with communication problems and at the same time they automatize their existing L2 knowledge. The second argument is that learners are able to acquire new L2 knowledge as a result of taking part in communication. They 'pick up' knowledge from the input they are exposed to through interaction.

One the issues addressed by classroom process research is the extent to which classrooms are able to afford opportunities for authentic communication (e.g. Riley, 1977; Edmondson, 1985). The study of the teacher's and the learner's language and of the discourse they jointly construct have shown that the communication that takes place in the classroom is usually very different that which takes place outside. The asymmetrical role relationships between teacher and learners together with an educational ideology that views the process of teaching–learning as one of transmission result in a distorted form of communication. A number of questions arise. One concerns whether the distortion has a negative effect on L2 learning. Another concerns how the distortion can be overcome (e.g. through talk in small-group work).

The key question regarding the role of meaning-focused instruction concerns how interaction contributes to the acquisition of new linguistic knowledge. According to one view comprehensible input is necessary. Krashen (1985) has emphasized the importance of the teacher simplifying input to ensure that learners are able to understand. Long (1983a) has argued the importance of negotiation of meaning when there is a communication difficulty. This helps to make input which contains new linguistic material comprehensible and so facilitates its acquisition. According to another view learner output is important.

Swain (1985), for instance, argues that learners need the opportunity for 'pushed output' (i.e. output that stretches their linguistic capacity) in order to avoid stopping learning some way short of native-speaker competence. A theory of classroom language learning needs to consider the role of meaning-focused instruction. It needs to explain the respective contributions of form-focused and meaning-focused instruction and to provide a principled basis for how the two can be combined.

Conclusion

The goal of this book is the construction of a comprehensive theory of classroom L2 learning. This chapter has had three main purposes: to define the term 'classroom language learning', to identify and describe the types of information to be drawn on in the process of building a theory and to outline some of the major issues which the theory will have to address.

The study of classroom language learning can proceed in different ways. It can draw on the theories and methods of different disciplines – linguistics, sociology, psychology and education. This book does not aim to promote the claims of any one discipline over those of the others. If it gives greater attention to psycholinguistic enquiry, this is not because this is considered the 'right' way to go about building a theory but because it reflects the personal interests of the author. Nor is it intended to suggest that a psycholinguistic theory is the 'best' kind of theory upon which to base pedagogic practice. The relationship between research and theory on the one hand and pedagogy on the other, however, does need careful consideration. It will be examined in chapter 8.

NOTES

1 The distinction between formal training and apprenticeship in language teaching is mirrored in Stern's (1981) pedagogic distinction between an 'L' approach (characterized as linguistic and analytical) and a 'P' approach (characterized as psychological and experiential). Howatt (1984) distinguishes a 'rational' and a 'natural' approach.

2 Klein (1986) distinguishes classroom and naturalistic acquisition in a similar way. He describes the former as 'spontaneous' and the latter as 'guided'. 'Guidance' is evident in both the choice of what to teach (syllabus) and how to teach it (methodology).

3 Chomsky continues to maintain that language constitutes a separate faculty which cannot be explained with reference to a general cognitive system (cf. Chomsky, 1986). He rejects, therefore, explanations of language learning within a Piagetian framework.

4 The fifties and sixties were not devoid of empirical research, of course. In

particular, there were numerous studies of language aptitude (e.g. Pimsleur, 1960; Carroll, 1963). However, these were experimental in nature and extrinsic to the classroom. No attempt was made to enter the classroom and observe what happened there.

5   I am, of course, ignoring the history of language teaching prior to the advent of audiolingualism. My reason for this is that before audiolingualism there was no *explicit* attempt to justify pedagogic techniques by reference to the way a L2 was learnt. Grammar—translation, for instance, made no mention of how languages are learned. The learning theory that underlay the oral approach was ill-defined, to say the least (cf. Richards and Rodgers, 1986: 36—7).

6   There is, in fact, no one 'cognitive theory'. Rather there are a number of separate theories which are broadly similar in that they recognize similar distinctions — such as that between declarative and procedural knowledge — and draw extensively on research into information processing.

7   It is important to note, however, that the idea of a 'natural order hypothesis', in the L2 acquisition of grammatical structures is a controversial one. Not all studies lend support to this. The hypothesis and the research are considered in chapter 3.

8   Krashen's later work (e.g. Krashen, 1985) draws on studies of both naturalistic and classroom learning. The Monitor Model, however, was constructed on evidence supplied predominantly from research into naturalistic acquisition.

9   Long (1985a) argues that it is not necessary to demonstrate a direct relationship between interaction and the acquisition of specific linguistic features. He suggests that the link can be demonstrated indirectly by showing that the negotiation of meaning promotes comprehension which in turn promotes acquisition. This proposal is discussed in detail in ch. 5.

10   In fact, though, many of the studies of formal instruction are not really classroom research in the strict sense of this term, i.e. they did not involve going inside the classroom. Comparative studies of naturalistic and classroom learning, for example, have been conducted by collecting data outside the classroom.

2 Behaviourist Learning Theory and Classroom Language Learning

Introduction

The dominant language-teaching method of the fifties and sixties was audio-lingualism. This method originated from the 'scientific' descriptions of language provided by American linguists such as Bloomfield and Fries, both of whom belonged to the structuralist school, which sought to identify and describe the formal patterns of a language in an explicit and rigorous manner. Subsequently, language-teaching methodologists such as Brooks and Lado drew extensively on behaviourist psychology as a means of justifying the prescriptions of the method they advocated. Thus, audiolingualism drew on linguistics in the first place, extrapolating from the theoretical claims of general psychology only at a later date.[1] This chapter begins with a brief account of the emergence of audiolingualism.

Several behaviourist accounts of learning were drawn on as a warrant for audiolingual principles of teaching. Methodologists drew liberally and eclectically on available theories to justify their own views about teaching. However, it is probably true to say that the views on learning advanced by Watson and more especially Skinner constituted the primary source for extrapolation. No attempt will be made here to describe in detail particular behaviourist theories of learning. This is not necessary, as the main purpose of this chapter is to identify the views of L2 learning that underpinned audiolingual teaching. The chapter, therefore, will examine the assumptions about L2 learning found in audiolingualism, borrowing from and extending a list which Rivers (1964) drew up. Where some background theoretical knowledge is needed in order to make sense of a particular assumption this will be provided.

The assumptions of audiolingualism were subjected to a critical evaluation in the early sixties on the grounds that language learning is a process to which the learner actively contributes. The central idea that learning could be directed from the outside by manipulating the behaviour of the learner was rejected by nativists, who argued that learners themselves control the course of language learning. This chapter examines the objections which have been levelled against audiolingual learning theory. In so doing it stands back from the preoccupations of the day to ask whether audiolingual learning theory offers any insights of value for an understanding of classroom L2 learning.

The Emergence of Audiolingualism

Audiolingualism was a method of teaching that grew out of the **structural approach** developed by a number of American linguists — notably Fries. The method originated in the attempts to provide training to army personnel during the Second World War. It was designed to develop oral fluency in a L2 in nine months. An outline of the approach was later described by Fries (1948) in an article written for the first issue of *Language Learning*. First, linguists drew up descriptions of the patterns of the L2, using native speakers of the language as informants. Second, applied linguists carried out contrastive descriptions of the learners' L1 and the target language. These served as a basis for the selection and grading of the patterns which were to be taught. The applied linguists then prepared teaching materials to practise the patterns. Finally, the materials were implemented. Howatt (1984:267) noted that the structural approach lacked a set of clearly defined methodological principles; it was based on 'the cult of materials' derived from 'sound linguistic principles.'

The **structural approach** served as the basis for the Foreign Language in the Elementary School (FLES) programmes that began throughout the United States in the fifties. The new techniques held out the promise that children could quickly and easily master a L2. Whereas the **grammar−translation method**, which the audiolingual method replaced, had emphasized intellectual and literary study, the new approach rested on techniques of mimicry and memorization ('mim−mem') designed to develop the ability for oral communication. As such, it was seen as appropriate for teaching young children and of greater practical relevance to society.[2] McLaughlin (1985) reports that by 1960 there were over a million children in the FLES programmes.

The late fifties and early sixties in the States saw a number of books on applied linguistics and language-teaching methodology, stimulated by the rebirth of interest in foreign language teaching in American education. In 1957 Lado published *Language across Cultures*. This provided a lucid account of the principles and methods involved in contrastive descriptions of two languages. In 1960 *Language and Language Learning* by Brooks was published, followed in 1964 by Lado's *Language Teaching*. In 1961 the staff of the Modern Language Materials Development Center published teaching manuals for the major foreign languages. A feature of all these — and other — publications was reference to the principles of learning propounded by behaviourist psychologists such as Watson and Skinner. It is perhaps significant that, as attention was given to actual classroom practice, as opposed to the specification and ordering of teaching content, reference was made to psychological principles.

Audiolingualism was very much an American method. In its purist form it was never very popular in Britain and Europe, where less attention was paid to teaching the formal patterns of the L2 and more to the situational uses of the L2.[3] In general, approaches to language teaching in Europe have treated theories of learning provided by psychologists or second language acquisition researchers with suspicion. Thus Catford (1959) in a review of the teaching of English as a foreign language in Britain paid lip-service to the need for language teaching to seek guidance from both linguistics and psychology but, in fact, made scarcely any reference to learning. However, many of the audiolingual assumptions regarding the way language is learnt can be found in the pedagogical prescriptions of British and European methodologists writing at this time (cf. early issues of *English Language Teaching*).

Assumptions about L2 Learning in the Audiolingual Approach

In this section the term *foreign language* (FL) learning will be used throughout as audiolingual methodologists held that foreign or classroom language learning was different in kind from naturalistic or second language learning and were concerned only with the former.

Assumption 1: Foreign language is the same as any other kind learning and can be explained by the same laws and principles   This assumption was basic to all the other assumptions. Skinner (1957:10) made his position on this point quite clear: 'We have no reason to assume ... that verbal behavior differs in any fundamental respect from non-verbal behavior, or that any new principles must be invoked to account for it.' This claim was the basis for extrapolating from a general theory of learning. Skinner, in fact, went further and argued that laboratory experiments designed to investigate how animals such as rats could be trained to perform specific sequences of behaviour served as a basis for making claims about the way language learning took place.

Assumption 2: All learning is the result of experience and is evident in changes in behaviour   All bevahiourist theories were based on observable behaviour. For Watson (1924) there was no such thing as 'mind' or 'consciousness'. The sole criterion he used for determining whether something existed was whether it could be observed. Other behaviourists – such as Skinner – accepted the existence of mind, but rejected any explanation of human behaviour in terms of feelings or mental processes.

Learning, then, consisted of changes in behaviour that were brought about through experience. It followed that learning could be effected by manipulating the environment to provide the required experiences. This is exactly what Skinner attempted to do in his animal experiments. It is also what audiolingual techniques set out to do with the language learner. One of the great attractions of audiolingualism was the conviction that FL learning could be manipulated and induced by ensuring that the learners produced the appropriate behaviours.[4] If learning was behaviour it could be taught by inducing the correct behaviour (Politzer, 1961:2).

One of the results of treating learning as behaviour was that 'meaning' was excluded from consideration, as Politzer (1961:19) indicates: 'The other possibility ... that has been proved feasible ... is to eliminate meaning almost totally from the initial phase of language instruction. It is entirely possible to teach the major patterns of a foreign language without letting the student know what he is saying.' The exclusion of meaning was considered particularly important in the early stages of learning.

Assumption 3: Foreign language learning is different from first language learning   According to behaviourist theories of learning, the mechanism by which all language learning took place was the same. All language was 'verbal behaviour', so it followed that both L1 and foreign language (FL) learning consisted of developing the correct behavioural responses.

However, language teaching methodologists were often at pains to point out the differences between L1 learning and FL learning. They were well aware that FL learning posed difficulties which the child learning an L1 did not face. As Mackey (1965:107) put it: 'The learning of one language in childhood is an inevitable process; the learning of a second language is a special accomplishment.' Brooks (1960) also emphasizes the differences. Despite an otherwise strong adherence to behaviourist orthodoxy, he speaks mentalistically of the 'vital force' which characterizes the newborn baby and which enables it to 'break the code' of the L1.[5]

However, despite the recognition that the two types of learning differed, the relevancy of a general theory of learning to L2 learning was not seriously questioned. Comparisons between L1 and FL learning were undertaken with two purposes in mind. The first was to emphasize the relative ease of L1 learning and to make out a case for commencing FL instruction as early as possible in order to tap the natural language-learning capacity of the young child. Brooks recommended starting at eight years old. Arguments such as this were used to justify setting up FLES programmes. The second purpose was to dispute the view that the classroom should try to imitate 'real life'. L1 learning took place successfully in 'real life', but FL learning required setting up the 'optimal conditions' for learning in order to overcome the various problems.

Assumption 4: Foreign language learning is a mechanical process of habit formation   This assumption lay at the centre of audiolingualism. Brooks (1960:49) wrote: 'The single paramount fact about language learning is that it concerns, not problem solving, but the formation and performance of habits.' Methodologists recognized two different ways in which habits could be formed. According to the theory of **classical conditioning**, a stimulus present in the environment comes to be closely associated with a particular response such that whenever the stimulus occurs the response is automatically produced. **Instrumental learning**, as described by Skinner (1957), worked somewhat differently. Responses were emitted rather than elicited. **Operants** were produced randomly in the first place as a result of some ill-determined inner drive. Selected responses, however, were then subjected to reinforcement. Through the process of rewarding responses produced on a trial-and-error basis new habits were formed.[6]

Both theories of habit formation are evident in the writings on audio-lingualism. Classical conditioning fitted in nicely with the structuralists' view of language as a set of patterns. Each pattern, once identified, could be practised through stimulatus−response drills until it became a habit. Behaviourist psychologists, such as Thorndike, had carried out experiments to determine the optimal conditions for habit-formation. Lado (1964) and others refer to a number of 'laws of learning' which had been derived from these experiments. For example, the **law of effect** stated that if an act was followed by a satisfying state of affairs, the probability of its occurrence in a similar situation increased. In the case of the pattern-drills the 'satisfying state of affairs' was brought about by the learner knowing that he had produced the correct response. Another key law was the **law of intensity**, according to which the more intensely a response was practised, the better it was learnt and the longer it was remembered. The audiolingual emphasis on repetition, imitation and simple substitution on the part of the learner and systematic reinforcement on the part of the teacher was intended to reflect these laws of learning.

For learning to be effective habits had to become automatic. This is what Bloomfield (1942) had in mind when he claimed: 'Language learning is over-learning. Anything else is of no use.' Only if the patterns of the L2 had been 'over-learnt' was it possible for the learner to produce them correctly in real communication. Stimulus−response associations had to be learnt so that they could be accessed when the attention was on content and this required developing 'bundles of habits below the threshold of awareness' (Lado, 1964:34).

Skinner's account of instrumental learning was used to provide a principled explanation of how learning could be shaped by dividing the learning target into a series of minimal steps and arranging these in a carefully ordered sequence. The idea here was to effect efficient learning by making sure that each step in the learning process lay within the capabilities of the learner. In language teaching this was reflected in designing drills that exposed learners to **minimal differences** between patterns and, especially, in programmed instruction designed to lead the learner towards some predetermined criterion in an optimal fashion.

Audiolingual methodologists rejected 'total language experiences' such as those provided by normal communication on the grounds that these were beyond the capacity of the learner. Forcing the learner to adopt 'a normal language set' would result in imperfect experiences and, therefore, faulty or non-learning. Audiolingual teaching, therefore, was based on providing 'partial experiences'. Success in a partial experience provided a platform for more complicated behaviour. Thus Skinnerian principles of operant conditioning lay behind the audiolingual conviction that learners should not engage in meaningful communication before they were ready.

Assumption 5: Language learning proceeds by means of analogy rather than analysis   The grammar–translation method emphasized the value of deductive learning through formal explanations of L2 rules. In contrast, the audiolingual approach emphasized inductive learning through pattern-practice. This contrast is often referred to as that of **analysis** vs. **analogy** (cf. Brooks, 1960). **Analysis** involved 'problem solving'[7] rather than 'habit-formation'. Metalingual knowledge was no guarantee of the ability to use a grammatical feature correctly. Indeed, metalingual knowledge was worse than useless as it was a source of potential interference in the process of developing FL habits: 'The learner who has been made to see only how language works has not learned any language; on the contrary, he has learned something he will have to forget before he can make any progress in that area of language' (Brooks, 1960:49). Thus, as Valdman (1966a) puts it, the use of grammatical rules as 'predictors' of linguistic behaviour was outlawed.

Two uses of analysis were allowed, however. First, Brooks thought that giving an analytical explanation could help to 'clear the track' with learners who were used to deductive teaching. Brooks emphasized, however, that 'clearing the track' was not the same as advancing along the track. Second, Politzer (1961) suggested that rules could be provided as 'summaries of behaviour'. Politzer seems to accept that learners must undergo some kind of conscious realization of what a pattern consisted of during pattern practice and that this could be consolidated by providing a grammatical explanation.

The central process in forming habits was **analogy**. This involved discrimination and generalization. The learner needed to identify the underlying structure of a pattern by perceiving its similarities and differences with other patterns. Also the learner was expected to reproduce a pattern in similar but not identical situations, using different vocabulary. Substitution and cue drills were intended to foster both discrimination and generalization.

Assumption 6: Errors are the result of L1 interference and are to be avoided or corrected if they do occur   The patterns of the learners' L1 and the FL would be the same in some cases and different in others. Where they were the same, it was assumed that the learning of the FL would be faciliated because all the learner had to do was to transfer L1 habits. However, where they were different, learning difficulties arose as a result of **proactive inhibition** – the inhibition of new habits by previous learning. The learner's L1 interfered with the acquisition of new, FL habits. As a result errors appeared in the learner's responses which were directly traceable to the L1.

Audiolingualists recognized other sources of error (e.g. random responses or overgeneralization of a pattern resulting from incomplete learning'[8]) but considered L1 interference by far the most serious.

The goal of language teaching was to develop the FL as a **coordinate system**, independent of the learner's L1 rather than a **compound system**, in which the mother tongue accompanied and dominated attempted behaviour in the L2. To achieve a coordinate system it was necessary to prevent learners from speaking their L1 in class — although they might occasionally be allowed to hear it. More important still was the need to prevent L1 interference occurring. The avoidance of error was one of the central precepts of audiolingualism. Statements like the following from Brooks (1960:58) were common in the literature: 'Like sin, error is to be avoided and its influence overcome, but its presence to be expected.' Error prevention necessitated massive pattern-practice by means of mechanical drills which had a low probability of error and which could ensure use of the L2.

Errors would be prevented more easily if they could be predicted. To this end, the **contrastive analysis hypothesis** was formulated. In its strong form (cf. Wardhaugh, 1970) this stated that all L2 errors could be predicted by identifying the differences between the target language and the learner's L1. On the grounds that linguistic difference constituted learning difficulty a number of contrastive studies between English and the major European languages were carried out in the United States at the newly formed Center for Applied Linguistics (e.g. Stockwell and Bowen, 1965; Stockwell, Bowen and Martin, 1965). These studies were designed to identify the patterns which were most likely to cause difficulty so that materials writers could give precedence to them.

Despite all the preventive measures some errors were bound to occur. They had to be dealt with. Students were not to be allowed to discover and correct their own mistakes (Modern Language Materials Development Center, 1961:28). The recommended method was immediate correction by the teacher followed by further opportunity to produce the correct response. Such an approach to error treatment was compatible with the central tenet of operant conditioning, namely that correct responses received positive reinforcement and negative responses negative reinforcement.

An Evaluation of Audiolingual Learning Theory

These six assumptions constitute the theory of FL learning that underpinned audiolingualism. Of course, the learning theory was not monolithic. Politzer (1965:14), for instance, was not convinced that learning was simply a matter of method: 'It is not the method that performs the trick, it is the learner.' Valdman (1966a) queried the general assumption that learning was over-learning, referring to such a view as a 'simplistic model'. Even Lado (1964), one of the main proponents of audiolingualism, was cautious in the claims he made for his theory of FL learning. 'The theory is in the nature of a proposed explanation whose status is still partly conjectural' (p. 39). Nevertheless, the six assumptions reflected the confidence placed in behaviourist accounts of learning. They also reflected a preparedness to apply theory to practice or, more accurately perhaps, to justify practice with reference to theory.

Attacks on audiolingual learning theory came from two directions. First, applied linguists such as Rivers (1964) and Carroll (1966:101) took a close look at some of the principal assumptions from the perspective of developments in general learning theory. Carroll, in particular, was sceptical of the kinds of claims about FL learning advanced by Brooks and Lado: 'we do not yet have either a good general theory concerning the conditions under which learning takes place or a general theory of language behavior that would enable us to select optimal components of a foreign language teaching system for any given case.' He argued that the audiolingual habit theory was not linked to any contemporary theory of learning and had, in fact, only a 'vague resemblance' to an early version of association theory. He also noted the absence of any relevant research that could lend support to the theory. Rivers adopted a similar approach. She drew on the neo-behaviourist theories of Osgood and Mowrer which gave recognition to the mediational and emotional processes inside the learner. Her main point was that any approach to teaching which failed to recognize the contribution of the learner was inadequate. The basis of the first kind of attack on audiolingual learning theory, then, was to argue that the theory was no longer abreast of recent developments.

The second source of attack came from the paradigm shift in the psychology of language brought about by Chomsky's (1959) attack on Skinner's *Verbal Behavior*. Chomsky challenged the very basis of behaviourism by arguing that language was not a set of habits but a set of abstract rules and that language was not acquired through imitation and repetition but rather was an innate inheritance triggered off by minimal environmental exposure. Chomsky's arguments were lent further support by Lenneberg (1967), who provided experimental and clinical evidence that language development was biologically rather than environmentally determined. This position, which contradicted the assumption that all learning was the result of experience (see Assumption 2), soon began to be reflected in discussions of language-teaching methodology (cf. Newmark, 1963; Corder, 1967; Chastain, 1969). It is dealt with in detail in the next chapter.

The pedagogic proposals that derived from these two sources of attack were very similar. However, the sources were different in a significant way. Carroll and Rivers still sought to extrapolate from general theories of learning to FL learning. No consideration was given to the possibility that FL learning was different in kind from other types of learning. Chomsky and Lenneberg, however, took up just such a position. They argued that language was a specifically human faculty and that, therefore, it was not possible to extrapolate from general theories of learning.[9] A language-specific theory was needed.

This constituted a direct attack on the principal assumption (i.e. Assumption 1) of audiolingual learning theory.

Here is an account of the main objections raised against some of the other assumptions of audiolingual learning theory.

FL Learning vs. L1 Learning

According to audiolingual learning theory FL and L1 learning were both similar and different. Interest in the similarities and differences has continued since (cf. Cook, 1969; Ervin-Tripp, 1974; Ellis, 1985b). The differences which audiolingual theory assumed to exist as a result of L1 interference and age have been challenged, although not conclusively. The basis of the assumed similarity (habit-formation) is no longer accepted, but the idea of similarity itself lives on. The L2 = L1 hypothesis (Dulay and Burt, 1974a) was proposed on the grounds that the process of L2 development was essentially the same in both types of learning (see chapter 3).

The assumption that differences existed was largely motivated by the recognition that whereas success in L1 learning was guaranteed, this was not the case in FL learning. It is probably true to say that the conditions that govern FL learning are still seen as less favourable than those governing L1 learning. The search for the 'optimum conditions, for classroom language learning – the main goal of the audiolingual approach – continues (see chapter 5).

Habit-formation

Language learning cannot be convincingly treated as a process of mechanical habit-formation. Rivers (1964) disputes the 'mechanical' part of the assumption, arguing that a habit is developed only when the learner has a communicative need and is in a relaxed state. Chomsky (1959) disputes the concept of 'habit' itself. He argues that the concepts of 'stimulus' and 'response' are vacuous where language behaviour is concerned. We do not use language in response to clearly delineated behavioural stimuli. Also no behaviourist theory of learning can account for the speaker-hearer's ability to understand and produce sentences which are not merely novel in terms of lexical choice but also in their underlying pattern.

With these kind of arguments the whole edifice of audiolingualism began to collapse. In particular, the belief that learning could be controlled from the outside was eroded. As Dakin (1973:16) put it, 'though the teacher may control the experiences the learner is exposed to, it is the learner who selects what is learnt from them.' Implicit in audiolingual learning theory was the belief that patterns and items could be learnt in the order they were practised. The criterion used to determine the order of presentation was that of linguistic difficulty. No thought was given to the inherent learnability of specific linguistic features. Indeed such a notion was unthinkable in a theory that equated learning with behaviourally induced habits. The essence of both neo-behaviourist and nativist theories of learning was that the learner played an active role in determining both what was learnt and when it was learnt. Learnability became a central issue.

Can a case still be made for language learning as habit-formation? In so far as memorization has a part to play, the methods by which 'habits' are formed may contribute to at least some aspects of classroom L2 learning (e.g. vocabulary or ready-made phrases). They may also enable the learner to automatize new knowledge. Current cognitive theories of learning distinguish declarative and procedural knowledge (see chapters 1 and 8). Pattern-practice may be a means of helping the learner to proceduralize declarative knowledge. This is, in fact, the usual justification offered today for the continued use of pattern-practice in language teaching (Gower and Walters, 1983). Such a view is controversial, however. Johnson (1988:91), for instance, argues that mistake-correction can only take place if there is 'an opportunity to practise in real conditions'. Pattern-practice does not afford such conditions. How L2 knowledge is acquired and how it is automatized have become central questions in the study of classroom L2 learning. It is doubtful whether the notion of habit-formation can provide adequate answers.

There was one theory of language learning – originating from Russia – which integrated mentalist and behaviourist perspectives. Belyayev (1963) distinguished 'knowledge', 'skills', and 'habits'. In terms of language, 'knowledge' consisted of declarative facts about linguistic rules. 'Habits' were actions that can be performed without conscious thought, such as the pronunciation of a particular sound or the choice of lexical items. 'Skills' were communicative actions carried out consciously, such as the stylistic use of language for particular effects. Belyayev was critical of both teaching based on explanations of grammatical rules and teaching that required endless repetition of correct sentences. Although 'knowledge' and 'habits' could provide a basis for learning, the goal was to develop 'skills' in relation to communicative language use. He argued that teaching could promote learning if it included activities designed to develop all three aspects. Belyayev's theory with its recommended balance between accuracy and fluency teaching was not so very dissimilar to that proposed in England by Palmer (1921) or, more recently, by Brumfit (1984).

Analogy vs. Analysis

A number of arguments were advanced to refute the assumption that analysis was of no value in language learning. One of the most compelling was that voiced by Dakin (1973:19): 'if no public explanation is given, the learners will often form their own private explanation.' Rivers (1964) argued that explanations served to prevent practice becoming blind. The explanation helped the learner to recognize and focus on those elements in the pattern that were the goal of the lesson. The **cognitive code method**, which came to rival audiolingualism in the late sixties and seventies, gave emphasis to the importance of metalingual knowledge and the intellectual activity needed to acquire it. However, the status of metalingual knowledge has continued to be uncertain in theories of classroom L2 learning and there is continuing debate about its usefulness.

Error Avoidance and L1 Interference

Nativist theories of language learning have led to a complete revision in thinking regarding the role of error. Errors have come to be seen as part of the learning process. They are inevitable and provide evidence that acquisition is in fact taking place. The next chapter considers these views in some detail.

The theory of transfer was closely tied to the belief that FL learning consisted of habit-formation. Attacks on the latter were also attacks on the former. If proactive inhibition was discounted, L1 interference could no longer be treated as a major source of error. A number of attacks were mounted on the **contrastive analysis hypothesis**. It was pointed out that linguistic difference could not be equated with learning difficulty in any simple, straightforward way. Wardhaugh (1970) argued that the strong form of the hypothesis (which stated that errors could be predicted by identifying the linguistic differences between the learners' L1 and the target language) was untenable, although the weak form (which stated that contrastive analysis might be used to explain some of the errors that were seen to occur) was still possible.

Transfer has continued to be a problematic area in L2 acquisition research, not least because of its associations with behaviourist learning theory. There can be little doubt, however, that the learner's L1 does play a significant part in L2 learning and, in particular perhaps, FL learning (Marton, 1981). One of the major problems in determining exactly what this role is lies in the difficulty of distinguishing transfer that occurs in conscious translation from transfer that results from subconscious processes. Corder (1978a) talks of the former as a **communication strategy** and the latter as a **learning strategy**. The 'transfer debate' continues in full flow today (cf. Gass and Selinker, 1983; Kellerman and Sharwood-Smith, 1986). Discussion now takes place within the framework of cognitive or linguistic rather than behaviourist learning theories. The term **crosslinguistic influence** is often preferred to that of transfer.

Conclusion

Audiolingualism rapidly lost popularity in the United States, partly as a result of the strong theoretical arguments that were advanced against it, but also because the results obtained from classroom practice were disappointing. The method required highly skilled teachers who were not always available. Many learners found pattern-practice boring and lost interest in FL learning. Even learners who were 'motivated' to persevere found that memorizing patterns did not lead to fluent and effective communication in real-life situations. Older learners found little appeal in a method that denied them opportunity to use their cognitive skills in a more rule-governed approach to language learning.

Nevertheless, the premises of behaviourist psychology continue to influence many teachers thinking about how a L2 is learnt. Brumfit (1979) contrasted a traditional language teaching methodology (present → controlled practice → free practice) with a communicative methodology (communicate → present → controlled practice). There was a role still for controlled practice in a communicative methodology − presumably as a way of enabling the learner to acquire and use linguistic features which are not yet part of her repertoire. The theoretical justification for controlled practice − implicit or explicit − remains behaviourist ideas of habit-formation. These are rarely acknowledged these days, however.

Audiolingual learning theory is an inadequate explanation of classroom L2 learning. Its value is that it offered a number of explicit claims about the nature of learning which were open to challenge. The theory, therefore, instigated the discussion of a number of questions of central importance for understanding instructed language learning:

1   To what extent is it possible to control the course of L2 development by the external manipulation of the linguistic environment?
2   What role does controlled production of L2 forms play in their acquisition?
3   Does classroom L2 learning consist of the incremental acquisition of discrete linguistic features?
4   To what extent are the errors produced by instructed learners the result of L1 interference?
5   What role do errors play in the process of classroom L2 learning?
6   What role does metalingual knowledge play in classroom L2 learning?

Audiolingual learning theory offered definite answers to these questions. It soon became clear that they were the wrong answers but they provided clear reference points for subsequent thinking and research. What was missing from the theory was a recognition that language learning is a developmental process. Only a theory that paid due attention to the contribution of the learner − as opposed to the environment − was capable of addressing this major lacuna.

NOTES

1   It is probably true to say that most approaches to language teaching − in Britain at least − have owed more to linguistics than to psychology. The so-called **communicative approach**, for example, derives primarily from functional descriptions

of English (Wilkins, 1976). Language teaching in the United States, however, has paid more attention to psychology. The humanistic approach (cf. Stevick, 1976; 1980) owes much to a particular view about the nature of learning.

2 In fact, the methodological procedures remained the same irrespective of the age of the learner. None of the language-teaching handbooks of the time saw any need to modify the approach to take account of the cognitive differences between young children and adolescents/adults.

3 Structuralist linguistics − the origins of audiolingualism − were never as popular in Britain as the United States. Firthian linguistics, which emphasized the relationship between context and language, encouraged a different view of language, one that gave greater importance to meaning.

4 The ideal learner was an 'automaton'. Consider what Morton (1964:3) had to say about learning L2 pronunciation: 'It can be accomplished most quickly if the student makes a conscious effort to 'automatize' himself − turn himself into a non-thinking 'machine' whose only responsibility is to respond immediately, mechanically, AUTOMATICALLY to an external, physical stimulus.'

5 Brooks also makes the point that classroom L2 learners will approach the task in a formal way as a result of their previous experiences of what it means to learn in a classroom. When students have their first taste of FL learning they will have already developed a learning 'set' as a result of their earlier experiences of studying other school subjects. They bring this 'set' to the task of FL learning.

6 Skinner's account of operant conditioning was developed to explain L1 learning. No language-teaching methodologist advocated a 'trial-and-error' approach. Lado specifically dismissed such a possibility. In order to ensure that there were optimal conditions for learning it was necessary to elicit responses. Thus, mainstream audiolingualism conformed more to theories of classical conditioning, although operant conditioning was drawn on as a justification for 'shaping' learners' responses in stages.

7 The term 'problem solving' appears to be used to refer to any learning activity that required intellectual effort (e.g. understanding a grammatical explanation or translating).

8 'Incomplete learning' occurred when the teaching was unsatisfactory in some way. Implicit in the audiolingual method was the belief that as long as the teaching provided optimal conditions, complete learning would take place and errors be avoided.

9 Chomsky also argued that language was separate from other cognitive systems and therefore could not be explained by means of a general theory of human learning such as that developed by Piagetian psychologists. A number of applied linguists have found such a theory attractive, however. Dakin (1973), for example, provides a cognitive account of learning, the main points of which are: (1) learners need real-life experience, (2) learning involves assimilation and accommodation and (3), as a result of (2), learning takes place in stages.

3 Naturalistic Language Acquisition and Classroom Language Learning

Introduction

In the last chapter we saw that one of the factors contributing to the rejection of the audiolingual theory of foreign-language learning was the emergence of a powerful theory that addressed head-on how language is learnt. This theory was derived from a particular view of language, one that emphasized the mentalistic nature of linguistic knowledge and was, therefore, diametrically opposed to the structuralist linguists' view of language as a set of habits. The theory initially addressed how children acquired their mother tongue (L1), generating a number of studies of L1 acquisition. The theory and the empirical research provided a basis which was used by applied linguists to support two different views about the nature of classroom L2 learning. One view held that classroom language learning was essentially the same as L1 acquisition and would proceed most effectively if no attempt was made to interfere with the natural processes of learning. This view of learning was used to justify a set of pedagogical proposals which have become known as the **cognitive anti-method**. The other view drew on Chomsky's distinction between competence and performance. A number of applied linguists argued that as the real goal of classroom language learning was competence, learners should be encouraged to engage in the conscious 'analysis' of linguistic forms. This view led to the **cognitive code method**. This chapter begins with an account of these two views of learning. This leads into a fuller consideration of the L2 = L1 hypothesis, which we touched on briefly in the last chapter.

Towards the end of the sixties interest in the nature of second language (L2) acquisition began to gather steam. This interest manifested itself in three major directions. First, researchers began to examine the errors which L2 learners produced, collecting corpora of learner language, identifying the errors and then seeking to describe and explain them. Second, a number of studies of naturalistic L2 acquisition were undertaken. These were of two kinds: longitudinal case studies of individual learners and cross-sectional studies of large groups of learners. Both the error-analysis and naturalistic studies were motivated initially by the need to determine to what extent L2 learning was different from L1 learning, in particular as a result of transfer and age. Third, theories of L2 acquisition began to appear. This period – from the late sixties up to the end of the seventies – provided a rich source of descriptive information about the nature of L2 learner language and the processes of naturalistic acquisition together with a theoretical framework, which has become known as **interlanguage**. Although much of the research was speculative, incomplete and did not investigate classroom language learning directly, it was used to justify a number of radical proposals about how teaching should proceed.

This chapter also considers Krashen's Monitor Model. This was first described in a series of papers that appeared in the late seventies, subsequently brought together in *Second Language Acquisition and Second Language Learning*, published at the beginning of the eighties. Krashen drew extensively on studies of naturalistic acquisition (both L1 and L2) to advance a theory that has had considerable impact on language teaching. Krashen himself has never been shy to apply his model to the classroom. Together with Terrell (1983) he has proposed a method (the 'Natural Method') which he claims is based on a thoroughly tested set of principles of L2 acquisition. Krashen – more than any other researcher – has been prepared to stick his neck out and commit himself to a highly controversial view of the teaching–learning relationship. Krashen's influential work represents the attractions and the dangers of an approach that rests on the application of non-classroom based research.

Finally, in the conclusion to the chapter, the legitimacy of an approach to classroom L2 learning based on the application of the results of research into naturalistic acquisition is questioned. This is an issue that has been hotly debated with strongly divergent views.

The Applications of L1 Acquisition Research

The impetus for the L1 acquisition research which took place in the sixties and early seventies came from Chomskyan linguistics. This provided a radically different view of language from that of the structuralist school. Whereas the latter saw language in terms of the surface patterns that make up speech and emphasized the differences between languages, Chomsky emphasized the abstract nature of the rules that constitute the individual speaker-hearer's underlying competence and the universal nature of these rules. These differences in the way language was viewed were matched by corresponding differences in how language acquisition was thought to take place. As we saw in the last chapter, behaviourist psychologists maintained that language was learnt as a set of habits in which particular stimuli were associated with particular responses through reinforcement. This position was challenged by a generative theory of language which emphasized the abstract nature of linguistic knowledge. Chomsky has consistently argued the impossibility of a child arriving at the rules of the target language grammar solely on the basis of primary linguistic data. In other words, **competence** could not be achieved simply by attending to **performance** because the available input data were simply insufficient to enable the child to discover the 'hidden' rules.[1] The child's task – as seen by Chomsky – was to devise an appropriate grammar given imperfect primary linguistic data. This was possible only if the child was credited with a **language-acquisition device** consisting of innate knowledge of grammatical principles: 'As a precondition for language learning, he [the child] must possess, first, a linguistic theory that specifies the form of the grammar of a possible human language, and, second, a strategy for selecting a grammar of the appropriate form that is compatible with the primary linguistic data' (Chomsky, 1965:25).

The task of the linguist was to specify the nature of the 'linguistic theory' that enabled the child to learn language. Although the details of the linguistic theory have changed over the years, Chomsky's initial premise has not. The search for an adequate description of the **Universal Grammar** which makes the learning of a particular language possible continues today (cf. Cook, 1988).

Empirical studies of L1 acquisition were instigated as a means of testing Chomsky's claims about language and language learning. One of the important issues was whether the speech produced by children provided evidence of habit-formation or of innate linguistic knowledge. Another important issue was whether there was any evidence of developmental progression in the way children's competence evolved – and, in particular, whether this progression conformed to the specific proposals of generative grammarians such as Chomsky. For example, Chomsky (1957; 1965) distinguished **phrase structure rules** which generated abstract base or deep structures and **transformational rules** which converted these into the surface structures observable in actual speech or writing. Researchers were interested in whether children began the process of acquiring language with a 'simple' grammar composed only of base structures and then added the transformational component later (cf. McNeill, 1970). The sixties and early seventies saw a number of child acquisition projects involving both longitudinal studies (e.g. Brown, 1973; Bloom, 1970) and cross-sectional studies (e.g. Villiers and Villiers, 1973). These provided evidence that children passed through a series of stages *en route* to adult competence.[2] The progression was evident both in the gradual increase in the **mean length of utterance** in children's speech and also in the order of acquisition of grammatical features such as progressive (-ing, plurals), copula ('be', and 3rd person -s). Thus, children's utterances grew increasingly longer as they acquired first one grammatical feature, then another and so on. Evidence was also forthcoming that the child revised grammatical rules as acquisition took place; for example, the past tense of irregular verbs, such as 'went', showed a U-shaped pattern of development, with 'goed' replacing the correct 'went' in an intermediate stage. These findings provided support for

Chomsky's arguments that language acquisition was internally rather than environmentally driven.

Applied linguists responded rapidly both to Chomsky's view of language and to L1 acquisition research. The teaching manuals that now appeared (e.g. Rivers, 1968; Jakobovits, 1970; Chastain, 1971) reflected the rejection of audiolingual theory and argued the case for a teaching approach that gave recognition to the learner and the abstract nature of linguistic competence. There was, however, far less conviction regarding both how an L2 was learnt and how it should be taught. This was understandable, given the feeling that all the old certainties had gone: 'The theoretical foundations of our assumptions about the nature of language and how it is acquired have been badly shaken if not actually destroyed' (Donaldson, 1971:123) and that nothing clear-cut had taken their place. Applied linguists spoke of 'psycholinguistic upheaval', 'uncertainty' and 'current ferment' and they were aware that the new proposals they put forward were tentative. As Wardhaugh (1971:16) put it: 'Perhaps a new method will develop which will achieve the same kind of general approval as the Audiolingual method, but at the moment there is no consensus as to what it would be like.'

The general feeling was that the new linguistics and language acquisition research could not be used to justify confident prescriptions about pedagogic procedures but could only serve to provide 'insights' about the teaching—learning relationship. These insights took the form of the cognitive anti-method and the cognitive code method, both drawing on different aspects of Chomsky's 'cognitivism'. It is probably true to say that the theories of classroom language learning upon which these methods were based lacked the cohesiveness of audiolingual learning theory. The cognitive code method had little impact on classrooms. Cognitive anti-method was also peripheral, although its principal assumptions were incorporated into subsequent theories of classroom language learning derived from L2 acquisition research. At the time definitive new practical directions were lacking (Smith, 1971). It is perhaps for this reason that Richards and Rogers (1986) include neither method in their admirable survey of language-teaching approaches and methods.

The Cognitive Anti-method

The cognitive anti-method was articulated in a series of articles published by Newmark and Reibel in the sixties. Very similar views were also expressed in Corder (1967) and Jakobovits (1970). The theory of classroom learning which supported the method is outlined below.

Assumption 1: Second-language learning is controlled by the learner rather than the teacher This assumption is central to the theory. Newmark and Reibel (1968), for instance, talk disparagingly of 'the excessive preoccupation with the contribution of the teacher' and argue that this has 'distracted the theorists from considering the role of the learner'. Kennedy (1973:76) gives expression to the new belief that it is the learner who is in charge: 'in the final analysis we can never completely control what the learner does, for *he* selects and organises, whatever the input.' The learner is seen as a problem-solver who contributes hugely and actively to the learning process.

Assumption 2: Human beings possess an innate capacity for learning language Chomsky's arguments that children made use of a biologically endowed language-acquisition device for acquiring language were widely accepted. Newmark (1966) saw L1 acquisition as a model of successful learning and argued that L2 learning in the classroom could proceed in much the same way as long as the teacher avoided 'interfering'. Newmark and Reibel (1968) saw the adult as 'a potentially magnificent language learner'. They went on to argue that the foreign language (FL) learner's capability was 'qualitatively' the same as the child's – although, possibly, 'quantitatively' different. In other words, they credited both the child and adult L2 learner with continued access to the child's language-acquisition device. It should be noted, however, that this was contentious; other applied linguists were less sure that adults in particular could learn a L2 in the same way as children acquired their L2.

Assumption 3: It is not necessary to attend to linguistic form in order to acquire a L2 The cognitive anti-method shared one assumption with audio-lingual learning theory – namely that linguistic analysis was not necessary. Newmark (1963: 217) argued: 'Systematic attention to the grammatical form of utterances is neither a necessary condition nor a sufficient one for successful language learning.' Newmark pointed out that L1 acquisition took place very successfully without any analysis and he noted that many classroom learners were unsuccessful despite it. He advised special caution about applying the descriptions from transformational generative grammar to the classroom, arguing instead that there was a need to 'liberate language teaching from grammatical theory'.

Assumption 4: Classroom language learning is not an additive process Perhaps the most radical departure from audiolingual learning theory was Newmark's (1966) claim that classroom language learning, like child L1 acquisition, was not an additive process, i.e. the learner did not acquire linguistic features incrementally but rather learnt 'whole chunks' at a go. Newmark considered the isolation of parts from wholes 'artificial' and recommended the provision of 'natural contexts' where no attempt was made to select and grade the input for the learner.

Assumption 5: Errors are a concomitant of the learning process and are therefore, inevitable Empirical studies of L1 acquisition showed that many of the utterances produced by children were unique. Utterances such as the following could not be found in the input data to which the children were exposed (Brown, 1970):

Mommy sock
Allgone rattle
Sweater chair
Walk street

This finding was important because it provided strong evidence against behaviourist claims that language learning involved imitation of parental speech. Another finding was that the child's unique utterances were highly systematic, reflecting the existence of underlying rules. This led researchers such as McNeill (1966) to propose that the child derived utterances from an internally consistent grammar which was constructed in the process of acquisition. When the child produced deviant utterances − such as those above − she was testing out hypotheses about the rule system of the language. In McNeill's (1966:2) terms the child was trying 'to discover how a more or less fixed concept of a sentence is expressed in the language to which he has, by accident, been exposed'.

This view of L1 acquisition led to a re-evaluation of the role of error in L2 learning in what was, perhaps, the most significant advance in thinking about classroom language learning. Jakobovits (1970) argued that learners should not be forced to produce well-formed sentences. He pointed out that the production of deviant sentences in L1 acquisition did not prevent the child from going on to produce well-formed sentences later. Corder (1967) suggested that it was much more important that L2 learners be allowed to discover their own errors rather than be corrected by the teacher.

Assumption 6: L1 interference is the result of ignorance Newmark and Reibel (1968) accepted that L1 interference did take place. However, they did not consider it a significant factor in classroom language learning. They argued that interference was more likely to occur if the learner's attention was drawn to the contrasts between her L1 and the L2 − as was the case in both grammar−translation and audiolingualism. They suggested that the conditions that produced interference should be minimized by reproducing the learning environment of L1 acquisition in the classroom. In short, they viewed the 'problem of interference' as a 'problem of ignorance'; the solution was simply 'more and better training in the foreign language'. This could not be provided by drilling the points of difference but only by 'observation and exercise of particular instances of the language in use'.

These six assumptions constituted a radical alternative to audiolingual learning theory. Whereas the latter emphasized the importance of controlling the course of L2 development by manipulating the linguistic environment, the cognitive anti-method rested on the belief that the innate language-learning capability of the student was sufficient. This would work best if the conditions of learning found in L1 acquisition were reproduced in the classroom. Newmark and Reibel's proposals were before their time but, as we shall see, they bear a striking resemblance to those advanced a decade later by Stephen Krashen.

The Cognitive Code Method

The cognitive code method was far less radical. Carroll (1966:102) describes it as 'a modified, up-to-date grammar translation theory'. It was for this reason, perhaps, that it was taken more seriously than the cognitive anti-method by the teaching profession. As we saw earlier, it motivated a major comparative method study (Smith, 1970) designed to establish whether it led to more successful language learning than audiolingualism. The method is described most fully in the work of Chastain (1971).

The principal assumption of cognitive code learning theory was that perception and awareness of second language rules preceded the use of these rules. It was in this respect that it differed most strongly from audiolingualism. Audiolingual learning theory discounted the contribution of metalingual knowledge, except as 'summaries' of acquired behaviour; cognitive code learning theory saw conscious grammatical knowledge as essential to the learning process. This assumption derived in part from the competence/performance distinction. Donaldson (1971:123) commented: 'We have discovered rather late that we have been teaching *speech* and not *language*.'

Thus competence (i.e. 'language') was equated with explicit knowledge of grammatical rules, while performance ('speech') was equated with practising their use. The learners' first task was to lay the foundations of their linguistic knowledge; only when this had been achieved could they 'perform'. Thus according to theorists such as Chastain (1971) learning proceeded from competence to performance. He argued that the presentation of grammatical rules should precede the provision of opportunities for practice. Whereas audiolingual learning theory emphasized inductive learning, the cognitive code learning theory placed considerable store on deductive learning, at least as a basis for practice.

Although applied linguists lent their support to the explicit teaching of grammar, they were careful to emphasize that they were not advocating a return to the bad old days of the grammar—translation method. They argued that learners needed to understand what they were learning and that they ought to be allowed to make use of their cognitive skills to help them achieve comprehension of grammatical structure. 'Rules can obviously provide a short-cut to learning,' argued Prator (1969).

The other major difference from audiolingualism lay in the recognition that language learners needed opportunities to use the language innovatively and creatively. One of the principal objections to the audiolingual learning theory was that language use was innovative and stimulus-free. As Chomsky

(1966:153) stated: 'Ordinary linguistic behavior characteristically involves innovation, formation of new sentences and new patterns in accordance with rules of great abstractness and intricacy.' Language learning, therefore, could not be accounted for in terms of the memorization of a fixed set of patterns. 'The use of language resembles more writing a play than performing one,' McNeill (1965) claimed.

The rejection of stimulus−response association as the basis of language learning led to a reconsideration of the role of practice. Jakobovits (1968) and Chastain (1971) rejected mechanical practice as a means of forming grammatical rules. According to them new grammatical forms were not acquired through imitation and not stamped in through practice. The starting point was 'concept attainment', which resulted from verbalizing grammatical relations. Practice was useful, however, once a grammatical concept had been acquired. Jakobovits recommended transformation exercises on the grounds that these dealt with deep structure and, except for pronunciation, rejected pattern drills which only dealt with surface structure. Chastain emphasized the importance of providing opportunities for the learner to create language in 'language-demanding situations'. These opportunities needed to be 'linguistically unique'.

These, then, were the principal views of learning upon which the cognitive code method was based. The emphasis on rule perception and conscious analysis set cognitive code learning theory off against both audiolingual learning theory and the position adopted by Newmark and Reibel. The recognition that learners needed an opportunity to use the L2 meaningfully was shared with cognitive anti-method but contrasted with audiolingualism. In many respects cognitive code learning theory was a half-way house between the received opinion of audiolingualism and the radical proposals of the cognitive anti-method.

Cognitive code learning theory was problematic in a number of respects. Applied linguists such as Chastain were too ready to extend terms like 'competence' and 'performance' beyond the theoretical boundaries in which they were formulated. Equating an understanding of grammatical rules with competence and speaking with performance was a distortion of Chomsky's position. In fact, Chomsky made it clear that both understanding and speaking were aspects of performance since the same non-linguistic variables (memory span, attention etc.) affected both. Also, competence for Chomsky was not explicit knowledge but rather the abstract knowledge that underlies the speaker-hearer's use of language. It makes no sense, therefore, to talk of competence (= explicit knowledge) preceding performance (= language use). Nor, in fact, does it make much sense to insist that language instruction should be concerned primarily with competence, as learners clearly need to be able to perform successfully in a L2.

Another problem concerned the sequencing and grading of linguistic items. In audiolingualism there were clear criteria for determining the order of presentation (e.g. difficulty). Cognitive code learning theory continued to view L2 learning as an incremental process but offered no rationale for deciding in which order items should be dealt with. One proposal was that the teaching syllabus should follow the natural sequence of acquisition observed in L1 acquisition. McNeill (1970) hypothesized that children begin with a 'base', not dissimilar from the base proposed in early models of generative grammar, and then go on to acquire various 'transformations'.

This led Chastain (1971:91) to suggest that L2 learners might do the same: 'One would suspect that, since first-language learners first produce base structure, second-language learners should also begin with base structure.' However, he was not certain that a L2 should be learnt in the same manner as the L1, admitting that the best way of establishing the relationship between base structure and surface structure was still unclear. Jakobovits (1970:23) put forward the proposition that the learner should be exposed to utterances which are 'grammatically progressive at each stage but which fall short of having the complexity of well-formed sentences'. In other words, an attempt should be made to follow the L1 learner's developmental route by teaching appropriate learner-rules at each stage. McNeill (1965) also felt that it might be worth while teaching adult L2 learners child grammar so that they first learn base structure. Jakobovits, however, recognized that this kind of proposal was likely to be resisted by most teachers. He acknowledged that not enough was yet known about whether such finely tuned input facilitated acquisition or not. These various suggestions testify to the uncertainties about what to teach and when to teach it, which were so evident in accounts of the cognitive code method.

The cognitive code-learning theory represents an uneasy attempt to incorporate the new ideas provided by generative linguists and L1 acquisition researchers. It maintained the view that classroom learning could be externally manipulated – 'interfered with', as Newmark and Reibel would have it – by presenting and practising discrete linguistic features. But it did introduce the important idea that there were constraints to do with the nature of language learning which had to be taken into account if instruction directed at specific items was to work.

Neither the cognitive anti-method nor the cognitive code method made much of an impact on language teachers. The former was probably too radical and the latter insufficiently distinct from audiolingualism. The methods are of historical interest because they reveal the initial attempts of applied linguists to attend to the way language is acquired when they formulated pedagogic proposals. They reflect the attempt to obtain insights from an understanding of how L1 acquisition took place. Newmark and Reibel accepted the equation of L1 and L2 acquisition with confidence. Jakobovits (1968:275), however, voiced the kind of doubt that most applied linguists felt at the time when he said that 'the fastest method of acquiring a second language need not be one that replicates the conditions existing under "natural" language acquisition.'

It is now time to consider in more detail the basis of the L2 = L1 hypothesis.

The L2 = L1 Hypothesis

Applied linguists of this period found themselves in something of a quandary. On the one hand they wished to use the evidence of L1 learning to support arguments for a more cognitive approach to language teaching. On the other hand, they recognized the obvious differences that existed between L1 and classroom L2 learning. Most applied linguists rejected the 'natural approach' advocated by Newmark and Reibel. They wished to maintain their advocacy of a 'structured content' (Prator, 1969) for L2 learning (i.e. selection and grading).

The arguments in favour of the non-equivalence of L2 and L1 learning seemed overwhelming. They were frequently rehearsed in a number of publications (e.g. Prator, 1969; Cook, 1969; Kennedy, 1973). They are summarized in table 3.1. It should be noted that the differences all related to the **conditions** of learning or to the **learner** and concerned the physical, cognitive and affective domains of learning. However, there was no consideration of whether the **process of learning** in the linguistic domain was the same in both types, despite the fact that this was really the central issue.

It became common to distinguish **acquisition** and **learning** (cf. Corder, 1973; Wilkins, 1974). These terms were defined with specific reference to the conditions of learning:

> The term *acquisition* is used here for the process where language is acquired as a result of natural and largely random exposure to language, the term *language learning* where the exposure is structured through language teaching. (Wilkins, 1974:26)

The basis of this definition contrasts with that of Krashen's (1981) later definition. Krashen emphasized the differences in the way linguistic knowledge is internalized and stored, i.e. process differences.[3]

There were two responses to the differences in learning conditions. Some applied linguists assumed that they were inevitable. Prator (1969:143) commented: 'There is actually no way whereby the circumstances under which a child learned his mother tongue can ever be reduplicated for learning a second language.'

Others, however, felt that L2 conditions were not immutable and that much more could be done to make the classroom environment resemble that of L1 learning. Kennedy (1973), for instance, suggested that a structured content could result in an artificial learning context which was counterproductive. Both Cook (1969) and Kennedy felt that avoidance of errors might inhibit hypothesis testing and communication. Thus, although the presence of differences in the conditions of learning were widely acknowledged, their inevitability was also beginning to be challenged.

Table 3.1   Differences between L1 and classroom L2 learning

Aspect		*Points of difference*	*Comments*
A. Conditions	1	Amount of time	L1 learner has much more time at disposal; classroom L2 learner has very restricted time.
	2	Structured content	L1 learner is exposed to naturally occurring language; L2 learner is presented with carefully selected and graded input.
	3	Avoidance of errors	In L1 learning errors permitted and, if they do occur, they are usually not corrected; in classroom L2 learning errors are avoided and corrected.
B. Learner	1	Age	L1 learner has innate capacity for learning language; 'critical period' for this capacity may have passed for L2 learner, who is also cognitively more mature.
	2	Motivation	Child has strong motivation to learn L1 because of importance of communication for satisfying basic needs; L2 learner's motivation is necessarily weaker.
	3	Linguistic knowledge	L1 learner has no previous knowledge of language; L2 learner approaches task already knowing a language and potentially transfers this knowledge.
	4	Cultural knowledge	The L1 learner acquired cultural norms in the process of acquiring language; the L2 learner has already acquired a set of cultural values and may experience anomie as a result of learning L2.

Source: based on Prator (1969); Cook (1969); Kennedy (1973)

Applied linguists of this period were clearly reluctant to claim that the child's language-acquisition device was still available to the adult learner. Even those who leaned in this direction did so uncertainly. Cook (1969:109), for example, concluded with the warning that the soundness of the analogy between L1 and L2 learning still had to be proved. There were two main reasons for this hesitancy; L1 transfer and age.

Applied linguists were doubtful whether L1 and L2 learning involved similar processes because they remained convinced that language transfer was a major factor in L2 learning. Prator (1969:151) believed that linguistic interference was 'so obvious that it hardly seems necessary to consider it further'. Other commentators such as Chastain (1971) continued to recognize the role of the learner's L1 but saw it in a more positive light, arguing that learning could be facilitated by concentrating on areas of structural similarity between mother tongue and target language. Jakobovits (1970) thought that transfer might be more a feature of performance than competence and also speculated that different performance factors (understanding, speaking, reading, writing) were affected to different extents. But it was not clear how transfer could be reconciled with the idea of an innate capacity for learning languages. Only in recent years has the idea of language transfer been satisfactorily incorporated into a nativist model of L2 learning (cf. Kellerman, 1984). For example, it has been suggested that the learner resorts to her L1 in cases of indeterminancy, i.e. where the language-acquisition device fails to specify narrowly the syntactic rule of the L2 (Zobl, 1983).

The other major impediment to grasping the innate capacity nettle was age. There were both folk beliefs and scientific arguments to support the idea that the language-learning device atrophied with age. It was a well-known fact that children picked up their L1 effortlessly, whereas adults had to struggle ineffectively with a new language. Neurophysiological evidence seemed to support such a belief. Penfield and Roberts (1959) advanced the *critical period hypothesis* according to which the ability to learn a language naturally and effortlessly was linked to cerebral plasticity, which terminated around the age of ten years when puberty set in.[4] This occurred as a result of lateralization of the language function in the left hemisphere of the brain. Lenneberg (1967) provided clinical evidence to support the hypothesis. For example, children who underwent surgery on the left hemisphere recovered total language control, whereas adults did not.

The critical period hypothesis continues to be hotly debated today. Seliger (1978) has put forward the view that there might be different critical periods for different aspects of language. Long (1988c) suggests that the critical period for acquiring a native-speaker pronunciation is around six years, while puberty is the key age for the acquisition of L2 grammar. In general, it is accepted that whereas children are able to access their language-acquisition device in L2 learning, adults make use of strategies of learning of the kind employed in general problem-solving. Bley-Vroman (1988), for example, disputes the L2 = L1 hypothesis on the grounds that adult language learning is more like general skill-learning than L1 acquisition. However, it has also been argued that the adult's use of problem-solving strategies does not preclude the possibility that L2 acquisition proceeds in the same way as L1 acquisition. Other researchers (e.g. White, 1985) maintain that adults have continued access to the language-acquisition device and that the overall process of acquisition is the same in L1 and L2 acquisition, irrespective of age.

In the sixties L1 transfer and the critical period hypothesis provided powerful reasons for believing that the process of L2 acquisition must be different from that of L1 acquisition. However, as we have seen, there were those who began to argue otherwise. Newmark (1966), for instance, put forward the **ignorance hypothesis** to account for L1 interference (see p. 00). Newmark's view was that 'the cure for interference is simply the cure for ignorance:learning'. The ignorance hypothesis was compatible with an innate acquisition device in L2 learning. Macnamara (1973) queried the critical period hypothesis. He pointed out that there was no evidence that a language could not be learnt just as well after puberty as before. Nevertheless, the received opinion was that knowledge of a previous language and age made L2 learning qualitatively different from L1 learning.

The uncertainty of the L2 = L1 hypothesis prevented a quantum leap away from the well-tried assumptions of the audiolingual learning theory. It lay behind the tentativeness and incompleteness of the cognitive code learning theory and the peripheral status of the cognitive anti-method. The uncertainty could only be resolved if a number of questions were answered. What role did the learner's L1 play? Was the child's language-acquisition device available for use in L2 learning? Could the classroom replicate the conditions of L1 learning? These were the questions that motivated the first empirical studies of L2 acquisition.

The Applications of Naturalistic L2 Acquisition Research

It would be incorrect to say that there were no empirical studies of L2 acquisition until the late sixties. McLaughlin (1978a) in a review of early research into child L2 acquisition mentions a number of early studies. But it is true to say that there was a sudden explosion of studies at this time. This was stimulated by the theoretical questioning of behaviourist theories of language learning and the need to obtain answers to the questions listed at the end of the previous section. It was made possible by the methodological techniques developed by L1 acquisition researchers.

The vast majority of the studies examined either pure naturalistic or mixed L2 acquisition. There were very few studies of pure classroom learners. This might seem surprising given that most of the research was frequently motivated by the desire to find out how classroom learning could be facilitated and was carried out by researchers-cum-teachers. There were, however, a number of reasons. The main one was the desire to explore to what extent L2 acquisition was different from L1 acquisition. It made better sense if the comparison was made between learners who experienced similar learning conditions. Another was that much of the research took place in **second** rather than **foreign** language settings (e.g. learners of L2 English in the United States or learners of L2 German in Germany). Also the methodological techniques of L1 acquisition research transferred easily to naturalistic L2 acquisition research.

It was several years before these techniques were applied to classroom language learning. Allwright (1980) lamented that the case-study approach – foremost in early studies of naturalistic acquisition – was spurned in classroom research.[5]

The purpose of this section is not to review the findings of the research. A number of reviews are already available (e.g. McLaughlin, 1978a and 1985; Ellis, 1985a; Long and Larsen-Freeman, forthcoming). Instead, there will be a brief account of the different types of enquiry and an outline of the theory associated with it – interlanguage theory. This will be followed by a discussion of the main conclusions that were reached regarding the applications of the research to the classroom.

Types of Enquiry

There were three distinct types of enquiry: error analysis, performance analysis and form–function analysis. These are described below. Also some of the methodological problems of each technique are considered so that the limitations of the research are clearly understood before the applications are considered.

Error analysis   Error analysis was not new. There had been a number of earlier studies of errors in L2 learner-language (e.g. French, 1949). These, however, consisted of lists of typical errors made by learners from different language backgrounds. Error analysis in the late sixties and seventies was used for different purposes – in particular to investigate the contrastive analysis hypothesis. If it could be shown that many L2 errors were not traceable to the L1 this would provide strong evidence against the audiolingual learning theory. Also, if it could be shown that many of the errors were developmental (i.e. reflected the stage of development of the learner) this would constitute evidence that the process of L2 and L1 acquisition were similar.

The error analysis movement never lost sight of the classroom. Corder (1967) claimed that errors were significant in three different ways and the first of these was of value to the teacher – they indicated how far the learner had progressed towards the final goal. The other two concerned the researcher (errors provided evidence of how language is learned) and the learner (errors were used to test hypotheses). The steps involved in error analysis also reflected the close relationship between this technique and pedagogy. Els et al. (1984) identify the steps as:

1   identification of errors
2   description
3   explanation
4   evaluation
5   prevention/correction

The last two steps make a direct link between analysis and teaching. Evaluation involved considerations of error gravity (James, 1974) and communicative efficiency. It was concerned with the attempt to identify which errors most warrant pedagogic attention. Prevention and correction were explicitly pedagogic.

The results of error-analysis studies were important because they provided empirical support for the some of the theoretically derived claims. The majority of learner errors were **intralingual** (i.e. caused by the structure of the L2 itself) rather than **interlingual** (i.e. the result of L1 transfer). Dulay and Burt (1974a) claimed that only 3 per cent of the errors produced by their subjects could be explained by interference. Studies of errors, such as that carried out by George (1972), showed that the learner herself made a substantial cognitive contribution to the learning process — just like the child in L1 acquisition.

However, the technique was open to a number of criticisms. Long and Sato (1984) list six. Error analysis ignored what learners were doing correctly. The classification of errors was subjective and unreliable. Analyses were unquantified. Explanations of errors were 'impressionistic and vague'. The samples they were based on were often biased so that valid generalizations were not possible. No account was made of the learner's avoidance of certain structures (Schachter, 1974). Some of these criticisms could be overcome by improving the methodology but others could not; they indicated the need for an alternative technique.

Performance analysis   Performance analysis started a little later than error analysis and came to dominate L2 acquisition research in North America in the seventies. Performance analysis differed from error analysis in that it aimed to provide a description of the L2 learner's language development and, therefore, looked not just at deviant but also at well-formed utterances. As such it provided a much more powerful analysis.

The analytical tools were borrowed from L1 acquisition research. Brown (1973) used the concept of an **obligatory occasion** to determine to what extent a child had acquired a specific grammatical feature. An obligatory occasion consisted of any context for the use of a specific grammatical feature which a learner incidentally created in the course of using the language. The procedure consisted of first identifying all such contexts for a functor and then establishing whether the feature was supplied in each one. The percentage of accurate suppliance was then calculated. In order to determine whether the feature was actually acquired it was necessary to decide on a **criterion level of suppliance**. The actual level chosen varied from researcher to researcher, but approximated to 90 per cent. Thus a functor was considered 'acquired' if it was supplied in 90 per cent or more of the contexts requiring it.

Performance analysis was used in both cross-sectional and longitudinal L2 studies. In the case of the former, the accuracy order of a number of different grammatical features was calculated and this order was then equated with the order of learning. Thus, there was an a priori assumption that the accuracy order corresponded to the acquisition order. The seventies saw a number of cross-sectional studies that followed this procedure. These became known as the **morpheme studies**. They investigated a common set of English grammatical morphemes. The results were used to claim that there was a more or less invariant order of acquisition which was independent of L1 background and age (see figure 3.1). Although this order was slightly different from that found for the same morphemes in L1 acquisition research, it provided evidence against the contrastive analysis hypothesis and in favour of the existence of universal cognitive mechanisms which enabled learners to discover the structure of a particular language. This view of L2 acquisition became known as **creative construction** (Dulay and Burt, 1975). However, the evidence provided by the morpheme studies needs to be treated circumspectly as the methodological procedure was seriously flawed. Also, despite some of the claims made for the consistency of the findings, a number of studies produced different accuracy orders (e.g. Hakuta, 1976). Lightbown (1984:248) comments at the

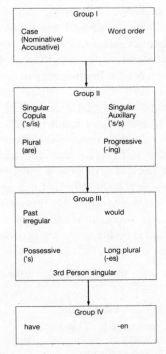

Figure 3.1 L2 acquisition hierarchy for thirteen English grammatical morphemes
   Note: The hierarchy consists of groups of morphemes representing different
          overall levels of accuracy and, therefore, of acquisition. The
          morphemes were grouped in this way in recognition of the fact that the
          difference in accuracy between some morphemes was too small to
          claim that they were acquired at different times.
   Source: Based on Dulay and Burt (1975)

end of a review of performance-analysis studies which provided evidence of an invariant order of accuracy/acquisition:

> This research has been very persuasive, but it can be shown to be limited in generalizability. For every one of the examples given above, there are other studies which provide counter-evidence, usually related to the influence of the first language on SLA, but also to variation in input or even in the degree of social integration.

In other words, the so-called 'natural' order of acquisition of L2 English morphemes was not as fixed and definite as some researchers claimed.

Performance analysis was also used in longitudinal studies of individual L2 learners. Some of these studies also examined grammatical morphemes (e.g. Rosansky, 1976), but others looked at syntactical sub-systems such as English negatives and interrogatives (e.g. Cazden et al. 1975; Wode, 1976). The results of these latter studies indicated that learners passed through a series of overlapping stages *en route* to the full target language system (see table 3.2). Minor variations in the sequence of development did occur as a result of the learners' L1 background, but in general the route they followed was very much the same. In the late seventies and eighties work on the L2 acquisition of German word order in naturalistic learners (Meisel, Clahsen and Pienemann, 1981) provided strong evidence for the presence of highly regular acquisitional sequences. These longitudinal studies constitute the strongest evidence to date in support of a nativist theory of L2 acquisition.

Performance analysis research was a major breakthrough in the study of L2 learning. It gave us − for the first time − evidence of what happened when learners set about acquiring an L2. The case-study data, in particular, enabled us to see the process at work. There were a number of problems identified with this technique, however (Hatch, 1983a; Long and Sato, 1984). Some of the main ones will be mentioned here. Obligatory context analysis ignored occasions when the learner overgeneralized. It was possible that a learner could supply a feature like verb-ing on every occasion that called for it and

Table 3.2 Summary of stages of acquisition for auxiliary verbs in L2 English

Stage	Description
1	Verbless utterances (e.g. 'This kite')
2	Base form of verb with no auxiliary; some learners use 'dummy' verbs such as 'get', and 'wanna'.
	Almost concurrently V-ing appears without 'be'.
3	'be' auxiliary appears − first as 'is' and later as ''m' and ''re'.
4	'do' auxiliary appears in negative form only ('don't').
	Modal verbs begin to appear but order varies from learner to learner.
5	'do' auxiliary is acquired in its various forms and functions.
6	'have' auxiliary is acquired late − rarely seen in first 2 years.

Source: Based on Hatch (1974)

thus be credited with having acquired it. However, the same learner might also use verb-ing in contexts that did not require it. To say that this learner had 'acquired' verb-ing would clearly be misleading. A feature is not fully acquired until the learner has mastered the particular grammatical functions that it serves. Performance analysis is also based on the assumption that the 'rules' which a learner internalizes correspond to the 'rules' of a fully competent native speaker. This need not be the case, however; the learner may construct highly idiosyncractic systems consisting of unique rules not found in the native speaker's competence. Bley-Vroman (1983) talks of the **comparative fallacy**; he argues that instead of measuring L2 acquisition using the yardstick of the target language, we need to illuminate the inner logic of learner grammars by examining them in their own right.

Form—function analysis More recently form—function analyses of L2 learner language have been undertaken in order to overcome the kinds of problems in performance analysis referred to above. The basis of this approach is the study of the different functions which a specific form performs at different stages of development.

Researchers have often commented on the high degree of variability evident in learner language. Cancino et al., for example, (1978) talk about 'the constant development and concomitant variation' in their subjects' speech. They found that their subjects alternated in the use of different negative forms (no + V, don't + V, aux.—neg. and analysed don't) with two or more of these forms apparent in their speech at any one time. Wagner-Gough (1975) studied the L2 acquisition of Homer, a six-year-old Iranian boy. She found variation in his form—function mapping of V-ing. In addition to marking progressive aspect, V-ing was used to refer to immediate intention, distant future, past time and process-state. Homer also used simple V to perform the same range of functions. In other words, V-ing and V were used in apparent free variation.

Variability is, in part, a reflection of inconsistent form—function mappings. The learner frequently uses two or more forms to perform the same set of functions. The learner needs to discover the functional restrictions that apply to each form and only when this has been achieved can acquisition of the forms be said to have taken place. The study of form—function relationships, therefore, has been seen as methodologically necessary by a number of researchers (e.g. Huebner, 1979; Ellis, 1985d).

It is important to study these relationships for another reason. The studies by Cancino et al. and Wagner-Gough suggested that the variation is often random. However, a careful form—function analysis can often reveal hidden systematicity. An example will make this clearer. Let us imagine that a learner produces the following negative utterances:

No play football today.
Me no see Mariana.
Don't look my card.
Don't talk to that one.

The first two utterances make use of the 'no + V' pattern, while the second two make use of 'don't + V'. An obligatory occasion analysis of these data would show a 50 per cent level of accuracy for negatives. However, a closer look reveals that 'no + V' is used in statements, while 'don't + V' is used in commands. The two negative forms are being used systematically to perform different functions.

Form–function analyses, then, help to show the inner logic of the learner's mental grammar. Studies by Huebner (1979; 1983) and Schachter (1986) have revealed the hidden system of learners' grammars, once a form–function analysis is applied. For example, Huebner shows how an uninstructed Hmong-speaking adult uses an article system at different stages of development of L2 English. Initially, the learner used 'da' to mark nouns as specific and known to the hearer. Nouns that constituted the topic of an utterance were not marked, however. Next, the learner used 'da' more widely with all nouns, while later still, he used 'da' in conformity with native-speaker usage. Huebner was able to show how the system was gradually revised so that it accorded with the form–function distribution of English. He refers to form–function analysis as 'the dynamic paradigm' and observes: 'Although an approach which looks at only those morphemes found in Standard English obligatory contexts can tell us *when* morphemes are acquired with respect to one another, it may not be the most insightful approach to the question of *how* they are acquired' (Huebner, 1979:22). Huebner is right. Form–function analyses provide us with windows for viewing the **process** by which learners build their grammars. Arguably, however, a full understanding of interlanguage development requires both the order-of-acquisition approach afforded by performance analysis and Huebner's dynamic paradigm.

The empirical research carried out using these techniques helped to provide answers to important questions. It showed that L1 transfer was not necessarily the dominant factor in L2 acquisition and it also showed that the process by which learners construct their knowledge of a L2 was not substantially affected by age. In other words, the main objections to the L2 = L1 hypothesis discussed above were removed.

Interlanguage Theory

The theory that motivated and fed off the empirical research become known as **interlanguage theory**, after the term coined by Selinker (1972). It is a constantly evolving theory, having changed considerably since its initial formulation. It is, therefore, not any easy task to produce an accurate account of the theory. The aim here is to provide a brief and composite account of the central premises of early interlanguage theory. The reader who wants a more detailed description together with an account of differences in the positions adopted by individual researchers and the way these have evolved is referred to McLaughlin (1987).[6]

The main premises of interlanguage theory are:

(1)   The learner constructs a system of abstract linguistic rules which underlies comprehension and production.

The system of rules is referred to as 'an interlanguage'. The learner draws on these rules in much the same way as the native speaker draws on linguistic competence. The rules enable the learner to produce novel sentences. They are also responsible for the systematicity evident in L2 learner language. An interlanguage is 'a linguistic system ... in its own right' (Adjemian, 1976). As such it is a natural language and is entirely functional.

(2)   The learner's grammar is permeable.

The grammar that the learner builds is incomplete and unstable. It is amenable to penetration by new linguistic forms and rules, which may be derived internally (i.e. by means of transfer from the L1 or overgeneralization of an interlanguage rule) or externally (i.e. through exposure to target language input).

(3)   The learner's competence is transitional.

As a result of the permeability of an interlanguage system learners rapidly revise it. They pass through a number of stages in the process of acquiring the target language. Each stage constitutes 'an interlanguage' − or, in Corder's (1967) terms a 'transitional competence'. The series of stages together comprise the 'interlanguage continuum'. Of course the stages are not discrete but overlap because every part of an interlanguage is subject to constant revision.

Interlanguage can be seen as a **restructuring** or a **recreating continuum** (Corder, 1978b). According to the former the starting point of L2 acquisition is the L1; the learner gradually substitutes target language for mother-tongue rules. According to the latter, the learner starts from some basic simple grammar which is independent of the L1. Most interlanguage theorists see interlanguage as a recreating continuum, although they do not eliminate the possibility of transfer.

(4)   The learner's competence is variable.

At any one stage of development the language produced by learners will display systematic variability. This variability reflects the particular form−function correlations which comprise the rules of the learner's grammar at that stage of development. The learner's competence must be viewed as heterogeneous rather than homogeneous (cf. Tarone, 1983).

This principle is more contentious than the previous ones. There is in fact considerable disagreement about how best to characterize the nature of an interlanguage system. Adjemian (1976) and, more recently, Bialystok and Sharwood-Smith (1985) and Gregg (forthcoming) reject a variable competence account of interlanguage. Nevertheless, this principle is able to account for the insights provided by form−function analyses.

(5) Interlanguage development reflects the operation of cognitive learning strategies.

The process by which interlanguages are constructed has been explained in various ways. One type of explanation identifies a number of cognitive learning processes such as L1 transfer, overgeneralization and simplification (Cancino et al., 1974). According to this view, the L2 learner does not necessarily utilize the same language-acquisition device as the child. The similarity between L1 and L2 acquisition lies in the process of hypothesis-formation and testing. Hypothetical rules, formulated on the basis of learning strategies, are tested out in comprehension and production and amended if understanding is defective or if the utterances produced fail to communicate.

An alternative account credits the L2 learner with a language-acquisition device. According to this view, L2 learning, like L1 learning, involves the learner discovering how the general principles that constitute any learner's innate knowledge of language are realized in the target language (cf. Cook, 1985).

(6) Interlanguage use can also reflect the operation of communication strategies.

When learners are faced with having to communicate messages for which the necessary linguistic resources are not available, they resort to a variety of communication strategies (Tarone et al., 1976). These enable them to compensate for their lack of knowledge. Typical communication strategies are paraphrase, code-switching and appeals-for-assistance.

(7) Interlanguage systems may fossilize.

Selinker used the term **fossilization** to refer to the tendency of many learners to stop developing their interlanguage grammar in the direction of the target language. Instead they reach a plateau beyond which they do not progress. This may be because there is no communicative need for further development. Alternatively it may be because full competence in a L2 is neurolinguistically impossible for most learners (Selinker and Lamendella, 1978). Fossilization is a unique feature of interlanguage systems.

Interlanguage theory provided an explanation for how both children and adults acquired a L2. Together with the empirical research which it supported and was supported by, it led to a number of specific proposals that had a considerable impact on language pedagogy.

The Applications

Most of the applications proposed on the basis of the results of interlanguage studies were not revolutionary. They corresponded quite closely to the kinds of implications drawn from L1 acquisition research found in Newmark and Reibel's proposals. This was not surprising, given that the central premises of interlanguage theory (i.e. that L2 learner language is rule-governed and that learners pass through a series of developmental stages as they test out hypotheses about the target language) paralleled the premises of L1 acquisition theory. However, the proposals based on interlanguage theory had a far profounder effect on language teaching than did those of Newmark and Reibel.

The basis for the application of interlanguage theory was the conviction that it was necessary and possible to conduct teaching in such a way that it corresponded to the way L2 learners learn. Corder (1976) commented: 'Efficient language teaching must work with rather than against natural processes, facilitate and expedite rather then impede learning. Teachers and teaching materials must adapt to the learner rather than vice-versa.' In other words, there was a strong conviction that classroom learning would be more successful if it more closely resembled naturalistic L2 learning. The main proposals related to three aspects of language teaching; (1) remedial procedures, (2) error treatment and (3) the organization of the syllabus. These are discussed in turn below.

Remedial procedures　The use of error analysis as a basis for remedial language teaching was nothing new. Language teachers had for a long time carried out informal error analyses as a means of assessing what their students had learnt and of diagnosing areas of continuing difficulty as a basis for later remedial activity. This generally consisted of re-teaching the problem areas using the same methods and even the same materials as in the initial teaching. As Corder (1974) pointed out, there was no obvious reason why the re-teaching should work when the first teaching had failed. What was missing from this informal approach was any understanding of the nature of the learners' difficulties. Corder argued that it was insufficient simply to describe and classify the errors. It was also essential to identify the psycholinguistic causes of the errors.

The procedure that Corder advocated, however, was not so very different from existing practice. Error analysis was to be used to provide a detailed description of the learner's interlanguage at a particular developmental point. This description could then be compared with a standard description of the target language and the differences identified. Corder claimed: 'It is the account of the precise nature of these differences which gives us the information which enables us to 'correct' the language learner's errors in a systematic fashion in our remedial teaching' (1974:54).

Corder admitted that such a procedure was limited because it provided no indication of the gaps in the learner's **communicative competence**, as error analysis only dealt with the language **code**. There were other major problems, however, which Corder's proposal did not consider. How was the teacher to undertake the re-teaching of problem areas in a way that took account of the psycholinguistic causes of the learners' errors? How was the teacher to take account of the inter-learner variation that would almost certainly be revealed by the error analysis? These were major issues, which the remedial teaching movement never really came to grips with.[7] It became apparent that remedial language teaching would make no headway until the more general problem of how to treat learner errors was dealt with.

Error treatment   Whereas remedial language teaching involves a *post-hoc* attempt at dealing with errors, error treatment − as the term is generally used − refers to attempts to handle errors concurrent with their appearance in learner language.

Traditional treatments of learner error consisted of the immediate correction of any utterance containing a deviant form by the teacher (see chapter 4). Interlanguage researchers argued that it was pointless correcting errors which were the result of the learner's attempts to communicate beyond her existing resources i.e. those errors that were the result of communication strategies. They also argued that errors were inevitable and an integral part of the process of L2 acquisition, reflecting the active way in which the learner tested out hypotheses about the nature of L2 rules. As such they should not just be tolerated, but welcomed in order to encourage learners to take risks.[8]

One view, therefore, was that errors should be ignored. Another, more commonly held view, however, was there should be selective correction of errors. A number of proposals were made regarding which errors ought to be corrected:

(1)   Distinguish mistakes and errors and treat differently.

Corder (1967) distinguished **mistakes**, accidental lapses in performance resulting from inattention from **errors**, deviations from the target language norms that occurred as a result of a lack of knowledge. Learners should be encouraged to correct their own mistakes. The teacher should take responsibility for dealing with errors − through further teaching.

(2)   Correct global, not local errors.

Burt and Kiparsky (1974) distinguished **global** and **local** errors. The former violated rules involving the overall structure of a sentence, while the latter involved mistakes in a particular constituent of a sentence. James (1974) made a similar proposal. He developed the concept of **error gravity** based on the number and the nature of the rules that were transgressed. The graver an error, the more it warranted correction.

(3)   Correct errors that affect the overall comprehensibility of an utterance.

This suggestion was closely related to (2), in so far as the motivation for recommending correction of global and grave errors was the belief that they interfered with communication more seriously. The criterion of 'comprehensibility', however, is broader. Even local and non-grave errors can cause communication breakdown in some contexts.

(4)   Correct stigmatized errors.

Native speakers respond differently to different errors. Certain kinds of errors can be considered stigmatized because they invoke highly negative responses from negative speakers (e.g. double negatives).

(5) Correct errors relating to the learner's next stage of development.

The assumption underlying this proposal was that the learner would be able to respond to such corrections because she was developmentally ready to discover the target language rule. There was, of course, the problem of determining whether a particular learner was ready or not.

In addition to these proposals regarding what errors to correct, there were others relating to when and how to correct (cf. Hendrickson, 1978, for an excellent overview of error treatment).

Researchers who emphasized the variable nature of interlanguage took a special interest in error treatment. Dickerson (1975), for example, applied the results of her study of the systematic variability of the phonological rules acquired by Japanese learners of L2 English by suggesting that teachers needed to recognize that learners' production of specific sounds will vary according to the linguistic context of the sound and also according to the task they are performing. She encouraged teachers to expect variability, as this was the norm, not the exception. Teachers were also advised to abandon the notion that an utterance was 'right' or 'wrong' and to acknowledge that there were degrees of attainment.

Syllabus organization The most radical proposals based on interlanguage theory concerned the organization of the teaching content. The recognition that the learner passed through a series of developmental stages brought into question the traditional principles of selection, grading and sequencing. There seemed little sense in ordering the teaching content according to external criteria of linguistic difficulty if the resulting order did not conform to the built-in syllabus of the learner. A more sensible approach was to design a teaching syllabus that was compatible with the learner's syllabus.

One proposal for achieving this was to sequence the content of the syllabus so that it mirrored the learner's developmental sequence. Nickel (1973) was one of the first to suggest that the syllabus should accommodate the progressive complication evident in interlanguage by teaching the sequence of approximative systems. Bailey et al. (1974) and Valdman (1978) put forward similar ideas. In order to implement this proposal, however, it would be necessary actually to teach erroneous forms, as the early stages of interlanguage involve the construction of simplified rules not found in the target language. Most applied linguists considered this proposal pedagogically unworkable, because it was contrary to both the teacher's and the learner's concept of teaching – learning. Widdowson (1975) – drawing on Labov's studies of stylistic variation – pointed out that it was natural for teachers and learners to refer to norms of correctness in the classroom as this constituted a formal situation.

The second proposal was far more workable and, in fact, has had considerable impact on language pedagogy. It was argued that classroom teaching should be focused exclusively on communication and that no attempt should be made to teach specific parts of the code. The syllabus should attempt to control the level of difficulty of the communicative demands placed on the learner but the learning of grammar was to be left to the learner. Corder (1976:78) commented: 'Instead, then, of grading the linguistic material that we expose the learner to, we should consider grading the communicative demands we make on him, thereby gently leading him to elaborate his approximate system.' This was in agreement with Newmark and Reibel's earlier proposals that language teachers should stop 'interfering' with the process of language learning. As Corder frequently pointed out, the proposal was also compatible with the educational arguments that were being advanced for group work and discovery learning. Teaching based on communication activities in contrast to language exercises seemed especially suited to learner-centred instruction.

Corder was, in fact, recommending a return to a 'natural method' i.e. the use of language in real situations to perform authentic communicative functions. This was justified on other grounds quite apart from interlanguage theory. It reflected the growing conviction among applied linguists that Chomsky's view of language was too narrow and that the real goal of language teaching should be **communicative competence**, not just **linguistic competence**. That is, language teaching needed to ensure that learners could not only use English correctly but also appropriately and that they could perform in a variety of situations requiring different types of discourse. By claiming that a knowledge of grammar grew in response to communicative needs, Corder was simply helping to push the teaching profession where it was going in any case. When provided with opportunities for communication, the learner would not only learn how to communicate but, in the process, would also acquire a knowledge of the linguistic system.

It is difficult to assess the contribution of interlanguage studies to language teaching. Language pedagogy was changing in any case, in response to theories of language that emphasized language use over linguistic form. It is probably true to say, however, that the interlanguage research of this period functioned as a catalyst to the process of change. It also contributed to the construction of a theory of L2 acquisition – the Monitor Model – which was much more cohesive and complete than early interlanguage theory and which was to have a direct and substantial effect on language teaching. We turn now to the contribution of Stephen Krashen.

The Monitor Model

The Monitor Model is undoubtedly the best known theory of L2 acquisition. It has been popularized in a number of articles in various journals – both academic and educational − and in four books (Krashen, 1981; 1982; 1985: Krashen and Terrell, 1984). For a while the theory dominated the field of L2 acquisition to such an extent that researchers felt compelled to measure their results and theoretical positions against those covered by the Monitor Model. This is a testimony to the lucidity, simplicity and explanatory power of Krashen's theory.

Table 3.3 An overview of the Monitor Model

Hypothesis	*Description*
1 Acquisition−learning	Acquisition is the subconscious process by which linguistic competence is developed as a result of using language for real communication. 'Learning' is the conscious process by which metalingual knowledge of a language is developed through study. 'Acquired' and 'learnt' knowledge are stored separately; 'learnt' knowledge cannot be converted into 'acquired' knowledge.
2 Natural order	Grammatical structures are 'acquired' in a predictable order, which is the same for adults and children and for learners with different L1s. It is evident whenever the focus is on communication. However, it is not evident in language activities such as grammar tests when the focus is on form.
3 Monitor	'Learnt' knowledge can be used to edit utterances generated by means of 'acquired' knowledge either before or after they occur in the output. Monitoring can only take place when there is sufficient time, the focus is on form and the rule is known. Monitoring is restricted to relatively simple rules such as regular past tense or 3rd person -s.
4 Input	This explains how 'acquisition' takes place. When learners are exposed to input that contains grammatical features a little beyond their current level, those features are 'acquired'. Krashen emphasizes that 'acquisition' is the result of **comprehensible input** and not production. Input is made comprehensible because of the help provided by the context. Krashen also emphasizes that the input only needs to be roughly and not finely tuned (i.e. there is no need to try deliberately to expose the learners to samples of a specific grammatical feature).
5 Affective Filter	This concerns attitudinal variables that affect 'acquisition'. Learners with optimal attitudes have a low affective filter. This means they try to get more input and are more receptive to the input they get. The affective filter controls the rate and ultimate level of success of 'acquisition'.

No attempt will be made here to provide a thorough account of the model (cf. Ellis, 1985a; Mclaughlin, 1987), the details of which have changed over the years in response to criticisms. A summary of the five hypotheses which constitute the core of the theory is given in table 3.3 for those readers who are not already familiar with the model. In accordance with the main aim of this chapter, the focus will be on the view of classroom language learning and teaching that Krashen derived from the theory and the theoretical objections which the model aroused.

Krashen's View of Classroom Language Learning and Teaching

Krashen has always maintained a keen interest in classroom language learning and teaching. The Monitor Model was constructed with the classroom in mind, even though it was developed to account for the results of studies of naturalistic L2 acquisition in the main. Krashen has expounded the applications of the model to language teaching–learning in considerable detail (cf. in particular Krashen, 1982 and Krashen and Terrell, 1984). His main proposals are:

(1)   The principal goal of language teaching is to supply comprehensible input in order to facilitate 'acquisition'.

Krashen (1982:64) writes that 'the defining characteristic of a good teacher is someone who can make input comprehensible to a non-native speaker, regardless of his or her competence in the target language'.

Optimal input is supplied when the teacher engages the learner in real communication which the learner finds interesting. Krashen draws on research into the role of motherese in facilitating L1 acquisition to describe the characteristics of simplified input that aid comprehension and, through this, 'acquisition'. The application of the input hypothesis to classroom learning and teaching is considered in greater detail in chapter 5.

(2)   Teaching should be seen as a preparation for 'acquisition' in the wider world.

Krashen argues that it is doubtful if the classroom can supply sufficient comprehensible input to ensure successful L2 acquisition. The classroom is more important to the beginner and the FL learner, who often are unable to secure adequate comprehensible input in the outside world. One of the aims of teaching must be to equip the learner to manage real-life conversations. This can be done by teaching 'conversational competence' in the form of a few well-chosen routines, discourse devices for getting the native speakers to explain their meaning, back-channel cues and topic-changing devices.

(3)   The teacher must ensure that learners do not feel anxious or are put on the defensive.

The basis of this proposal is the affective filter hypothesis. The learner has to feel relaxed and confident to ensure that the filter is down so that comprehensible input gets in. Krashen argues that if teachers insist on learner production too soon or if they correct errors in communicative activities, the learner will be inhibited from learning.

(4)   Grammar teaching should be restricted to simple forms and its goal is to enable the learner to monitor.

Grammar teaching of any kind (inductive or deductive) is of limited value because it can only contribute to 'learning' and never to 'acquisition'. Krashen argues that only a limited sub-set of the total rules of a language are 'learnable'. Complex rules such as WH questions or negatives cannot be learnt by most students. Krashen also considers that monitoring has a limited role in language production: 'Not everyone Monitors. Those who do, only Monitor some of the time and use the Monitor for only a sub-part of the grammar ... the effects of self-correction on accuracy is modest' (Krashen, 1982:112). Grammar can also be taught as 'subject matter', but this is not to be confused with the main goal of language teaching.

(5)   Errors should not be corrected when the goal is 'acquisition' but should be corrected when the goal is 'learning'.

Error correction has no role in 'acquisition' which only occurs as a result of the learner processing comprehensible input. However, error correction can help the learner to 'learn' a simple rule. Given that the main goal of teaching is 'acquisition', error correction is generally to be avoided.

The 'Natural Approach' (Krashen and Terrell, 1984) was based on these proposals. Its main principles (1984:58) can be summarized as:

1   The goal is communicative skills.
2   Comprehension precedes production.
3   Production emerges when the learner is ready.
4   Acquisition activities are central.
5   The affective filter needs to be kept low.

Krashen's proposals represent a radical move away from audiolingualism. In many respects they constitute a logical development of the pedagogic ideas first voiced in the theory of L2 learning that supported the cognitive anti-method and then by applied linguists who drew on interlanguage theory. The 'Natural Approach' rejects any attempt to shape the main process of acquisition through the systematic presentation and practice of the linguistic code.

The Monitor Model has been subjected to increasing criticism (McLaughlin, 1978b; Sharwood-Smith, 1981; Gregg, 1984; Barasch and James, forthcoming). One of the chief criticisms is that several of the hypotheses are not falsifiable. In particular, it is not clear how Krashen's claim that 'learnt' knowledge does not contribute to the development of 'acquired' knowledge can be empirically tested. Similarly it is difficult to see how the input hypothesis can be properly tested, given the vagueness of Krashen's idea of 'input containing structures just beyond those in the learner's current grammar' (see chapter 5 for a fuller discussion of this criticism). The Monitor hypothesis has been criticized on the grounds that it is far too restricting; learners are capable of learning and using metalingual knowledge to a far greater extent than Krashen allows for. From the point of view of Krashen's pedagogic proposals these three hypotheses are central. If 'learnt' knowledge is convertible into 'acquired' knowledge, if production is important for development (contrary to Krashen's insistence that only comprehension counts) and if monitoring is widespread, the theoretical foundations of the proposals are destroyed. As we will see in subsequent chapters, there are strong grounds for questioning these hypotheses.

The Monitor Model is inadequate in a number of ways and the pedagogic proposals based on it cannot be fully supported. Nevertheless, Krashen has done the teaching profession a service. He has provided a coherent set of ideas firmly grounded in L2 acquisition research. His work has stimulated not only a discussion of key issues in language pedagogy but, most important, has contributed to the growth of the empirical study of classroom L2 learning itself.

Summary and Conclusion

The aim of this chapter has been to examine a number of views about classroom language learning which were derived from the study of naturalistic language acquisition. A secondary aim was to provide a historical perspective for understanding both why certain beliefs about classroom L2 learning came about and what motivated much of the research into classroom L2 learning discussed in the next section of this book. It was for this reason that attention has been focused on the opinions current in the late sixties and seventies. Naturalistic language learning, of course, has continued to serve as a basis for theorizing about classroom language learning in the eighties and doubtlessly will do so in the future. The main ideas derived from it, however, have not significantly changed.

The chapter began with an account of the theory of L1 acquisition that resulted from Chomsky's views on the nature of language and the empirical studies which this theory stimulated. The cognitive anti-method drew directly on these views in presenting a radical alternative to audiolingualism. It emphasized the centrality of the learner and proposed that classroom language learning would take place most efficiently if the conditions of L1 acquisition were reproduced. There was to be no direct attempt to teach the language code. Cognitive code learning theory also drew on Chomsky's ideas of language but it maintained several of the key assumptions of audiolingualism — namely that the L2 code needed to be explicitly taught and that the classroom should not try to replicate the conditions of natural learning. The theory differed from audiolingualism in that it gave primacy to the deductive learning of linguistic knowledge and to opportunities for meaningful language practice. Neither the cognitive anti-method nor the cognitive code method had much impact on classroom teaching, however. They are of interest because they represent the first attempts to challenge the certainties of audiolingual learning theory and because, in so doing, they addressed two issues of central import-ance: the role of metalingual knowledge and the value of form-focused instruction.

This chapter also reviewed the various kinds of empirical studies into L2 acquisition that were carried out in the sixties and seventies and the inter-language theory with which the research was associated. The research lent support to the view that adult L2 learning was not so very different from child L1 acquisition in that transfer did not appear to be the major factor it was previously assumed to have been and the sequence of acquisition was not affected in any major way by age. It helped to reinforce the view of classroom language learning articulated by the advocates of the cognitive anti-method. Applied linguists drawing on L2 acquisition research emphasized the role of the learner and began to make radical proposals regarding both syllabus design and classroom methodology. In particular, the idea of attempting to control the order in which learners acquired knowledge of the linguistic code was further questioned. Instead it was suggested that learning should be allowed to take place naturally in the course of using the L2 for communication. Naturalistic L2 acquisition was seen as a model of successful learning; the goal of language pedagogy was to reproduce the conditions that made it successful. This led to questioning the value of a linguistic teaching syllabus and also the efficacy of error correction.

Finally, this chapter considered the Monitor Model and its applications to language teaching. Krashen's proposals represented a complete break with audiolingualism. The main goal of teaching was to provide comprehensible input for 'acquisition' – the spontaneous process of picking up linguistic knowledge from attempts at communicating in the L2. There was only a limited role for productive practice of specific linguistic forms; there was no role for explicit grammatical rules where 'acquisition' was concerned and only a very limited role in the case of 'learning'.

This chapter, then, has examined the various proposals about classroom language learning which were derived from the study of naturalistic acquisition. But how valid is this approach? This chapter concludes with a discussion of the legitimacy of such extrapolation.

A number of researchers have expressed misgivings about applying the results of language-acquisition studies to the classroom. Chomsky (1966), himself, was doubtful whether either psychology or linguistics had achieved sufficient understanding to support 'a technology of language teaching'. For Lightbown (1985a:180) the position was no better after several years of empirical research into L2 acquisition: 'Many of the recommendations based on second-language acquisition research have been (a) premature, (b) based on research which was extremely narrow in scope, (c) based on overinterpret-ations of the data, (d) based largely on intuition or (e) all of the above.' She goes on to argue that the research should not be used to prescribe *what* should be taught because the available evidence about acquisitional sequences is incomplete and often contradictory. She agreed, however, that it could inform about *how not* to teach.

Hughes (1983:1−2) is even more pessimistic about the utility of research: 'It must be said at the outset that it is not at all certain that at the present time there are any clear implications for language teaching to be drawn from the study of second language learning.' There is general agreement, however, that language teachers need to keep informed about the insights and understanding provided by the research and that language pedagogy needs to be consistent with the results that have been obtained.

Other researchers − like Krashen − have taken a stronger stance and argued that the study of naturalistic language acquisition provides a sound basis for making recommendations. Corder (1980:1) believes that 'we always have an obligation to attempt to answer practical questions in the light of the best available knowledge', although he too is prepared to offer only 'tentative proposals'. Perhaps the best reason for going ahead with applications is that there never will be a time when there is a generally agreed theory of L2 acquisition based on solid and enduring research. Theory constructions is a never-ending affair. Applying the results of research, then, should take place, although not with the expectancy that a single, incontrovertible account of the teaching−learning relationship will arise.

The research discussed in this chapter has dealt only with naturalistic acquisition. It resulted in 'a more reciprocal relationship between psychology and language pedagogy' (Stern, 1983) − a distinct advance on the relationship evidenced in the audiolingual learning theory where language learning was treated as the same as any other form of learning. However, the situational differences between naturalistic and classroom domains are bound to give rise to doubts about whether the results of research in the former are fully applicable to the study of the latter (doubts which received expression in the cognitive code learning theory). It is true to say, however, that the seeds of classroom research − the subject of the next few chapters − would never have been sown but for the essential preparation of the ground by the naturalistic research and theoretical perspectives discussed in this chapter. These helped to raise questions about the nature of instructed language learning which could only be answered by entering the classroom itself.

NOTES

1   The inability of the input to provide the child with the data needed to arrive at a grammar of the language has become known as the **poverty of the stimulus** argument. Initially Chomsky argued that the input was impoverished on the

grounds that parental speech to children was degenerate (i.e. consisted of sentence fragments etc.). Subsequent research into motherese has shown that it is, in fact, remarkably well formed (Cross, 1977). The poverty of the stimulus argument can still be maintained, however, by claiming that discovery of certain highly abstract rules is not possible without **negative feedback**, which is in fact only rarely supplied by parents.

2 Chomsky himself was dubious about whether the study of child language acquisition was of any great value. He distinguished **development** − the real-time learning of language − and **acquisition** − language learning unaffected by other factors such as memory and processing capacity. Acquisition in this sense is something abstract, not amenable to direct enquiry through the analysis of performance data.

3 In other words, for Wilkins *acquisition* and *learning* were synonomous with *informal* and *formal* language learning contexts. Krashen (cf. Krashen and Seliger, 1976), however, argued that 'acquisition' and 'learning' (defined in process terms) could both occur in both contexts.

4 The age at which cerebral plasticity is lost as a result of lateralization is controversial. Krashen (1973) reviewed the research which has investigated this issue and arrived at the conclusion that cerebral dominance was largely complete by the age of 5 yrs − well before puberty.

5 There are still only a few case studies of classroom learners (e.g. Ellis, 1984a). One of the inhibiting factors is the problem of obtaining adequate data in a classroom setting. Individual tutored learners say very little and what they do say is often not genuinely 'communicative'.

6 McLaughlin (1987) points to two current developments in interlanguage theory. One involves the comparison of the process of L2 acquisition with that of the creolization of pidgins and emphasizes the universality of strategies of simplification and complexification. The other follows developments in Universal Grammar in arguing that the learner's L2 knowledge derives from the process of setting the parameters of abstract linguistic principles.

7 In fact, remedial teaching has fallen out of fashion. Current attempts at applying L2 acquisition theories make no mention of it.

8 It was often pointed out that the term 'error' was misapplied, as the learners' utterances were 'grammatical' with reference to their own transitional competences.

4 Classroom Process Research

Introduction: A Historical Perspective

Classroom process research is concerned with the careful description of the interpersonal events which take place in the classroom as a means of developing understanding about how instruction and learning take place. As Van Lier (1988:71) puts it: 'Second-language classroom research, in studying the processes and circumstances of second-language development, aims to identify the phenomena that promote or hamper learning in the classroom.'

The principal method of studying L2 classroom activity is observation, defined by Allwright (1988a:xvi) as 'a procedure for keeping a record of classroom events in such a way that it can later be studied'. Much of the research (particularly the early research) reported in this chapter has not been theory-led; rather it has been exploratory and illuminative in nature. However, as Van Lier points out, observation cannot take place unless prior decisions have been taken about what to look for. There is no such thing as atheoretical research.

Classroom process research owes much to observational research in education and the social sciences. Researchers interested in the L2 classroom drew heavily on the instruments and techniques developed by educationalists and sociologists. The rejection of 'method' in favour of the detailed study of actual classroom behaviour had taken place in general educational research some time before it did in L2 classroom research. Grittner (1968, cited in Allwright, 1988a), for instance, pointed out that large-scale studies of the kind carried out by Scherer and Wertheimer (1964) and Smith (1967) had lost favour in educational circles. He summarizes their failure in this way: 'In short, a half century of such 'research' has told us almost 'nothing' about the relative superiority of one educational strategy or system over another.' Thus, as Allwright (1983) has noted, the study of language teaching–learning has tended to lag behind general educational research.

Developments in educational research involved a switch from a faith in measurement to a faith in observation. This was motivated initially by a desire to identify the characteristics of different teaching styles (often with a view to prescribing those behaviours that constituted the 'best' style) and, increasingly, by the recognition that very little was known about what actually happened inside a classroom. As Stubbs (1976:69) put it: 'There was an enormous psychological literature on 'learning theory' based largely on experimental situations, but very little is known about what and how children learn in schools. The only way to discover this is to observe children in classrooms.'

Initially, observational research was carried out by means of **interaction analysis**. Numerous observational instruments were designed for coding what teachers and pupils said and did in the classroom. Simon and Boyer (1967) refer to over seventy such coding schemes. Increasingly, this method was abandoned as a research tool (but not as a resource in teacher training) in favour of anthropological or ethnographic research (e.g. Mehan, 1974). The emphasis here was on detailed fieldwork of the kind that anthropologists undertook in documenting and understanding the beliefs and behaviours of remote tribes. In another branch of classroom research, educationalists set out to discover the structure of classroom dialogue (e.g. Bellack et al., 1966), describing the various 'moves' that made up teaching 'cycles' and identifying the hierarchical nature of classroom discourse.

Sociologists have also shown an interest in classrooms, focusing on the different types of social organization found there and the ways in which social control and personal relationships are enacted (e.g. Walker and Adelman, 1972). The difference between the norms of social interaction in home and classroom situations have been identified and described and the potential effects this difference has on educational success discussed (Labov, 1969). The complex nature of classroom social settings is emphasized. Much of what takes place can only be understood if the researcher has access to the same 'shared context' as the classroom participants themselves.

Classroom process research reflects all these various types of enquiry. As in educational research, interaction analysis was the first method employed, perhaps because it involved less of a break with measurement. But researchers were quick to take advantage of the new tools provided by anthropologists, discourse analysts and sociologists. The seventies and the eighties saw an increasing array of research techniques directed at describing and understanding the L2 classroom.

Although the techniques employed by L2 classroom researchers owe much to those used in education and social science, the questions which researchers sought to answer were more parochial; they were derived from views about language teaching and learning. Much of the early research focused on investigating specific pedagogic practices. For example, Politzer (1970) used observation to try to establish whether behaviours such as 'direct reference to textbook', 'use of visual aids' and 'student/student interaction' counted as 'good' or 'bad' teaching practices. Teacher trainers developed instruments to help them assess teachers' teaching and also tried to develop instruments that would provide them with a technical language to 'designate the teaching behaviour in second language settings' (Fanselow, 1977). The aim was to facilitate 'technical instruction'. Many of the initial descriptions of the language classroom were made by teacher trainers rather than by researchers and the tools they developed reflected their particular needs.

It would be wrong to suggest that the research in the early seventies was uninformed by views of how L2 learning took place, but it is probably correct to assert that learning took second place to teaching. Allwright (1988a:197) describes the classroom observation that took place during this period as 'a procedure looking for a purpose'. It was not until the late seventies and eighties that researchers began to address more directly issues arising out of work in L2 acquisition. Researchers became less interested in evaluating pedagogic practice than in providing comprehensive and accurate accounts of aspects of classroom behaviour which were deemed significant on the basis of L2 acquisition theory. There were detailed studies of aspects of the teacher's language – for example, the treatment of learner error (e.g. Allwright, 1975) and of teacher-talk (e.g. Henzl, 1973; Gaies, 1977). Studies of the student's language were less common – partly because the teacher was still seen as central and partly because in many classrooms there was not much student-talk to study – but one study often cited is Seliger's (1977) investigation of the role of language practice. In the late seventies and early eighties attention switched to the study of discourse in L2 classrooms, motivated again by work done in L2 acquisition. This suggested that interaction served as the matrix in which grammatical competence was acquired. It should also be noted that L2 acquisition research provided not only the research topics but, increasingly, the actual categories of analysis (Allwright, 1988a:239).

A great variety of classrooms have been investigated – foreign language classrooms, ESL classrooms, immersion classrooms, bilingual classrooms, mainstream classrooms containing limited-proficiency students. The learners in these classrooms have come from widely differing backgrounds and the teachers have been varied in experience. Amongst this diversity it is possible to identify common ground with regard to both the general approach and the classroom language behaviours that have been studied. The approach emphasizes description but not as an end in itself, rather as a means to understanding the factors that contribute to L2 learning in a classroom context.[1]

The rest of the chapter provides a review of a selection of classroom process research. No further attempt to adopt an historical perspective will be made. The chapter begins with a brief account of the principal research procedures used and then examines, in turn, what has been discovered about the teacher's language, the learner's language and classroom discourse.

The Methodology of Classroom Process Research

Long (1980) published a comprehensive review of the different methodological approaches for investigating classroom processes. He distinguishes two broad approaches: interaction analysis and anthropological observation. The former typically leads to quantitative research involving the measurement of the frequencies with which classroom events of various kinds occur. The latter involves relatively unstructured observation of classrooms in the sense that what is observed is not predetermined by the researcher but depends on the observer's developing understanding of what is significant.

Interaction Analysis

Interaction analysis involves the use of some form of schedule consisting of sets of categories for coding classroom behaviours. In a **category system** each event is coded each time it occurs. In a **sign system** each event is recorded only once within a fixed time-span irrespective of how many times it actually occurs. A **rating scale** is used after the period of observation to estimate how frequently a specific type of event occurred.

Initially, the schedules used were those that had been developed for content classrooms. The best known was that of Flanders (1970). This included categories of teacher behaviour (e.g. 'Teacher asks questions' and 'Teacher accepts feelings') and also learner behaviour (e.g. 'Pupil responds'). Shortly afterwards, expanded interaction schedules for use in the language classroom were developed (e.g. Moscowitz, 1970) in order to take account of the special kinds of behaviours found in language instruction. The content of these early interactional systems was not motivated by any strong theory that predicted which behaviours were important for language learning. Instead, it reflected opinion then current about what processes ought to occur. For example, the Marburg form (reported in Freudenstein 1977) included categories such as 'phases of instruction' in which it was assumed that the basic pattern of a lesson would consist of 'warming up', 'presentation', 'learning' and 'using'. Subsequent schedules (e.g. Fanselow, 1977; Allwright, 1980) were more sophisticated. They aimed to provide a much more comprehensive description of classroom interaction and were less tied to a particular view of how teaching should take place. Observation schedules continued to become more complex as they tried to take account of the findings of more theoretical analyses of classroom discourse (e.g. Sinclair and Coulthard, 1975). Such schedules attempted to preserve the discourse structure of a lesson, rather than segmenting it into discrete units (e.g. Riley, 1977).[2]

The increasing complexity of observational schedules was the result of two factors. First, one of the original motivations for observing classroom behaviours was teacher training. The observational categories, therefore, derived from the prevailing views about what should happen in a language lesson and were designed to sensitize teacher trainees to the kinds of behaviours they should incorporate into their own teaching. The other factor that led to an increase in complexity was the use of audio and video recordings of lessons. The early schedules were designed for use in 'real time'. That is, the observers sat in on lessons and coded each event as it occurred. It was essential that the schedules were manageable under such conditions and, therefore, they contained a small number of 'low inference' categories. Later schedules were designed for use with recorded or transcribed data. It became possible to code larger numbers of categories and also to develop much more explicit descriptions of the categories used. Systems that attempted some kind of discourse analysis (e.g. Allwright, 1980; Bowers, 1980) necessitated retrospective interpretation.

Interaction analysis systems are useful in teacher training. Also the task of designing a schedule has itself proved valuable in opening researchers' eyes to the nature of classroom processes. There has been a proliferation of systems, however. Long (1980) lists twenty-two and there have been new ones since. The status of many of the categories is questionable. Long (1980:10) comments: 'The value of analytical systems must ultimately depend on the significance for teaching and learning of the categories they contain.' Each category constitutes an untested claim about teaching — learning. Also the categories tend to focus on the teacher's behaviour and to neglect the learner's. A more serious criticism is voiced by McLaughlin (1985:149), who notes that because the behaviour of the teacher and the learners is treated separately, information is lost about 'the sequential flow of classroom activities' and how participants provide each other with feedback. The product of interaction analysis is disconnected tallies of behaviours without any general picture of how the classroom process is negotiated.

Anthropological Observation

Anthropological observation provides a more qualitative approach to the description of classroom processes. The general aim is to describe every aspect of those experiences considered significant, in as much detail and as openly as possible. Emphasis is placed on building up a holistic picture. The idea is to observe classroom events in the same way as anthropologists observe primitive societies. Anthropological observation typically involves the collection of massive amounts of data which then have to be sifted and reported in a coherent manner.

A number of procedures are to be found (cf. Long, 1980). **Participant ethnography** involves the researcher taking a regular part in the activities under study. This approach is evident in the journal records of classroom learning experiences kept by learners (cf. Bailey, 1983). **Non-participant observation** sets the researcher outside the classroom events being observed. A variety of techniques can be used to obtain data — note-taking, interviewing, administering questionnaires, eliciting personal opinions by means of ratings and rankings and analysing relevant documents (e.g. students' homework and teachers' handouts). This approach has been used by researchers in the United States interested in examining the behaviours of ethnic minority children in mixed classrooms (e.g. Phillips, 1972). **Constitutive ethnography** aims to make explicit the way in which classroom participants succeed in creating and managing the events in which they take part. Mehan (1979) employed repeated viewings of videotaped lessons and also solicited the participants' reactions to the events that took place, in order to examine the way behaviour is organized and how the interactions were accomplished. **Microethnography** focuses on 'particular cultural scenes in key institutional settings' (Erickson and Mohatt, 1982; quoted in Mitchell, 1985). It has a similar aim and employs similar techniques — such as the detailed analysis of audiovisual records of instructional events — to those used in constitutive ethnography, but restricts the object of study to delimited contexts of activity which are recognized as real by the participants (e.g. 'getting ready for a break' or 'setting homework'). Anthropological studies of these kinds generally present their results in a discursive and illustrative manner.

Anthropological research involves more than observation. It also typically includes collection of introspective and retrospective accounts of classroom events. This is motivated by the desire to obtain different perspectives on the same phenomena. Researchers in this tradition recognize that there is no single 'true' interpretation of an event. The teacher's, the learner's and the researcher's views about what took place may all differ. Classroom processes, therefore, can best be understood if the principle of triangulation is adhered to. Anthropological research is distinguished from interaction analysis not only in the manner in which observation is carried out but also by the use of verbal report data (Cohen, 1987).

There are several advantages of anthropological research. Gaies (1983a) lists three: (1) it can account for learners who do not participate actively in class; (2) it can provide insights into the conscious thought processes of participants; and (3) it helps to identify variables which have not been previously acknowledged. However, the anthropological approach also has a number of limitations (Long, 1980). It depends to a great extent on the skills of the researcher, it is time-consuming and it is difficult to generalize the results obtained because we can never be certain what is idiosyncratic and what is common to many classrooms. Ogbu (1981; referred to in McLaughlin, 1985) also criticizes anthropological studies of classroom interaction on the grounds that they ignore the social status of the learners and thus fail to acknowledge that minority children often develop survival strategies which are 'more or less incompatible with the demands of classroom teaching and learning'. Ogbu was concerned with second- rather than foreign-language classrooms, but his general point — that anthropological research neglects superordinate variables — may also hold true for the latter.

A distinction is often drawn in classroom process research between objective research based on observation schedules designed to provide an accurate and reliable record of behaviours and subjective research that emphasizes the interpretative, value-laden nature of all description and seeks to guard against partial accounts by means of painstaking research from a number of different perspectives. Objective research is characterized as hypothesis-testing and subjective research as illuminative (Allwright, 1983). In a field of enquiry as complex as classroom language processes, this distinction becomes blurred. The research to be considered in this chapter — whether based on interaction systems or anthropological techniques — has often been *ad hoc*, unmotivated by a well-defined theory of teaching—learning. It would be more honest, therefore, to treat the information it has supplied as illuminative in nature, irrespective of whether the research purports to be objective or subjective.

The Teacher's Language

The teacher typically dominates classroom interaction. Holmes (1978) provides a lucid account of how this takes place. The role relationship between the teacher and the pupils is asymmetrical. Teachers have a superior status because they are older and because they are presumed to know more about the subject they are teaching. Teachers also have ultimate responsibility for managing classroom interaction — ensuring that it proceeds in an orderly way despite the large number of participants. Because of these factors, teachers talk more than the other participants (around 70 per cent of the time). They also typically control the turn-taking by adopting a role similar to that of a chairperson in a formal meeting. They control the topic of the discourse by means of questions. It is not surprising, therefore, that much of the research into classroom language processes has focused on the teacher's language.

This chapter will consider three aspects of the teacher's language: error treatment, 'input' features and 'interactional' features. The term 'input' is used to refer to the formal adjustments that teachers make to their speech when talking to L2 learners; 'interactional' features consist of the special functional properties of teacher talk (cf. Long, 1981).

Error Treatment

The teacher has a traditional right to provide learners with feedback regarding the correctness or appropriateness of their responses. In the case of the language classroom, the focus of the treatment is likely to be on the formal correctness of the learners' productions. Error treatment in language classrooms is often widespread. It is frequently not only welcomed but demanded by learners (Cathcart and Olsen, 1976).

The study of error treatment requires an operational definition. Researchers need to be able to identify incidences in a lesson. This has proved to be less easy than expected. One problem is that teachers do not correct every error that occurs. It is useful, therefore, to distinguish T-errors and U-errors (Edmondson, 1986). A **T-error** is any discourse act which the teacher treats explicitly or implicitly as erroneous, while a **U-error** is any learner utterance which deviates from target language norms. Researchers usually elect to examine T-errors (e.g. Allwright, 1975; Chaudron, 1977).

The search for an operational definition of error treatment is characteristic of much of the research to date. Long (1977) proposes a distinction between 'feedback' and 'correction'. He suggests that the term 'feedback' be used in the case of teachers' attempts to supply learners with information about the correctness of their productions, while 'correction' should be used to refer to the result of feedback (i.e. its effects on learning). Chaudron distinguishes four types of 'treatment':

1 Treatment that results in the learners 'autonomous ability to correct herself on an item'.
2 Treatment that results in the elicitation of a correct response from the learner.
3 Any reaction by the teacher that clearly transforms, disapprovingly refers to or demands improvement.
4 Positive or negative reinforcement involving expressions of approval or disapproval.

The broadest definition is provided by (3); (4) is very limiting as it restricts the object of enquiry to occasions when the teacher draws explicit attention to a learner error; (1) and (2) are concerned with the relationship between 'feedback' and 'correction'. However, (1) cannot be determined within the context of a single lesson as it involves investigating the effects of error treatment on long-term learning. Most researchers adopt (3) as a basis for research.

More recently, arguments have been put forward for widening the scope of error-treatment studies to cover the whole concept of **repair**. Such an approach, it is claimed, would provide 'a process-centred approach to error' in place of one that concentrates on the discrete products of linguistic failure (Bruton and Samuda, 1980). The study of repair derives from the work of Schegloff, Jefferson and Sacks (1977), who investigated how native speakers are able to sort out potential communication problems. They describe repairs in terms of the production of the trouble source, the initiation of repair and its completion. The trouble source can be located in the teacher or the learner, as can the initiation and completion of repair. Kasper (1985) found that repair in the language-centred phase of a lesson in a Danish gymnasium differed from that in the message-focused stage. In the former, trouble sources in the learners' utterances were identified by the teacher and were either corrected by the teacher or by another learner to whom the teacher delegated the task. In the latter, self-initiated and self-completed repair were preferred by both learners and teachers, although teacher-initiated and completed repair were still strongly represented. Van Lier (1988) points out that other repair (by the teacher) can be of two types, depending on whether it takes place while the trouble-source turn is in progress or in the next-turn position. Other repair that takes place during the learner's turn is a form of 'helping' and may be a special characteristic of the language classroom. It tends to focus on specific linguistic properties involved in the execution of a complex utterance. Other repair that takes place on the completion of a learner turn often involves some form of evaluation of the learner's performance on the part of the teacher.

One way of describing error treatment is by listing the various options available to the teacher (e.g. 'To treat or ignore', 'To treat immediately or delay', 'To transfer treatment or not') and the various features of the error treatment provided (e.g. 'Fact of error indicated', 'Blame indicated', 'Location indicated'). In other words, a kind of observation schedule specially designed for those parts of a lesson in which error treatment occurs is developed. Allwright (1975) − from whom the examples listed above come − and Chaudron (1977) have developed comprehensive taxonomies of this kind.

In another approach, discourse systems to show how corrective discourse is constructed have been developed. The emphasis here is not on isolated acts of treatment but on whole exchanges involving one or more learners and the teacher. Long (1977) provides a model of the decision-making teachers go through in providing feedback. Chaudron (1977) adapts the model of classroom discourse proposed by Sinclair and Coulthard (1975) and incorporates the various options listed by Allwright (1975) in an explicit description of error treatment. Van Lier (1988:205) provides a model of 'repair decisions'. He proposes that teachers respond initially to whether an utterance is 'intelligible', then to whether it is 'acceptable' and finally to whether it is 'correct'. Criteria of correctness often override criteria of acceptability in the classroom context.

A number of characteristics of error treatment have been noted. Holley and King (1975) found that graduate trainee teachers consistently overcorrected. If a student hesitated in producing a response, the teacher immediately jumped in to complete it. A student response that was deemed incorrect was cut off before completion. Holley and King found that it was possible to modify the trainees' treatment through training by encouraging them to delay filling in student pauses and to avoid correcting obviously incorrect answers. Other researchers have found that experienced teachers vary enormously in the extent to which they correct and, also, in their attitudes to error correction (Nystrom, 1983; Chaudron, 1986a). For example, some teachers feel that it is important to correct every linguistic error that occurs, while others feel that linguistic errors should be ignored and only content errors corrected. It has also been shown that native-speaker teachers tend to be more tolerant of error than non-native-speaker teachers (Hughes and Lascaratou, 1982).

Teachers also display inconsistency and lack of clarity in their treatment of error. Long (1977) notes that teachers often give more than one form of feedback simultaneously and that many of their feedback moves go unnoticed by pupils. Teachers use the same overt behaviour for more than one purpose. For example, a teacher repetition can occur after a learner error and serve as a model for imitation or it can function as reinforcement of a correct response. Teachers often fail to indicate where or how an utterance is deviant. Positive feedback is sometimes provided, even when the learner's response is incorrect. Teachers correct an error in one part of a lesson but ignore it in another. They also correct an error produced by one student but fail to correct the same error in another student's speech. McTear (1975) notes that teachers also frequently give up the task of correction. Nystrom (1983) sums it all up when she writes: 'the fact remains that each interactive situation is quite

complex, and teachers typically are unable to sort through the feedback
options available to them and arrive at the most appropriate response.' However,
there is disagreement as to whether this constitutes a desirable or undesirable
state of affairs. Long argues that teachers need to be consistent. Allwright
(1975) suggests that teachers may have a duty to be inconsistent in order to
cater for individual differences amongst their students.

One explanation for the teacher's inconsistency – apart from the complexity of
the task they face – may lie in differences in learner proficiency. Chaudron
(1986a) compared the corrections made by teachers in French immersion
classes in Canada on two different occasions, separated by a six-month
period. He found that the teachers corrected more morphological errors and
fewer discourse errors (e.g. errors involving the use of incomplete phrases or
speaking out of turn) at time two. Another factor accounting for inconsistency
is the nature of the teaching task. Teachers are less likely to correct linguistic
errors in tasks that call for real communication (Kasper, 1985).

There have been very few studies that have examined the effects on
learning. Chaudron (1977) investigated the relationship between different
types of corrective repetition and student uptake (i.e. the extent to which a
student incorporated the treatment into her next utterance). Reduced repetitions
containing emphasis on the key word were most strongly related to uptake.
Expanded repetitions without emphasis were the least successful. However,
students were often unable to produce the correct form after any kind of
treatment. Chaudron (1986a) found only a 39 per cent rate of success in the
three classes he studied.[3]

Even if the rate of success had been much higher, it is not clear that the
ability to uptake the teacher's correction is the same as learning. In order to
demonstrate that error treatment has a real effect, it is necessary to show that
learners are able to produce the correct forms autonomously (i.e. in their
own-initiated utterances) when they were unable to do so before treatment.
From what is known about the way interlanguage develops, error treatment is
unlikely to achieve such an effect. As Long (1977) points out, errors disappear
slowly. It is possible, of course, that error treatment helps to speed up the
process. Ramirez and Stromquist (1979) found a positive correlation between
the correction of grammatical errors and general gains in linguistic proficiency. It
should be noted, however, that this study did not examine the relationship
between the correction of specific errors and the elimination of these errors in
the learners' interlanguages. There is no definitive study showing that error
treatment promotes acquisition.

There are, however, plenty of strong opinions. Krashen (1982) emphasizes
the limitations of error correction. He argues that it puts learners on the
defensive and encourages them to avoid difficult structures and to focus on
form rather than on meaning, all of which are bad for 'acquisition'. He
concludes (1982:119): 'even under the best of conditions, with the most
learning-oriented students, teacher corrections will not produce results that
will live up to the expectations of many instructors.'

Van Lier (1988) also thinks that other-repair (by the teacher) may be less conducive of acquisition than self-repair (by the learner). In particular, learners may find classrooms where self-repair predominates more hospitable and less threatening than ones where teacher-repair is the norm. Edmondson (1985), however, argues that bringing errors to the learner's attention helps learning. He sees error treatment as contributing to the process of consciousness-raising which he deems important for language acquisition. All these arguments derive from theoretical positions rather than from empirical research.

Several researchers have noted that teachers can actually bring error into existence. Stenson (1975) describes how errors can be elicited by the way a teacher frames a question or an explanation of a grammatical rule. For example, the learner utterance:

* In this class there are any students who speak German.

resulted from the teacher saying that 'any' is used in negative constructions, which the learner understood as meaning that 'any' replaces the negative marker. Edmondson (1986) illustrates how teachers actually elicit error in the process of correcting. He observes that 'some teaching methods ... require the occurrence of error as a teaching tactic (1986:118). Thus teachers exert interactional pressure on learners to produce errors!

The research reported above has provided some valuable insights into the nature of error treatment. The general picture that emerges is that error treatment is not a manipulative process – as it was seen to be in audiolingual learning theory. Rather it is a process of negotiation, one of several ways in which the teacher and the learners collaborate in managing interactional tasks in the classroom. This is why treatment is often inconsistent and why error can be created in the very act of trying to correct. It is not clear yet to what extent, if at all, error treatment facilitates learning. Even less clear is which kinds of treatment are effective and which ones are not.

Input Features

The input features in teachers' language which have been studied include amount of talk, rate of speech, vocabulary, syntactic complexity and correctness. These studies have been motivated by a particular view of the language classroom – one that sees instruction in terms of the provision of input for acquisition rather than as attempts to achieve specific linguistic aims. They mirror studies of **motherese** in first language acquisition research.

Delamont (1976; quoted in Holmes, 1978) has noted that 'research reported from all over the world shows a similar pattern: in India, Belgium, Iraq, South America and New Zealand the teacher keeps on talking.' The dominance of the teacher's language is most evident in classrooms which are teacher-centred, where instruction proceeds with the whole class in lockstep. However, even in primary school classrooms, where a more child-centred methodology might be anticipated, the teacher has been shown to take up the main share of the talking time.

Also of interest is the amount of language directed at individual students. This has been examined with reference to mixed classrooms (i.e. classrooms containing both native-speaking children and L2 learners). Schinke-Llano (1983) found that teachers in her study of 5th and 6th Grade content classrooms in the United States interacted twice as much with the native speakers as with the L2 learners. Nearly half of the latter were not addressed directly at all, while this happened to only 14 per cent of the native-speaking children. There was, however, considerable variation among the teachers. Kleifgen (1985) found that kindergarten teachers varied the amount of speech they addressed to individual learners according to the students' needs in performing various tasks. Which learners teachers talk to most is likely to vary enormously according to the teacher's teaching style and the level and composition of the class. For example, Ellis and Rathbone (1987) found that teachers directed practice opportunities at those students who would be continuing their study of L2 German beyond the first year at the expense of those students who did not intend to continue.

Teachers typically reduce their rate of speaking when they are teaching L2 learners. Also they slow down in accordance with the learners' levels of proficiency. Chaudron (1985; 1988) has reviewed a number of studies which have examined this aspect of teacher input in either simulated or real instruction. He notes that 'the absolute values of speech to beginning learners are around 100 w.p.m.' while intermediate and advanced learners receive speech which is 30–40 w.p.m. faster. The importance of this research is that it shows that beginner learners receive speech which may help them to process input.

Adjustments in vocabulary also occur. Henzl (1979) found that when teachers were asked to tell a story in English to beginners, advanced learners and native speakers, they simplified their lexis according to level. With the beginners, lexical items with general meanings were substituted for items with narrow semantic fields (e.g. 'woman' was preferred to 'young gal'). The teachers also avoided colloquial items with beginners and tended to use stylistically neutral language. Both Henzl and Kleifgen (1985) found that the type–token ratio was higher with less proficient learners (i.e. fewer different items were used).

There is also variation in the syntactic complexity of teachers' speech. Chaudron (1985; 1988) again provides an excellent review of the relevant studies. He notes that the findings are contradictory. Whereas some researchers (e.g. Pica and Long, 1986; Wesche and Ready, 1985) found no difference in their chosen measures of syntactic complexity (e.g. tensed and non-tensed forms), other researchers (e.g. Gaies, 1977; Hakansson, 1986) have found quite marked differences. At the moment it is not clear why this contradiction occurs. One reason might be the different syntactic measures used.

In naturalistic conversations between native and non-native speakers, adjustments can result in ungrammatical input under certain circumstances (Long, 1983c). Hakansson (1986) found that the input of teachers of L2 Swedish contained a higher proportion of correct sentences than that found in either formal or informal Swedish addressed to native speakers. The ungrammatical input data consisted mainly of incompleted sentences and was the result of the teachers' attempts to prompt or prod the students into responding. She claims that ungrammatical input in teacher-talk is rare. However, it has been found to occur in communication sequences which are not overtly instructional. Hatch, Shapira and Gough (1978) found that a teacher in a beginners' class in an adult community school in Los Angeles always used standard English in drill practice, but resorted to ungrammatical simplifications in instructions and discussions, as in these examples:

> Is important.
> The writing not important.
> I say bye bye, I no want.

Ellis (1982) also found evidence of similar simplifications in the speech of teachers of a London language unit.

The research outlined above indicates that teachers are generally sensitive to their students' levels of proficiency. Probably teachers are not aware of the precise state of their L2 knowledge, but respond more generally according to their ability to understand. It is also unlikely that teachers have a very exact idea regarding gradations in the linguistic complexity of different structures (cf. Chaudron, 1986b) but rely on a general intuitive feel for what makes input simple or complex. An interesting question is what teachers use as a basis for determining the level of input adjustments to strive for in classes containing learners with mixed ability in the L2. Hakansson (1986) speculates that they may aim at some hypothetical average learner. In this case, the input may not be tuned very accurately to the level of either the less or more advanced learners. It is reasonable to assume that in the one-to-many interactions that occur in teacher-fronted lessons, the input which individual learners receive is not so well adjusted to their level of proficiency as is the case in the one-to-one interactions that are more common in naturalistic L2 acquisition. In homogeneous classes, however, it is reasonable to assume that learners receive input which is similar in complexity to that experienced by naturalistic learners (Pica and Long, 1986), although, as noted above, it is likely to be more grammatical.

Interactional Features

Interactional features of teacher-talk have attracted increasing attention from classroom researchers. We will consider them in greater detail in the next chapter when we will review the research that has derived from Long's claims regarding the role of negotiated input in L2 acquisition. Here we will sketch some of the main characteristics.

The functional nature of teacher-talk is largely a product of the discourse rights that are invested in the teacher. Gremmo, Holec and Riley (1978) list these rights. The teacher has the right to:

1   participate in all exchanges;
2   initiate exchanges;
3   decide on the length of an exchange;
4   close exchanges;
5   include and exclude other participants in exchanges;
6   open all adjacency pairs;
7   be the only possible addressee of any exchange initiated by another participant;
8   decide on the order of other participants' turns;
9   decide on the number of turns to be attributed to each participant.

Such a list is the testimony to the enormous power that the teacher can exert in classroom discourse. Of course, the teacher can elect not to use this power. Much depends on the nature of the role that the teacher chooses to adopt (Corder, 1977). If the teacher chooses to act as 'informant' or 'knower', she places the learner in a totally dependent position. In such a situation the teacher is likely to make full use of her rights. However, if the teacher acts as 'referee' or 'mentor' and the student plays the role of 'actor' or 'apprentice member of society', the learner has greater control over the discourse and, Corder argues, over the conduct of her own learning.

The reality of most classrooms is that the teacher is in control of most of the interactions that take place. This is reflected in the preponderance of teacher acts over student acts. Gremmo, Holec and Riley (1977) find a 2 : 1 ratio. Also teachers typically perform a greater variety of acts and their nature is different. Teachers open and close interactional exchanges, while students are restricted to replying. Teachers elicit and students supply responses. The nature of the acts found in teacher-talk also differs considerably from that found in foreigner-talk (i.e. the language used by native speakers to address non-native speakers in naturalistic contexts). Long and Sato (1983) investigated the language used by six ESL teachers in classes containing beginners and false beginners and compared it to the language used in native speaker/non-native speaker conversations. They found that statements accounted for most of the teacher-talk (54 per cent), followed by questions (35 per cent) and imperatives (11 per cent). In foreigner-talk conversations the percentages were statements (33 per cent), questions (66 per cent) and imperatives (only 1 per cent). In other words, questions were more frequent in foreigner-talk, although this might have been a reflection of the 'interview-style' conversations of which their data consisted.

We can expect considerable variation from teacher to teacher and also from class to class. Politzer, Ramirez and Lewis (1981) looked at classes where standard English was being taught to speakers of Black American Vernacular. They examined the proportion of teacher 'moves' that were eliciting, directing, informing, evaluating, expressing (i.e. social, personalized comments) and replying. Overall, they found that eliciting moves were the most frequent, followed by informing and evaluating moves. Replying moves were very infrequent. This result contradicts, in part, Long and Sato's findings.[4] However, they report that the frequencies of the different functions varied enormously from teacher to teacher and also from lesson to lesson. Quantitative studies of the kind reported above are likely to produce different results depending on a variety of factors.

There can also be variation within a single teacher's practice, according to the nature of the activity engaged in. Mitchell (1988b) found that teachers of elementary French in Scottish secondary schools varied in their use of English (the L1) or French (the L2) in different kinds of classroom-management discourse. The L2 was widely used in organizational instructions (i.e. utterances which dealt with telling the pupils how to group themselves, what materials to get out and what page to turn to etc.). The L2 was also employed in disciplinary interventions. But the L1 was generally preferred in activity instructions (i.e. utterances in which the teacher explained how to perform a pedagogic activity). The teachers in Mitchell's study had a high level of commitment to communicative language teaching and, therefore, were much more likely to try to use the L2 for management purposes than more traditional teachers.[5]

One of the interactional features that is a more or less universal characteristic of teacher-talk is questions. Questions serve as the principal way in which the teacher maintains control over the classroom discourse. They have attracted considerable attention from researchers of both content and language classrooms. Barnes (1969) reports on a study of teachers' questions in secondary school subject classrooms. He found a predominance of factual as opposed to reasoning questions. Also **open questions** (i.e. questions which permit a number of possible answers) were extremely rare, while **closed questions** (i.e. questions designed to have only one acceptable answer) were very common. The teachers used questions as a device for eliciting the information they wanted to transmit. Long and Sato (1983) found that 79 per cent of the questions which requested information from the students were closed (or, as they call them, display questions). This contrasted with the use of questions by native speakers in naturalistic discourse with non-native speakers, where display questions occurred only rarely. Long and Sato concluded:

> This result suggests that, contrary to the recommendations of many writers on SL (second language) teaching methodology, communicative use of the target language makes up only a minor part of typical classroom activities. 'Is the clock on the wall?' and 'Are you a student?' are still the staple diet, at least for beginners. (1983:280)

Such is the prevalence of closed questions that learners can actually become confused when the teacher asks an open question (McTear, 1975) and try to interpret it as if it were a closed question.

Another interactional feature of teachers' classroom speech derives from the attempt to solve the comprehension problems the learners experience. Mitchell (1988b) identifies a number of **communication strategies** which the teachers in her study employed in order to consolidate the learners' comprehension of unfamiliar items. She divides these strategies into those that maintained the L2 medium and those that involved use of the L1. Table 4.1 lists the various strategies employed and provides examples of each.

Teacher-talk in language classrooms is also typically context-embedded, at least with beginners. Kleifgen (1985) reports that the L2 learners in the kindergarten classroom she studied received more context-embedded language than the native-speaking children. Long and Sato (1983) found that six ESL teachers used verbs that were marked for present time significantly more than verbs marked for past time (71 per cent versus 29 per cent). Henzl (1979) found that teachers increased their use of explanatory gestures when talking to low-level learners. It would seem that the 'here-and-now' principle is adhered to fairly strictly in the classroom, even with adult learners. In foreigner-talk studies it has been found that this principle figures strongly in conversations with children but less so with adults (Hatch, 1978b; Scarcella and Higa, 1981).

The extent to which the teacher's language promotes or inhibits acquisition of the L2 remains largely a matter of speculation. Gaies (1977) suggests that teachers' language is characterized by similar 'training strategies' to those found in motherese (e.g. the use of repetitions, prompts, modelling and expansions) and for this reason may help learning. It should be noted, however, that the kind of modified language that characterizes teacher-talk is not necessarily ideal for language learning. Chaudron (1983) argues that some kinds of modification – in input and interaction – can result in either ambiguous oversimplification or redundant over-elaboration. In such cases the learner finds it more rather than less difficult to understand. Learners may also react negatively to simplified teacher language (Lynch, 1988).

Other researchers (notably Long and Sato) see the teacher's language – in particular her use of closed questions – as restrictive. There is a general conviction that teachers talk too much. Politzer, Ramirez and Lewis (1981) suggest that the more successful teachers in their study dominated classroom talk to a lesser extent than the more unsuccessful teachers, but they found no overall relationship between the number of teacher moves and learning outcomes.

However, not all researchers have taken such a bleak view of the teacher's contribution. Mitchell (1988b:166) concludes her study of elementary French teaching by drawing attention to the 'critical importance of the teacher as the central classroom resource'. She writes:

No functional syllabus, 'authentic' materials, or microcomputer program can replace the capacity of the live, fluent speaker to hit upon the follow-up topics of interest to particular individuals, continually adjust his/her speech to an appropriate level of difficulty and solve unpredictable communication difficulties from moment to moment . . . In all this, the teacher and his/her interactive skills are decisive.

Mitchell's comments are salutary in reminding us that teachers' efforts to teach the L2 are not always in vain!

Table 4.1   Teacher communication strategies

Strategy	Description	Example
A. L2-medium strategies:		
Repetition	The teacher (T) simply repeats the problematic item	T: Si vous commencez là et vous continuez tout droit ... Vous comprenez? Non? Ecoutez encore. Alain, si tu commences là et tu continues tout droit ...
Substitution	The teacher substitutes another, roughly equivalent item	T: Alors les Tuileries, c'est un jardin − vous comprenez, un jardin? C'est comme un parc.
Explanation	The teacher explains the meaning of the problematic item.	T: Patiner à roulettes, ça veut dire patiner, pas sur la glace, mais avec ... mais avec des roulettes comme ça. (*gestures*)
Contrast	The teacher contrasts the problematic item with others which in some way belong to a similar set.	T: Tout le monde comprend, les autobus? ... alors, si vous voulez faire un tour de Paris, vous pouvez prendre le métro, vous pouvez prendre l'autobus normal ...
Exemplification	The teacher exemplifies the problematic item.	T: Ecrivez dans votre cahier en anglais les mots que vous allez entendre. Par exemple, vous entendez 'janvier' et vous écrivez dans votre cahier 'January'.
Clue-giving	The teacher suggests an associated concept.	T: Vous comprenez l'Egypte? Vous comprenez les pyramides?
B. L1-based strategies:		
Pupil interpretation	The teacher invites other pupils to supply an L1 equivalent of a problematic item.	T: Alors voilà un chat (pointing to picture) 'Un chat', qu'est-ce que c'est, 'un chat'?
Teacher interpretation	The teacher supplies a translation of the problematic item	T: Choisis! Tu ne comprends pas 'choisis'? Ça veut dire 'to choose'.

Language switching	The teacher speaks bilingually, repeating messages in the L1 that were first said in the L2?	T: Tu vas préparer le test. Prepare ... tu as fait le test? Have you done the test?
Interpretation	In L1-dominant exchanges the quoted problem is the only L2 heard	T: What does 'Parle avec ton partenaire' mean?

Source: Mitchell (1988b)

The Learner's Language

We now turn to the learner's contribution to classroom processes. This varies greatly according to whether the learner is engaging in teacher-directed discourse or in the 'interlanguage talk' that results from small group work. The focus of this review will be on the former.

The restrictions that are placed on the learner's contribution in lockstep lessons as a result of the asymmetrical roles of teacher and students have already been commented on. Thus learners typically talk far less than teachers and perform a much narrower range of language functions. The crucial factor appears to be the extent to which the learner or the teacher controls the discourse. Barnes (1976) describes how a group of junior school children in Britain produced language that was marked by a rich vocabulary, complexity and a range of grammatical structures and long utterances. This occurred when the teacher ceased to control the moment by moment progress of the discussion. Barnes studied native-speaking children, but Cathcart (1986) reached similar conclusions in her study of the different kinds of communicative acts performed by eight Spanish-speaking children in a variety of school settings (recess; seatwork; free play; ESL instruction; playhouse; interview; storytelling). She found that situations in which the learners had control of the talk were characterized by a wide variety of communicative acts and syntactic structures, whereas the situations where the teacher had control seemed to produce single-word utterances, short phrases and formulaic chunks.

Learners learn how to take part in classroom discourse. Their performance in this type of discourse differs significantly from their performance in natural discourse. House (1986) reports an interesting comparison of advanced German learners of L2 English in a role-play situation and in a teacher-led discussion of transcriptions of the role-plays. She found that the learners confined themselves to an 'interactional core' in the discussion, omitting any non-essentials such as Topic Introducers (e.g. 'You know ...'), Grounders (i.e. supportive moves used by a speaker to justify a speech act such as a request) or Expanders (i.e. amplifications of a speech act). Instead they came to the point almost immediately. In contrast, the role-play conversations sounded much more natural because they did contain appropriate 'discourse lubricants'.

House argues that the asymmetry of the classroom discussions, where the teacher functioned as a manager of the talk, led to the learners adopting relatively passive roles.

The most common communicative act performed by the learner is that of replying to a teacher question. Politzer, Ramirez and Lewis (1981) report that 90 per cent of all student moves in their learner data were responses. The answers students give to closed questions are typically short. Brock (1986) found that learners' responses were longer and syntactically more complex when they followed referential (i.e. open) questions than when they followed display questions. The responses of university-level ESL students averaged 10 words in the case of the former and only 4.23 words in the case of the latter. Brock also found that referential questions resulted in responses with more sentential connectives. However, Long et al. (1984) did not find any significant differences in learner responses as a result of question types, although there was a tendency for display questions to elicit more student turns and for referential questions to elicit more and longer utterances. Any question − even an open one − exerts a form of control as it constitutes the first part of a question−answer pair. It is likely that learners' contributions will be more ample and syntactically complex if they have topic control (i.e. are not answering questions), as has been argued above. In other words, responses of any kind are likely to be sparser and leaner than speech acts that initiate discourse.

Although replying to questions is the main communicative act, students do perform other acts even in communication with the teacher. For example, in classrooms where the target language functions not only as a pedagogic norm but also as a means of conducting classroom business, learners have the opportunity to perform a wide variety of speech acts (see table 4.2). Also, when the teacher and a learner are jointly and collaboratively engaged in completing some task, the learner has the opportunity to initiate and greater variety of language results. Ellis (1981) illustrates how classroom learners can be given the same opportunity to talk as children in conversation with their mothers. He analyses a conversation between a group of L2 Asian children and a teacher while they are having a meal together in the classroom. The learners request permission, complain, make requests for goods, accept offers and make comments. Not all classrooms afford such occasions, however. The traditional foreign-language classroom is unlikely to provide opportunities for this kind of learner language.

Another approach to the study of learner language in the classroom is to examine **communication strategies**. These can be defined as attempts by the learner to overcome communication problems by compensating for a lack of linguistic knowledge (cf. Faerch and Kasper, 1980). There have been few studies of communication strategies in a classroom setting. Rosing-Schow and Haastrup (1982; as described by Holmen, 1985a) compared the performance of four advanced Danish learners of English in the classroom and in two-way interaction with a native speaker in a role-play activity. In the classroom, the

Table 4.2   Language functions performed by one L2 learner in speech
addressed to the teacher

Learner utterance	Context	Function
This one or this one?	Pointing at two pages in textbook	Request for information
You milkman.	It is near breaktime, when the teacher usually chooses a S to collect the milk.	Request for information
Me milkman.	As above.	Offer
Me no blue.	S is colouring but does not have a blue pencil.	Request for goods
Sharpening please.	S has taken his pencil to the teacher.	Request for services
Look me do.	Pointing at Christmas card which he has made.	Attracting attention
Me me.	The Ss are playing a game of rounders.	Demanding

Source: Based on Ellis (1980)

learners either resorted to a reduction strategy (i.e. gave up on their original communicative goal) or appealed to the teacher as a 'walking dictionary'. The authors concluded that the content and structure of most language classes do not encourage the use of a wide variety of communication strategies and therefore do not equip the learners for participation in ordinary face-to-face interaction. This conclusion is very similar to one House reached.

Mitchell (1988b), however, did find evidence of the learners' use of communication strategies in elementary French lessons in Scottish secondary schools. Some of the teachers she observed made efforts to equip the learners with the L2 means they needed to indicate that they were having comprehension problems. They taught such phrases as 'Je ne comprends pas' and 'Comment est-ce qu'on dit *x*?' The learners appeared to have mastered a number of such routines and showed a willingness to use them in the classroom. Ellis (1982; 1984a) also reports successful attempts by a teacher to teach ESL learners useful phrases such as 'I don't know'. Again, once they had learnt them, the learners made regular use of them. It would appear, therefore, that in both foreign and second language classrooms opportunities can be made for learners to learn and use the linguistic formulas needed to perform communication strategies. Whether these opportunities actually arise may depend on whether the teacher is committed to using the L2 for communication.

So far we have been considering learner language from the point of view of the learner herself. Gaies (1983b) examines 'learner feedback', which he defines as 'information provided by a learner to a teacher about the comprehensibility and usefulness of some prior teacher utterance(s)'. In other words he looks at learner language from the perspective of the teacher. Gaies argues that even in teacher-dominated lessons the learners negotiate the input they receive by providing feedback. He investigated twelve ESL dyads (teacher—student) and triads (teacher—student—student), collecting data from problem-solving tasks that required the teacher to describe graphic designs. The learners were instructed to provide whatever feedback they considered necessary in order to identify the designs being described. In the analysis Gaies distinguished learner utterances which were elicited by the teacher as opposed to those that were volunteered. The latter he divided into soliciting (i.e. the learners tried to obtain information), reacting (i.e. the learners indicated comprehension or non-comprehension) and structuring (i.e. the learners attempted to reorient or redefine the basis for subsequent interaction). The results revealed considerable variation from learner to learner in the amount of feedback provided. Not all the learners used the full range of feedback moves. Reacting moves were the most frequent and structuring moves the least. In the case of the triads one of the two learners always provided more feedback than the other. Gaies used the study to raise a number of interesting questions to do with the effects of the size of the learning group, the activity, learner characteristics and the teacher's language on the nature of learner feedback.

There are likely to be individual differences in learner language. One source of variation is the ethnic background of the learner. Sato (1981) compared nineteen Asian and twelve non-Asian university-level ESL students. The Asian students initiated fewer turns and were also nominated to speak on fewer occasions than the non-Asians. Irrespective of ethnicity learners vary in the extent to which they are prepared to risk themselves in front of the rest of the class. Diary studies (e.g. Ellis and Rathbone, 1987) show that some learners develop considerable anxiety when called upon to answer a question and avoid speaking if possible.

Holmen (1985b) suggests that learners can be placed on a continuum between very active and very passive. The older learners evidenced greater passivity than the younger learners she studied, a reflection of the different kinds of schools they attended. Schools with teacher-centred classrooms encourage more passive learners. However, Holmen recognizes that personality is also a factor. Some learners 'steal turns' and grab the teacher's attention whenever they can. Other learners contribute frequently because they have more teacher questions directed at them or because they have difficulty in making themselves understood — like Allwright's (1980) Igor.

Underlying much of the research that has been reported above is the assumption that production is an aid to learning. It is also felt that learners need the opportunity to perform a range of speech acts and communication strategies. The classroom is often seen as affording only limited opportunities for the kind of production that facilitates acquisition. It is, however an open question whether production is centrally important in all aspects of L2 acqui-sition. It is possible, for instance, that the development of linguistic competence owes more to comprehension than production (as Krashen argues). Production may be more important for the development of oral fluency and strategic competence. The next chapter takes a closer look at the role of learner participation.

Classroom Discourse

Much is lost by considering the teacher's and the learners' language behaviour separately. Classroom discourse is best seen as a cooperative enterprise. In this section of the chapter, then, we examine classroom discourse as a whole.

The Teacher's Paradox

The discourse that results from attempts to teach the target language is necessarily different from the discourse that occurs naturally outside the classroom. Edmondson (1985:162) refers to 'the teacher's paradox', which states:

> We seek in the classroom to teach people how to talk when they are not being taught.

This paradox results in a tension between discourse that is appropriate to pedagogic goals and discourse that is appropriate to pedagogic settings. On the one hand the teacher can create opportunities for discourse where the learner behaves as a learner, while on the other she can also offer opportunities for the learner to behave in other roles than that of the learner (i.e. by providing tasks that stimulate authentic communication). The classroom affords 'co-existing discourse worlds', depending on whether the participants are engaged in the act of trying to learn or trying to communicate.

This basic point about classroom discourse is reflected in the four types of language use which McTear (1975) observed in EFL lessons with adult Venezuelan students:

1   mechanical (i.e. no exchange of meaning involved);
2   meaningful (i.e. meaning is contextualized but there is still no new information conveyed);
3   pseudo-communication (i.e. new information is conveyed but in a manner that would be unlikely to occur outside the classroom);
4   real communication (e.g. spontaneous speech resulting from the exchange of opinions, jokes, classroom management etc.).

Table 4.3 Continuum of classroom interaction

	Instructional discourse	*Natural discourse*
Roles	Fixed statuses	Negotiated roles
Tasks	Teacher-oriented, position-centred	Group-oriented, person-centred
Knowledge	Focus on content, accuracy of facts	Focus on process, fluency of interaction

Source: Kramsch, (1985)

Pedagogic discourse is produced by (1) and (2), natural discourse by (4), while (3) falls somewhere in between.

It is perhaps wiser to treat pedagogic and natural discourse as two poles of a continuum rather than as alternatives. Kramsch (1985) discusses the factors that induce the discourse to lean one way rather than the other (see table 4.3). Instructional discourse occurs when the teacher and the students act out institutional roles, the tasks are concerned with the transmission and reception of information controlled by the teacher and there is a focus on knowledge as a product and on accuracy. Natural discourse is characterized by much more fluid roles established through interaction, tasks that encourage equal participation in the negotiation of meaning and a focus on the interactional process itself and on fluency.

Breen (1985a; 1985b) suggests how learning and the pedagogic discourse it produces can be reconciled with communication and the natural discourse it produces through metacommunication about the target language and the problems of how to learn it. In other words, the discourse worlds can be brought together through communication about learning.

Turn-taking

One aspect of classroom discourse which has received considerable attention – largely because marked differences from conversational discourse are often evident – is turn-taking. This refers to the systematic rules that govern how the roles of speaker and listener change (Coulthard, 1977). Sacks et al. (1974) identified a number of such rules in American English conversation and these have served as a yardstick for the study of turn-taking in the classroom. One of these rules is that only one speaker speaks at a time. Other rules relate to how speaker-change is negotiated. A speaker can select the next speaker by nominating her or performing the first part of an adjacency pair (e.g. asking a question which requires an answer). Alternatively, the speaker can allow the next speaker to self-select. Turns to speak are highly valued and there is frequently competition to take the next turn. There are also rules governing when a speaker can enter or re-enter the conversation. The general characteristics of conversational turn-taking as described by Sacks et al. are those of self-regulated competition and initiative.

Most researchers highlight the differences between turn-taking in natural and classroom settings (e.g. McHoul, 1978; Sinclair and Brazil, 1982). In classrooms there is a need to maintain centralized attention (usually directed at the teacher), the content of lessons is pre-planned, the actual sequence of utterances may be predetermined and the concern to maintain the 'official' topic inhibits small-talk. These factors can lead to a radically different pattern of turn-taking. Classroom discourse is often organized so that there is a strict allocation of turns to deal with potential transition and distribution problems. Who speaks to whom at what time is strictly controlled. This results in less turn-by-turn negotiation; competition and individual learner initiative are discouraged.

Lörscher (1986) is a good example of a study of turn-taking in the L2 classroom that highlights the differences between conversational and pedagogic discourse. Lörscher examined openings, turn-taking and closings using video-tapes of English lessons involving pupils in the age range of eleven to eighteen in different types of German schools. In the case of openings he found a number of differences between classroom and natural discourse. The former had a simpler structure, they were not negotiated or built up cooperatively, the topic was determined by the teacher and the students never attempted to postpone the topic. The turn-taking rules he identified were also different. In the classroom turns were allocated by the teacher, the right to speak always returned to the teacher when a student turn was completed and the teacher had the right to stop or interrupt a student turn. In the case of closings, there was no negotiation and 'possible pre-closings' − a feature of naturally occurring conversations − were very rare. Lörscher argues that these classroom discourse structures reflect the need for the communication partners to effect successful and economical pedagogical outcomes. They are determined by the nature of the school as a public institution and the teaching−learning process.

One of the possible effects of all this is that learners are robbed of 'an intrinsic motivation for listening' with the result that they do not attend fully to the input and thus L2 acquisition is impeded (Van Lier, 1988).

However, it is easy to overstate the lack of flexibility evident in L2 classroom turn-taking. Van Lier (1988) reports that in his data learners frequently do self-select and that 'schismatic talk' (i.e. talk that deviates from some predetermined plan) also occurs quite often. Teachers, too, perform many undirected utterances, thus allowing learners to self-select. The extent of the difference between turn-taking in conversation and classroom discourse is likely to be influenced by the teacher's perception of her role. If the teacher sees herself as a 'knower', transmitting L2 knowledge to the learners, then turn-taking is likely to be strictly regulated. If, on the other hand, the teacher sees herself as a 'facilitator' of self-directed L2 acquisition, the turn-taking is likely to be negotiated in a manner not dissimilar to that which occurs in ordinary conversation.

The Structure of Pedagogic Discourse

Pedagogic discourse manifests a particular structure. Sinclair and Coulthard (1975) found that the predominant **exchange** structure in teacher-controlled discourse was three-phase, involving a teacher elicitation, a student response and teacher feedback — IRF:

> Teacher: Ask Anan what his name is.
> Student: What's your name?
> Teacher: Good.

As long as the teacher is controlling the discourse, this structure is evident no matter whether the participants are focusing on linguistic form (as in the example above) or on meaning. Mehan (1979) found a similar structure. He distinguishes a 'basic sequence' which occurs when the learner provides the response the teacher wants and an 'extended sequence' which is found when the expected response does not occur. In this case 'teacher—student interaction continues until symmetry between initiation and reply acts is established' (1979:55). The three-phase structure of classroom discourse contrasts with the typical two-phase structure of natural discourse.

A series of exchanges form **transactions** (Sinclair and Coulthard, 1975). A transaction constitutes an episode in the lesson with a unitary purpose. Transactions are less tightly structured than exchanges. It is also possible to identify discourse organization at the level of lesson. Mehan (1979) distinguished three components: (1) an opening phase where the participants 'inform each other that they are, in fact, going to conduct a lesson as opposed to some other activity'; (2) an instructional phase where information is exchanged between teacher and students; and (3) a closing phase where participants are reminded of what went on in the core of the lesson. However, not all language lessons have such a pattern, perhaps because the content is 'language'. Some language lessons seem just to start and stop (i.e. consist entirely of an instructional phase).

Types of Classroom Discourse

A basic distinction has already been drawn between pedagogic and natural discourse — both of which can occur in the language classroom. A number of researchers, however, have attempted to produce more detailed descriptions of the types of interaction which can occur.

Ellis (1984a) describes classroom discourse in terms of two dimensions: (1) the interactive goal and (2) address. Three broad types of interactive goal are distinguished. 'Core goals' are reflected in the explicit pedagogical intentions of the teacher. These can be medium-centred (i.e. concerned with linguistic form), message-centred (i.e. concerned with the exchange of information) or activity-centred (i.e. directed towards the completion of some non-verbal task). 'Framework goals' are the interactional goals associated with the organization of classroom activity. 'Social goals' arise when the participants interact on everyday social matters. 'Address' types are determined with reference to one of four identities which a classroom participant can have (teacher, pupil, class member or group member) and her interactive role (speaker, addressee and hearer). The two dimensions form a matrix which can be used to classify classroom interactions.

Van Lier (1982; 1988) identifies four basic types of classroom interaction according to whether the teacher controls the topic (i.e. what is being talked about) and the activity (i.e. the way the topic is talked about). Type 1 interaction occurs when the teacher controls neither the topic nor the activity. Examples are small-talk with the teacher at the beginning of a lesson and private talk between students. Type 2 interaction involves teacher control of the topic but not of activity. This kind of interaction occurs when there is some information that needs to be transmitted or some issue that needs to be sorted out — for instance, when the teacher makes an announcement, gives some instructions or delivers a lecture. Type 3 interaction occurs when the teacher controls both topic and activity, as when some information needs to be transmitted in a specific way (e.g. teacher elicitation in the context of a language exercise). Type 4 involves teacher control of the activity but no control of the topic, as when the teacher sets up small-group work with prescribed procedural rules but allows freedom of choice of topic or when the teacher nominates a learner to ask a question of another learner.

The systems developed by both Ellis and Van Lier involve two dimensions. More complex descriptions have been developed involving several dimensions. Fanselow (1977), for example, set out to provide 'a technical, operationally defined set of terms' for discussing different kinds of teaching in terms of five dimensions: (1) source (i.e. who communicates); (2) move type (i.e. whether structuring, soliciting, responding or reacting); (3) mediums (i.e. linguistic, non-linguistic or paralinguistic); (4) content (i.e. language, life, procedure or subject matter) and (5) use (i.e. how the mediums are used to communicate content). Allwright (1980) attempts to characterize classroom interaction with reference to turns, topics and tasks.

Each system of classification represents the factors which its deviser considers important for understanding what takes place in classroom discourse. As Gaies (1983b:202) observes, the categories identified are not directly observable in actual data but rather 'reflect the particular order that a researcher chooses to impose on the data'. As such, the value of such systems lies in the insights they provide about potentially significant aspects of classroom behaviour. They should not be seen as comprehensive descriptions.

Interpreting the Research

Most of the studies reported above involved either a direct or an indirect comparison between classroom and natural discourse. In summary, it can be pointed out that the majority of studies emphasize the differences between the two types of discourse. However, some studies also acknowledge that classroom and pedagogic discourse are not entirely distinct, because the classroom can afford some opportunities for natural discourse.

The general position taken by most researchers is that the absence of natural discourse in the classroom inhibits language learning. Riley (1977), for instance, talks about the 'falsification of behaviour' and 'distortion' that occurs in pedagogic discourse. He argues that learners need to be exposed to discourse that has undergone the minimum of adulteration and interference. However, other researchers (e.g. Edmondson) acknowledge the inevitability of pedagogical discourse. They see it as the product of attempts to learn the target language and argue that such attempts are both logical and sensible. A somewhat smaller group of researchers (e.g. Mitchell, 1988b) bring evidence to show that teachers can provide opportunities for real communication and argue that the teacher functions as a valuable resource of L2 input. All these researchers share a common perspective: they see classroom discourse and the interaction through which it is constructed as the matrix of language learning–teaching – a radically different view from that discussed in the earlier chapters.[6]

Summary and Conclusion

This chapter has examined a range of classroom process research. This research was stimulated by the recognition that large-scale comparative method studies were unlikely to throw light on the factors that influenced L2 learning and that this could be better achieved by small-scale studies of teaching–learning behaviours. The principal aim of the research was to describe and understand the various behaviours that take place in the language classroom. Initially, the research was exploratory in nature,[7] but as time passed, researchers drew increasingly on the theoretical insights afforded by SLA studies. The principal method of classroom process research is observation. This has been carried out by means of interaction analysis, based on observation schedules for coding different types of behaviour, by anthropological or ethnomethodological studies of the social norms that govern classroom interaction and by the study of the structure of classroom discourse. Classroom process research has examined the nature of the teacher's and the learners' independent contributions and also classroom discourse taken as a whole.

There can be little doubt that the research has helped to increase our understanding of the activities from which learning derives. This understanding relates both to the general characteristics of the language classroom and also to the differences between classrooms – which should never be underestimated. The understanding that has been achieved is valuable in two ways. First, it is now clear that prescriptions regarding desirable teaching behaviours which have been generated by a particular method may not correspond to the actual behaviour that occurs in the classroom. Error treatment, for instance, has turned out to be much more complicated than was ever envisaged by advocates of audiolingualism. Second, a new way of conceiving the relationship between teaching and learning has developed. This is, that any learning that takes place must in some way result from the process of interaction the learner takes part in. Allwright (1984b) suggests two 'interaction hypotheses' to formalize this understanding. The first simply states that 'the processes of classroom interaction determine what learning opportunities become available to be learned from'. The second states more strongly that 'the process of interaction *is* the learning process'. By this Allwright means that interaction somehow produces linguistic development.

Classroom process research has done much to show us how learning opportunities are made available to the learner, but it has not been able to show how interaction results in L2 learning. As Van Lier (1988:91) points out:

> When observing an L2 classroom in action it is clear that no direct link can be made between observable behaviour and language development. Learning is not generally directly and immediately observable. In the first place, it is characterized by improved performance or increased knowledge, and manifested by the learner's behaviour at some time (unspecified) after the learning has occurred. Secondly, the learning itself may not be produced by one specifically identifiable event, but rather by the cumulative effect of a number of events.

For this reason classroom process research has had difficulty in describing what is 'good' or 'bad' for L2 learning. In order to establish a link between the observation of teaching–learning behaviours and the internal process of L2 acquisition researchers have had recourse to various theories of SLA. In this way they have felt able to make evaluative statements about what promotes and hinders acquisition. The next chapter examines a number of these theories.

NOTES

1 As pointed out in ch. 1, classroom process researchers have tended to emphasize social and sociolinguistic enquiry rather than psychological or psycholinguistic enquiry. That is, they have viewed the classroom as a social context and treated 'learning' as an interpersonal activity rather than as an activity that takes place in the learner's mind.
2 Recent interaction analysis systems have also been informed by research into L2 proficiency and language acquisition. The Communicative Orientation of Language Teaching (Allen, Fröhlich and Spada, 1984), for instance, was derived 'from current theories of communicative competence, from the literature on communicative

language teaching, and from a review of recent research into first and second language acquisition' (p. 223).

3   The failure of learners to incorporate teacher corrections into their next utterances is, of course, predicted by interlanguage theory. Learners will only be able to handle corrections of their 'mistakes', not of their 'errors' (see p. 54). Of course, they may be able to reproduce the teacher utterance containing the correction, but studies of learners' attempts at imitation (e.g. Naiman, 1974) suggest that in many instances they can only reproduce items that are already part of their competence.

4   One possible explanation for the contradiction is that the two sets of researchers used different operational definitions of such terms as 'questions', 'statements', 'eliciting' and 'informing'. One of the difficulties of comparing the results obtained from different studies rests in the lack of a widely accepted set of analytical categories.

5   Teachers' attitudes to the nature of the instructional task almost certainly act as a major determinant of classroom behaviour. However, there have been surprisingly few studies of the relationship between attitudes and behaviour in L2 classrooms.

6   There are two reasons for claiming that learners need the opportunity to engage in conversational discourse: (1) it enables them to develop discourse competence and (2) it facilitates the development of linguistic competence. It has also been argued (e.g. Ellis, 1984a; Van Lier, 1988) that the two are inextricably linked. That is, through the process of developing discourse competence learners come to extend their linguistic resources.

7   Ethnographic research is not only 'exploratory' and 'illuminative'. It is also theory-building – designed to provide a valid interpretation of the L2 classroom. However, it is probably true to say that much of the L2 classroom process research that has taken place has not been theory-building in the strict sense of this term. It has not produced a clearly articulated theory of L2 teaching–learning.

5 The Relationship between Classroom Interaction and Language Learning

Introduction

In this chapter and the one that follows we will explore a number of theoretical positions regarding classroom language learning. We will also examine some of the research which these positions have generated and which has been used to support them. It should be noted, however, that in many instances the theoretical positions described in both chapters are speculative and controversial in nature. There is no consensus among applied linguists as to which theory most adequately explains classroom language learning. No attempt will be made to advance the claims of one theory over those of another. Rather the approach adopted will be that of reviewing and evaluating each position and the associated research. Each chapter, though, will conclude with a more personal view of the teaching–learning relationship.

This chapter treats teaching as 'interaction' – the process by which samples of the target language become available to the learner for interlanguage construction through classroom interaction. In the next chapter teaching is viewed as 'formal instruction' – the attempt to intervene directly in the process of interlanguage construction by providing samples of specific linguistic features for learning.

These two ways of viewing teaching are not to be treated as alternatives. It is not intended to suggest that there are some classroom processes that can be classified as 'interaction' and others as 'formal instruction'. Everything that happens in the classroom involves communication of one kind or another. It is possible to view the same instructional sequence in two different ways – as 'interaction' and as 'formal instruction'.

An example may help to make this basic point clearer. Consider the following sequence:

T: R_____, what is _____?

L1: This is a book.

T: Wait. What is this?

L1: This is book.

T: 'A'.

L1: This is a book.

T: Right. Very good. What are these?

L1: What is _____
L2: These are _____

L1: This — these are rubbers.

T: Rubbers.

L1: Rubbers.

As 'interaction', this sequence is characterized by tight topic control, the use of display questions and evaluative and corrective feedback on the part of the teacher and minimal responses from the learners. A linguistic feature is the high frequency of third-person copula ('is' and 'are') in both the teacher's input and the learners' output. As 'formal instruction', the sequence involves an attempt to teach markers of plurality.

Not all instructional sequences can be viewed as both 'interaction' and 'formal instruction'. Meaning-focused sequences (see chapter 1), where, by definition, there is no attempt to teach specific linguistic items, can only be viewed as 'interaction'. It is form-focused sequences, such as the one above, which can be treated as both 'interaction' and 'formal instruction'. It should also be noted that the interactional characteristics of sequences which are meaning-focused are likely to vary greatly from those that are form-focused, as we discovered in the previous chapter.

This way of looking at classroom processes differs from that currently found in many teacher-training manuals, where 'communication' is contrasted with 'formal instruction', with the assumption that all teaching is one or the other. Such a contrast is misleading. We need to recognize that teaching intended as formal instruction also serves as 'interaction'. 'Formal instruction' does more than teach a specific item; it also exposes learners to features which are not the focus of the lesson. For example, participation in the above sequence may result in the acquisition of markers of plurality (the actual focus of the lesson) but might also facilitate the acquisition of other linguistic features such as third-person copula (which was not the focus of the lesson). In other words, learners may respond to form-focused instruction as 'interaction' and acquire features not envisaged by the teacher.

These two perspectives lead to very different kinds of questions being asked about the teaching–learning relationship. If we view teaching as 'interaction', we will be interested in the extent to which the different input and interactional features contribute to acquisition. We might ask, for instance, whether tight topic control helps L2 learning. If we view teaching as 'formal instruction', we will be concerned with whether the attempt to teach specific linguistic features results in their acquisition.

This chapter is concerned only with 'interaction' and the learning that derives from it. Interaction can be hypothesized to contribute to learning in two ways: (1) via the learner's reception and comprehension of the L2 and (2) via the learner's attempts to produce samples of the L2. Reception-based theories of L2 acquisition emphasize the importance of input, as opposed to learner output. The **frequency hypothesis** states that learners acquire linguistic features according to their frequency in the input; features which occur frequently are learnt before those which occur infrequently. The evidence for this hypothesis lies in quantitative studies which have correlated the frequency of input features with measures of acquisition. Krashen (1985) has advanced the **input hypothesis** (see p. 57) to account for how learners' interlanguages develop as a result of comprehending input that contains linguistic features one step beyond their current knowledge. Long (1983a) proposes the **interaction hypothesis**, according to which input is made comprehensible as a result of modification to the interactional structure of conversations when communication problems arise. Both the input and the interaction hypotheses have attracted considerable interest and have served as the basis for a number of strongly argued pedagogical prescriptions. For this reason, they will be considered in some detail.

There are also a number of production-based theories. Swain (1985) puts forward the **output hypothesis** which claims that learners need the opportunity to produce in order to develop native-speaker levels of grammatical proficiency. Ellis (1984c) proposes the **discourse hypothesis** to account for the link between input and production. Like Swain, Ellis argues that output is essential for learning. He suggests that the nature of the linguistic competence which learners acquire depends on the nature of the discourse in which they participate. The discourse hypothesis is closely linked to theories of L2 variability (cf. Tarone, 1983). Next, the role of **collaborative discourse** in assisting learners to produce new syntactic structures is considered. Studies which have explored this aspect of interaction have made use of 'discourse analysis methodology' (Hatch, 1978b; 1978c). Finally, the **topicalization hypothesis** is considered. This states that learners are more likely to obtain intake when they — rather than the teacher — initiate and control a topic.

This plethora of hypotheses (shown in figure 5.1) testifies to the importance which researchers have attached to investigating 'interaction' as the matrix of L2 acquisition. It also testifies to the lack of agreement regarding how classroom interaction contributes to the acquisition of new linguistic knowledge. We are a long way from being able to answer the two central questions: (1) What kind of communication is best for language learning? and (2) How much communication (of whatever kind) is needed for learning? This chapter concludes with a consideration of what constitutes an optimal mode of classroom communication for rapid and successful learning.

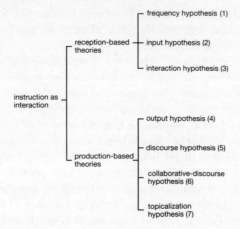

Figure 5.1 Theories of classroom learning based on instruction as interaction

Reception-based Theories

In this section we will consider a number of hypotheses based on the assumption that L2 acquisition occurs when the learner processes input data. Reception-based theories are of two kinds: those that emphasize *exposure*, such as the frequency hypothesis, and those that emphasize the need for *comprehension* of the input data, such as the input and interactional hypotheses.

It is helpful to begin by defining a number of key terms. **Input** refers to the target language samples to which the learner is exposed. It contains the raw data which the learner has to work on in the process of interlanguage construction. Corder (1967) distinguishes input and **intake**, the latter consisting of that portion of the input which the learner actually attends to and, therefore, uses for acquisition. Not all input serves as intake as only a subset of the total samples available are salient to the learner at any one stage of development. **Interaction** refers to the process of interpersonal communication; it involves the efforts of both the learner and the teacher. Input is supplied and made comprehensible through interaction.

The Frequency Hypothesis

The frequency hypothesis states that the order in which learners acquire L2 grammatical features is determined by the frequency of those features in the input; more frequent features are acquired before less frequent. The hypothesis makes no claims about the need for learners to comprehend the input. Input simplifications and interactional adjustments of the kind found in teacher-talk (see previous chapter) are important because these affect the frequency with which specific linguistic features occur in the input at different stages of the learner's development.

The frequency hypothesis has been tested by means of correlational studies.

These relate measures of the frequency of different linguistic features in the input to measures of acquisition of the same features, using statistical techniques. Table 5.1 provides a summary of the main classroom correlational studies. It will be seen that the results are very mixed. Larsen-Freeman (1976a & b), for instance, found a significant relationship between features in the input and output, but Long and Sato (1983) did not. There may be a number of reasons for this — for example, whether the learners are elementary or advanced. The studies also have design problems. Larsen-Freeman and Long and Sato correlated unrelated sets of input and output data.

It makes little sense to look for input—output relationships in data collected at the same time. Any effect that input might have will only become apparent at some point after the input has been supplied. In this respect, it is worthwhile reporting Wells's (1985) finding for L1 acquisition. He observed a rapid increase in adult caretakers' use of specific linguistic forms, such as auxiliary verbs, just before the emergence of the same features in the children's speech. Wells suggests that the frequency of more complex items might be kept low until the child is ready. Evidence for a similar delayed relationship in classroom L2 acquisition comes from Lightbown's (1983) study. She found that learners in Grade 6 ESL classrooms in Canada evidenced overuse of V-ing even though this feature was relatively infrequent in the classroom language at that time. However, they had received extensive exposure to this form during Grade 5. Lightbown also notes that the use of V-ing fell away in Grade 7. The possibility of instruction having a delayed effect is explored more fully in the next chapter.

The non-authenticity of classroom discourse has already been discussed, in chapter 4. It has implications for the frequency with which some linguistic forms are either under- or over-represented in the input. Lightbown (1985b) provides a number of examples of how this arises and the effects it has on acquisition. For example, she found that Grade 6 French learners of L2 English underused 'have' in their free speech. They even failed to produce the familiar error:

* I have twelve years old.

This could be explained by the absence of 'have' in the input in previous years. However, once 'have' was introduced, the learners rapidly switched to using it, including in sentences like the one above. V-ing is an example of a feature that is commonly over-represented. Lightbown argues that low or high frequency of a form in the input is a reflection of the distorted nature of classroom dialects and can result in pseudo-acquisition of that form.

There are two major problems with the frequency hypothesis. The first is that it is based on the assumption that linguistic items are acquired sequentially, i.e. it draws heavily on the idea of a 'morpheme order', which, as we have seen in chapter 3, is controversial. Second, the hypothesis does not really constitute an explanation of any kind. It does not tell us why input frequency should affect acquisition. Hatch and Wagner-Gough (1976) point out that there is an

Table 5.1 Correlational studies of classroom input and L2 learner production

Study	Design	Principal results
Larsen-Freeman, 1976a	Accuracy orders of ESL learners correlated with input frequency orders of same morphemes in the classroom speech of 2 ESL teachers.	The results reported are generally significant.
Larsen-Freeman, 1976b	L2 accuracy orders of grammatical morphemes correlated with order of frequency of the same morphemes in parental speech to children (based on Brown, 1973). The orders were calculated using data from a variety of tasks.	Significant relationships found for all accuracy orders except that derived from imitation task.
Hamayan and Tucker, 1980	The order of accurate production of nine French syntactic structures in the elicited speech of children speaking French as a L1 and learning French as a L2 was correlated with teachers' frequency of production of the same structures in the classrooms.	Significant rank order correlations reported for both L1 and L2. Also orders different for different classrooms but relationship between input and production orders remained significant.
Snow and Hoefnagel-Höhle, 1982	Achievement scores and gain scores of American children acquiring L2 Dutch in the Netherland correlated with (1) quantity of Dutch heard in the classroom, (2) percentage of speech directed specifically at them and (3) quantity of speech directed at individual learners.	No significant relationships reported.
Long and Sato, 1983	Krashen's (1977) average order of acquisition of grammatical morphemes correlated with the order of frequency of the same morphemes in ESL teachers' speech.	No significant relationship found. However, the teachers' production order did correlate with native-speakers' production order in conversations and this latter order correlated with Krashen's acquisition order.

Lightbown, 1983	Frequency of production of a number of grammatical morphemes (e.g. -s morphemes) by students in an oral communication game correlated with the frequency of same morphemes in samples of one teacher's speech and in the textbook used by the students. The study was longitudinal.	No direct relationship between input frequency and learners' morpheme order found at the same time. But there was evidence that a high level of frequency of some morphemes (e.g. -ing) resulted in *subsequent* overuse by the students. Frequency may, therefore have a delayed effect.

overlap between frequency, structural complexity and cognitive learning difficulty. The correlation between input and acquisition, therefore, is difficult to interpret, because other factors are confounded. It may not be frequency *per se* that counts but structural complexity. The hypothesis is descriptive rather than explanatory. It is of value from the point of view of language pedagogy, however, in that it highlights the need to consider instruction in terms of the *total* input to which the learner is exposed.

The Input Hypothesis

The other two hypotheses which are reception-based are explanatory in nature. They offer much more powerful accounts of how classroom input and interaction contribute to L2 acquisition.

The input hypothesis has already been briefly considered as part of the Monitor Model in chapter 3. It warrants a more detailed consideration, however. Its importance is reflected in the fact that Krashen has devoted a whole book to it (Krashen, 1985) and in the attention it has attracted from language teachers. A detailed description of Krashen's claims about the role of input follows, together with a review of the research which has been used to support them. Finally, the hypothesis is evaluated.

Description   Krashen provides a number of accounts of the input hypothesis, the most extensive of which is to be found in Krashen (1985). The hypothesis takes the form of a principal statement and two corollaries (see Table 5.2).

Long (1983a) makes some equally strong claims:

1   Access to comprehensible input is characteristic of all cases of successful acquisition, first or second.
2   Greater quantities of comprehensible input result in better (or at least faster) acquisition.
3   Lack of access to comprehensible input (as distinct from incomprehensible, not any, input) results in little or no acquisition.

Table 5.2   The Input Hypothesis

Principal statement:	Learners progress along the natural order by understanding input that contains structures that are a little bit beyond their current level of competence (i.e. i + 1).
Corollary 1:	Speaking is a result of acquisition, not its cause; it emerges as a result of building competence via comprehensible input.
Corollary 2:	If input is understood and there is enough of it, the necessary grammar is automatically provided; the teacher does not need to teach the next structure.

Source: Based on Krashen, (1985).

For Krashen the input hypothesis is the central hypothesis of the Monitor Model. He calls it the Fundamental Principle. This is because he sees comprehensible input as the necessary (although not sufficient) condition for 'acquisition'.[1] It is not possible to control *what* the learner acquires nor the *order* in which she acquires it. Both are determined by the internal language processor or language-acquisition device (LAD) which regulates what features in the input are attended to at each stage of development. However, the LAD can function properly only if the learner receives input that contains structures not yet learnt and if, despite this, the learner is able to understand the input.

Krashen describes two ways in which comprehension of input containing new linguistic material is achieved: the utilization of context by the learner and the provision of simplified input by the teacher. The learner makes use of context to infer the meaning of an utterance when existing linguistic resources are insufficient for immediate decoding. Three kinds of contextual information are available: extra-linguistic information, the learner's knowledge of the world and the learner's previously acquired linguistic competence. Krashen refers to a number of studies which demonstrate the 'dramatic effects' that contextual information can have on the comprehension of written texts; a study by Adams (1982), for example, was able to show a sixfold improvement in the comprehension of new lexical material when background information was made available.

Krashen does not illustrate how the learner makes use of context, although it is not difficult to think up examples. A passive sentence like 'Raza was given a pencil by Surjit' can be understood even though the passive is not yet part of a learner's interlanguage if it is accompanied with non-verbal behaviour which makes clear who the agent and patient are. A passive sentence like 'Raza was bitten by the dog' can be understood correctly even without extralinguistic information as the learner will know that the action of biting is performed by dogs on humans; this is part of her world knowledge. A passive sentence like 'Raza was hit' can be understood even without extralinguistic information or world knowledge if the learner's existing linguistic competence includes knowledge that 'hit' requires a patient; 'Raza' must perform the role of patient because it is the only argument of the predicate 'hit' in the sentence.[2]

Krashen also places great store on the provision of simplified input, although he acknowledges that input can be comprehensible without any simplification. He emphasizes that simplification is designed to promote communication rather than to teach and that it results in 'rough' rather than 'fine tuning'. By 'rough tuning' he means that the input is not exactly related to the learner's developmental level so that it does not contain precisely the next rule the learner is ready for. Thus the learner's 'next rule' is not present in every utterance. However, providing there is enough comprehensible input the learner is assured of exposure to the necessary grammar at the right time. Roughly tuned input makes the task of comprehension by means of inference easier. It ensures that the learner is not faced with input which overloads her processing and inferencing capacity by removing excess rules that are way beyond what is immediately acquirable. Also input to beginner learners typically relates to 'here-and-now' topics which facilitate comprehension by means of extralinguistic information. Krashen also argues that the simplified input found in **interlanguage talk** (i.e. communication between L2 learners) can promote learning.

Simplified input can be made available to the learner through one-way or two-way interaction. Examples of the former include listening to a lecture, watching television and reading. Two-way interaction occurs in conversations. Krashen acknowledges that two-way interaction is a particularly good way of providing comprehensible input because it enables the learner to obtain additional contextual information and optimally adjusted input when meaning has to be negotiated because of some communication problem. However, he rejects claims (of the kind made by the interaction hypothesis — see below) that two-way interaction is necessary for comprehensible input. According to Krashen, input can be comprehensible without any active participation on the part of the learner. Advanced learners can benefit from watching television. Also there is plenty of evidence to support the facilitative effects of extensive reading on acquisition.

Evidence Krashen offers no direct evidence in support of the input hypothesis. That is, he reports no studies which show that roughly tuned input containing 'i + 1' results in learners advancing to the next step in their interlanguage development. There are, however, various kinds of indirect evidence which lend support to the hypothesis. Some of the most important are considered below.

The input hypothesis predicts that learners will be able to learn specific grammatical features from classroom input irrespective of whether these are formally taught. Terrell et al. (1980) were able to show that classroom learners of L2 Spanish acquired the ability to produce interrogatives even though no explicit teaching was provided. Classroom input is presumably rich in interrogatives (see chapter 4) and these are often predictable and repetitive.

As a result they are readily comprehensible. Other studies have shown that the acquisition of some linguistic features is delayed in classroom L2 acquisition, possibly because they are absent from the input. For example, past tense forms occur infrequently in teachers' language and are acquired late by classroom learners (Ellis, 1982; Long and Sato, 1983).

A number of studies have shown a significant relationship between features of modified input and learner comprehension. These studies have all involved L1 acquisition, however. Cross (1977), for instance, reported significant correlations between the mean lengths of the caretaker's and child's utterances (a measure which gives an indication of general syntactic complexity) and an even higher correlation between the caretaker's Mean Length of Utterance (MLU) and the child's comprehension. Krashen − like Cross − interprets these results as indicating that caretakers adjust their input in rough accordance to the child's ability to comprehend and produce. Cross's study, however, was cross-sectional and could not be used to make claims for any causative effect of simplified input on learning. Other L1 acquisition studies have failed to show any relationship between formal characteristics of caretaker input and learning (e.g. Gleitman et al., 1984). Even if the L1 acquisition research was uniformly supportive of the input hypothesis it would still need to be shown that similar relationships occurred in L2 acquisition research. There has been a singular lack of such studies. However, given that Krashen (1985:27) accepts that learners may be able to learn from 'non-tuned' input (he refers to the Gleitman et al. study) providing it is still comprehensible, this lacuna is not very damaging to the hypothesis.

Long (1985a:378) has suggested that one way of demonstrating the relationship between comprehensible input and acquisition is to break the task down into three steps:

1 Show that (a) linguistic/conversational adjustments promote (b) comprehension of input.
2 Show that (b) comprehensible input promotes (c) acquisition.
3 Deduce that (a) linguistic/conversational adjustments promote (c) acquisition.

Evidence showing that simplified input aids comprehension can, therefore, contribute support to the hypothesis. However, the evidence available is quite limited. Chaudron (1985) in a review of the literature was able to find only one study (Kelch, 1985) demonstrating that a slower rate of speech led to increased comprehensibility. In this study slowing down from 200 words per minute to 130 w.p.m. resulted in significantly improved dictation scores. Long (1985a) investigated the effects of a number of modifications of lecture input on L2 university students' comprehension. The modifications included syntactic complexity, rate of speech and the addition of rephrasings and restatements − a mixture of input and interactional features. The problem with Long's study is that it is not possible to say whether it was the input or the interactional modifications that assisted comprehension. Pica, Young and Doughty (1987) carried out a study designed to investigate which type of modification was most effective. They compared the effects of pre-modified input in a lecturette with those of interactionally modified input that arose in two-way exchanges during a similar lecturette with no pre-modified input. They found that comprehension was assisted by the interactional modifications, whereas reduction of linguistic complexity in the pre-modified input had less effect. The importance of input modifications as an aid to comprehension cannot be considered proven by any stretch of the imagination. Even if it is finally demonstrated that they play their part, it is likely that other sources of comprehensibility (i.e. interactional modifications and contextual knowledge) will turn out to be more significant.

There have also been a number of studies which have investigated the relationship between the frequency of specific linguistic features in the input and in learner output. These are not considered here, however, as they throw no light on the input hypothesis. These studies demonstrate a role for *frequency* but not for *comprehensible input* (see the earlier discussion of the frequency hypothesis).

Krashen (1985) claims that the input hypothesis accounts for other research findings. Learners typically go through a silent period before they begin to produce in the L2; this serves as a means of building up competence through listening. Language classes have been shown to be important in the early rather than late stages of language learning; this is because the learner finds difficulty in obtaining comprehensible input in naturalistic contexts in the beginning. Methods that supply plenty of comprehensible input have been shown to be more successful than methods that are based on formal language study or practice.[3] For example, Asher's Total Physical Response – a method that requires the learner to respond non-verbally to instructions for a lengthy period before production is allowed (Asher, 1977) – produces consistently successful results. Immersion classes based on 'comprehensible subject-matter teaching' have met with tremendous success in Canada (Swain and Lapkin, 1982). Krashen argues that this is because they provide the learner with plenty of comprehensible input. The skill of writing has been shown to be fostered by large amounts of 'self-motivated reading' rather than by the deliberate teaching of writing skills.[4] Once again this is because reading provides plenty of comprehensible input containing the subtle grammatical and discourse features that characterize the written medium. For Krashen all this constitutes 'evidence' in favour of the input hypothesis.

Evaluation   Evaluation of the input hypothesis can proceed in two ways. First, the quality of the evidence which Krashen cites in favour of it can be considered. Second, the hypothesis can be subjected to theoretical appraisal.

The lack of direct supporting evidence has already been commented on. It is unlikely that such evidence will ever become available. An empirical study would need to show (1) that only *comprehensible* input promotes acquisition and (2) that it promotes acquisition of only that linguistic feature which is next in line along the natural route the learner is following. Krashen gives no suggestions for how such a study could be carried out, nor is it easy to envisage what it would look like.

The hypothesis can be tested, therefore, only indirectly − in the way that Long (1985a) suggests. However, to date there have been only a few studies which have shown that simplified input facilitates comprehension (see above) and these are far from conclusive. There is some evidence to suggest that simplified input can interfere with learning. Chaudron (1983), for example, illustrates how the pressure to achieve comprehension can lead to either ambiguous oversimplification or to confusing over-elaboration. For simplification to be effective the teacher needs to achieve a balance between these two extremes − no easy task, given that a class is likely to contain mixed-ability learners. There has also been very little research into the relationship between comprehension and acquisition. Faerch and Kasper (1986) in an article entitled 'The Role of Comprehension in Second-language Learning' fail to cite even one empirical study that has investigated this relationship. Even the indirect empirical evidence is, therefore, slim.

The other kind of evidence cited by Krashen relates to various findings about L2 acquisition which are compatible with the predictions of the input hypothesis (e.g. the results of immersion studies). The argument is a circular one, however. For example, Krashen (1985:17) states: 'The Input Hypothesis thus asserts that it is the comprehensible input factor that is responsible for the success of immersion' and at the same time argues that the success of immersion is evidence in favour of the input hypothesis. The hypothesis is used to *interpret* the research results which are then claimed as *evidence* in favour of the hypothesis. In addition, it should be noted that the kind of evidence provided by the immersion and other kinds of studies do not demonstrate that comprehensible input results in the acquisition of i + 1. At best, they only constitute evidence that acquisition in general benefits from the kind of linguistic environment provided in immersion classrooms. Later, we will find that even Krashen's claims regarding the success of immersion programmes is questionable.

The input hypothesis has also been subjected to a number of theoretical criticisms (cf. Gregg, 1984; Faerch and Kasper, 1986; White, 1987; McLaughlin, 1987). These are summarized briefly below:

(1)   The 'i + 1' construct is not operationally defined. This construct derives from another of the hypotheses of the Monitor Model − the Natural Order hypothesis − but not all researchers agree that L2 acquisition is characterized by a rigid sequence of development. Also it is not clear how input containing 'i + 1' can result in transitional structures of the kind found in the acquisition of negatives and interrogatives. These structures are deviant and yet constitute an advance in acquisition. Krashen sees learning as an incremental process by which one rule is added to another, but acquisition may be better viewed as a

process of constant restructuring of interim grammars involving the gain of new features, the functional re-employment of some old features and the eradication of other old features.[5] It is not clear how the presence of some unacquired feature in the input can generate such changes. White (1987) comments that what is needed is 'a theory of what precise aspect of the input interacts with what aspect(s) of the learner's existing system'. The input hypothesis does not constitute such a theory.

(2)   The relationship between comprehension and acquisition is not clearly spelled out. Faerch and Kasper (1986) point out that there is a distinction to be drawn between input functioning as intake for comprehension and input functioning as intake for acquisition. It is particularly difficult to see how understanding input can result in the acquisition of third person -s or many other grammatical morphemes, as these contribute no essential meaning to messages and are, therefore, redundant as far as comprehension is concerned.

(3)   Krashen's account of how comprehension takes place is inadequate. Faerch and Kasper (1986) provide an excellent summary of language-comprehension processes.[6] They emphasize that they consist of both 'bottom−up processes' and 'top−down processes'. The former are based more or less exclusively on the input and occur when the hearer is unable to activate contextual information (as, for instance, when one turns on the radio in the middle of a broadcast). The latter are based on the recipient's existing knowledge; some messages are so ritualized (as in service encounters) that they can be understood with almost no processing of the actual input. This distinction is of importance for the input hypothesis, as presumably acquisition of new linguistic material can only take place when the learner attends to actual input (i.e. when some degree of bottom−up processing occurs).

(4)   Simplified input may impede rather than facilitate acquisition. Gregg (1984:90−1) claims that 'no-one − certainly not Krashen − has shown that caretaker speech (CS) makes any significant contribution toward the acquisition of a grammar by a child, and no one has shown that the existence of CS has any bearing on second language acquisition'. White (1987) goes as far as to suggest that simplified input may in fact be detrimental. Interlanguage talk, for example, is likely to be lacking in just those features which the learner needs to acquire. White also argues that simplified input from native speakers can cause deprivation; for example, talking to learners in simple sentences deprives them of crucial input. Gregg and White overstate their cases. There is evidence to suggest that simplified input is involved in acquisition. Wells (1985), for instance, reports a marked increase of linguistic features in care-taker speech *shortly before* they first appear in the speech of children during L1 acquisition. This, of course does not prove that input causes acquisition but it is highly likely that it at least contributes to the process.

(5)   Some acquisition is not based on input at all. Krashen gives passing recognition to the fact that some changes in interlanguage are internally driven, i.e. result from the learner's current lexical and syntactical knowledge. This aspect of L2 acquisition is played down, however. There are two aspects of acquisition which are 'input-free'. The first concerns features which are triggered off by the acquisition of some other feature, which may be acquired from the input. For example, there is some evidence to suggest that exposure to input containing expletive pronouns ('There/It is . . .') provides the necessary evidence for learners to recognize that English does not permit pronoun drop (as in '*Is very busy'). The acquisition of pronouns appears to trigger off the acquisition of modal verbs, so that the learner does not require any input data relating to this grammatical feature. Zobl (1983) suggests that learners must possess a **projection device** to enable them to learn in this way.

The second aspect of acquisition which is input-free concerns the loss of deviant interlanguage rules. Researchers working within the Chomskyan tradition of Universal Grammar argue that the input does not typically supply the learner with the direct negative evidence (in the form of corrections, for instance) that is needed to 'unlearn' overgeneralizations. No amount of comparing such forms with the input will demonstrate to the learner that she is wrong. For example, if the learner produces sentences such as:

   * John donated the hospital some money.

by overgeneralizing from sentences like:

   John gave the hospital some money.

comprehending input will not help the learner to see that she is wrong. To unlearn this kind of overgeneralization the learner must either be equipped with innate knowledge or must receive direct negative evidence in the form of instruction. Neither has any role in acquisition according to the input hypothesis.

There are two other theoretical objections to the input hypothesis: (6) concerns Krashen's rejection of formal instruction as a basis for promoting 'acquisition' (as opposed to 'learning') and (7) concerns his rejection of output as a causative factor in acquisition. Both points are dealt with elsewhere. The next chapter covers (6), while (7) is considered in a later part of this chapter.

The input hypothesis is a bucket full of holes. It is an example of the 'tremendous leaps' which researchers make from 'low-level constructs about input itself to high-level constructs about their effects on L2 acquisition (Hatch, 1983b). As a basis for research the hypothesis is clearly inadequate, although, as White (1987) points out, there is still a need for *an* input hypothesis of a more precise kind. Krashen's input hypothesis is not without value for language pedagogy, however. It provides a statement of important principle, namely that for successful classroom acquisition learners require access to message-oriented communication that they can understand. It also provides a rough explanation of why this might be so. The main problem with Krashen's hypothesis is that it is nothing like as 'fundamental' as he claims. There is more to teaching than 'comprehensible input'.

The Interaction Hypothesis

Like the input hypothesis, the interaction hypothesis emphasizes the importance of comprehensible input. It also seeks to *explain* how acquisition comes about and makes claims regarding which kinds of interaction will best promote it. The interaction hypothesis has led to a substantial amount of classroom research, although, as we will see, this research has not been directed at falsifying the hypothesis. Rather, it has been based on the assumption that the hypothesis is correct.

Description The interaction hypothesis differs from the input hypothesis in the way it attaches importance to one particular method of making input comprehensible. There are three ways of making input comprehensible (Long, 1983a):

1 by means of input simplifications;
2 through the use of linguistic and extra-linguistic context; and
3 through modification of the interactional structure of conversation.

Long (1981) refers to (1) as **input features** and (3) as **interactional features** (see chapter 4, p. 70). In formulating the interaction hypothesis, Long argues that acquisition is made possible and is primarily facilitated when interactional adjustments are present.

The main interactional features which have been found to vary in foreigner-talk are described and exemplified in table 5.3. The presence of such features indicates that there is **negotiation of meaning** taking place. Long (1983c) identifies two kinds of negotiation: (1) negotiation aimed at avoiding conversational trouble and (2) negotiation aimed at repairing discourse when trouble occurs. Interactional modifications that derive from (1) reflect long-term planning by the native speaker and govern the way entire conversations are conducted. Long describes these modifications as **strategies**. Examples are 'Relinquish Topic Control', 'Select Salient Topics' and 'Treat Topics Briefly'. Interactional modifications that derive from (2) are spontaneous and mainly affect how topics are talked about. They are referred to as **tactics**. Examples include 'Request Clarification', 'Confirm own Comprehension' and 'Tolerate Ambiguity'. Other researchers have tended to restrict the term 'negotiation of meaning' to (2). Varonis and Gass (1985:39), for instance, define **negotiation exchanges** as 'those exchanges in which some overt indication that understanding between participants has not been complete and there is a resultant attempt to clarify nonunderstanding'.

Table 5.3 Interactional modifications involved in the negotiation of meaning

Interactional feature	Definition	Example
Clarification requests	Any expression that elicits clarification of the preceding utterance.	A: She is on welfare. B: What do you mean by welfare?
Confirmation checks	Any expression immediately following the previous speaker's utterance intended to confirm that the utterance was understood or heard correctly.	A: Mexican food have a lot of ulcers? B: Mexicans have a lot of ulcers? Because of the food?
Comprehension checks	Any expression designed to establish whether the speaker's own preceding utterance has been understood by the addressee	A. There was no one there. Do you know what I mean?
Self-repetitions: (1) repairing	The speaker repeats/ paraphrases some part of her own utterance in order to help the addressee overcome a communication problem	A: Maybe there would be— B: Two? A: Yes, because one *mother* goes to work and the other *mother* stays home.
(2) preventive	The speaker repeats/ paraphrases some part of her own utterance in order to prevent the addressee experiencing a communication problem.	A: Do you share his feelings? Does anyone agree with Gustavo?
(3) reacting	The speaker repeats/ paraphrases some part of one of her previous utterances to help establish or develop the topic of conversation.	A: I think she has *a lot of money*. B: But we don't know that? A: But her husband *is very rich*.
Other-repetitions: (1) repairing	The speaker repeats/ paraphrases some part of the other speakers utterance in order to help overcome a communication problem.	A: I think the *fourth family*. B: Not the *fourth family*, the third family.

| (2) reacting | The speaker repeats/
paraphrases some part of
the other speaker's
utterance in order to help
establish or develop the
topic of conversation. | A: | I think *she has three*
children. |
| | | B: | This is the thing. *She*
has three children. |

Source: Based on Pica and Doughty (1985a)

The interaction hypothesis also considers two-way communication of greater importance for acquisition than one-way. This is because negotiation of meaning is much more extensive when the learner is able to provide feedback on her success in understanding the native speaker. Negotiation of meaning, therefore, involves the learner as well as the native speaker/teacher. In this respect, therefore, the interactional hypothesis takes learner production as well as input into account. However, like the input hypothesis, it sees no direct role for output in promoting acquisition.

Figure 5.2 summarizes how interaction leads to acquisition, according to Long (1983a:214).

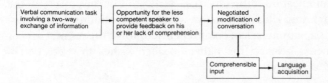

Figure 5.2 Model of the relationship between type of conversational adjustments and language acquisition

Evidence There have been no L2 studies investigating whether interactional adjustments promote acquisition. However, there have been more interesting results obtained from L1 acquisition research which has investigated the same question. Wells (1985) reports on the relationship between various input features and gains in acquisition by children. He found that children who received larger amounts of speech addressed to them showed larger gains in the mean length of their longest utterances, semantic complexity, noun phrase structure and clause structure. Not surprisingly, sheer quantity of exposure counts. The facilitative effect of a number of specific interactional features, however, was independent of the general effect for amount of speech. For example, both direct requests and 'extending utterances' (i.e. utterances which either added new propositional content to the topic or encouraged the child to do so) were related to progress in acquisition and were independent of the relationship between amount of speech and acquisition gains. In contrast, other interactional features (e.g. paraphrases and repetitions) tended to increase in proportion to amount of speech. There are obvious dangers in trying to apply the results of L1 acquisition research to L2 acquisition (see chapter 3), but it is somewhat surprising that research of the kind reported by Wells has received no attention from proponents of the interaction hypothesis. This research both gives general support to the claim that interaction facilitates acquisition (at least as far as rate is concerned) and also raises a number of interesting questions regarding which interactional features are the crucial ones.

The evidence cited in support of the interaction hypothesis is indirect in nature, consisting largely of theoretical argument. Two principal arguments can be identified. The first is based on research evidence which shows that foreigner-talk is characterized by interactional rather than input modifications. For example, Long (1981) carried out a study involving a comparison of conversations between sixteen native-speaker dyads and conversations between sixteen native and non-native-speaker dyads and found that whereas there were differences in only one out of the five input features he investigated, differences in ten out of eleven interactional variables reached statistical significance. In other words, there simply may not be much in the way of input modifications. If foreigner-talk is necessary for acquisition (as Long claims), then it must be because of the interactional features. The second argument concerns the interactional modifications that occur when there is some communication difficulty (i.e. tactics). For instance, in the example below (from Long, 1983c) the native-speaker's repetition (turn 3) is a response to the learner's apparent lack of comprehension, while the request for confirmation (turn 5) occurs because the native speaker wishes to make certain she has understood correctly:

1 NS: When did you finish?
2 NNS: Um?
3 NS: When did you finish?
4 NNS: Ten o'clock.
5 NS: Ten o'clock?
6 NNS: Yeah.

The modifications serve to make input which has proved problematic to the learner comprehensible. Through them, it is argued, the learner's attention is drawn to new linguistic material, which then becomes intake. Thus, in the above example the learner may be helped to focus attention on how past tense interrogatives are formed.[7]

Indirect support for the claim that negotiation leading to interactional adjustments results in more optimal input than do formal simplifications has been adduced from a study carried out by Scarcella and Higa (1981). They found that child learners received simpler input than adolescent learners. However, the latter participated more actively and generated more interactional adjustments from their native-speaker interlocutors. On the grounds that research has shown that adolescents learn more rapidly than young children (Snow and Hoefnagel-Höhle, 1978), it can be inferred that negotiation leading to native-speaker assistance in sorting out misunderstandings is more beneficial for learning than simplified input.

There is also some evidence to suggest that interactional adjustments facilitate comprehension. Reference has already been made to a study carried out by Pica, Young and Doughty (1987). They found that 73 per cent of the repetitions in the native speaker's two-way lecturette were triggered by interactional modification moves consisting of requests for clarification, confirmation checks and comprehension checks. Only 27 per cent were not triggered by some sort of interactional move. They consider it likely that comprehension was assisted by these interactionally motivated repetitions. Other interactional features have also been found beneficial. Chaudron and Richards (1986) examined the effect of different kinds of discourse markers on the comprehension of lectures by pre-university and university ESL students. They found that macro-markers (i.e. signals or metastatements about the major propositions in a lecture such as 'What I'm going to talk about today ...') aided the learners' retention of lecture content to a greater extent than micro-markers (i.e. signals of intersentential relations by means of connectors such as 'then', 'because', 'but'). Comprehension in conversations (as opposed to lectures) has been poorly researched, however, and doubts remain as to whether modifications to the structure of interactions help with comprehension (see below).

Classroom Research Based on the Interaction Hypothesis

The lack of research lending direct support to the interaction hypothesis has not inhibited researchers from basing classroom research on it. The general assumption is that the greater the amount of interactional modification there is, the more rapid and successful acquisition will be. A number of issues have been investigated:

1: Negotiation in classroom discourse vs. negotiation in naturally occurring conversations   The previous chapter reviewed a number of studies which have compared classroom and naturalistic discourse so there remains little to add here. One study − Pica and Long (1986) − has specifically examined the nature of interactional modifications in the classroom. It compared the classroom speech of ten ESL teachers with the speech of native speakers conversing with non-native speakers whom they had met for the first time (cf. Long, 1981). There was no difference in linguistic complexity but there were functional differences. Teachers produced more questions and imperatives and fewer statements. The teachers used more display questions and comprehension checks but fewer referential questions, confirmation checks and clarification requests.[8] Pica and Long conclude that there is less negotiation of meaning in classroom settings and suggest that, as a result, there is less comprehensible input.

2: The effect of task type on the amount of interactional adjustment that takes place   Crookes (1986) and Long (1988b) have both argued that L2 classroom research should be directed at 'psycholinguistically relevant design features'. Where tasks are concerned such a feature is 'one which can be shown to affect the nature of the language produced in performing a task in ways that are relevant to SL [i.e. L2] processing and SL learning' (Crookes, 1986:7). A number of such task characteristics have been investigated – in particular the difference between one-way and two-way tasks. One-way information-gap tasks are tasks that do not require participants to pool information; contributions from individual learners are a matter of choice. Two-way information-gap tasks are tasks that equip all the participants with information which they must share in order to solve a problem. Long (1983a) found evidence of more interactional modification in two-way than in one-way tasks in conversations between pairs of native speakers. However, not all studies have produced similar results. Gass and Varonis (1985) were unable to find any significant differences between the two types of task in interlanguage talk involving intermediate-level university students studying L2 English. The research is, therefore, not conclusive. This is a reflection of the difficulty of identifying and controlling variables that affect the interaction resulting from different tasks. For example, the intrinsic interest generated by a task may well be more important than whether the task is one-way or two-way. Also the distinction between one-way and two-way tasks is less clear-cut than Long's initial distinction recognized. As Gass and Varonis point out, the distinction represents a continuous rather than dichotomous variable.

Other researchers have been more hesitant to suggest that one particular task type is desirable and have argued that different task types contribute to acquisition in different ways. Tong-Fredericks (1984) compared learner output on three types of communication task: (1) a problem-solving task, (2) a role-play task and (3) an 'authentic interaction' task, requiring learners to find out from their partners what they had done the day before. Task (1) produced the highest number of turns per minute, but the turn-taking on this task was also the most disorderly, partly because the learners were thinking aloud. Self-corrections were more frequent on tasks (2) and (3). On task (1) the learners may have been too engrossed to bother with accuracy. No differences in speaking speed were found. Tong-Fredericks argues that one activity type is not necessarily better or more effective than another. Different tasks elicit different kinds of responses, which can promote acquisition in different ways.

Duff (1986) investigated divergent and convergent problem-solving tasks. The former requires learners to defend different viewpoints on an issue; the latter requires them to reach a mutually acceptable solution. From the point of view of negotiation of input, the convergent tasks worked better in pairs of Chinese and Japanese learners of English. However, Duff noted that the divergent tasks resulted in greater complexity of output. Like Tong-Fredericks, she concludes that the two task types may be complementary in pedagogic and psycholinguistic value.

In general, the results of research which has investigated the effect that different tasks have on classroom interaction have not been very conclusive, mainly because of the difficulty of identifying and controlling the task and learner variables that affect interaction.

3: Changes in the teacher's interactional modifications over time This issue has attracted less interest, although it is of considerable theoretical importance. If interactional modifications are the main source of comprehensible input, the quantity and perhaps also type of interactions ought to vary over time according to the learner's proficiency. Ellis (1985c) looked at the interactional modifications in one teacher's speech to two beginner learners on two occasions separated by a period of six months. He found that the teacher's speech contained fewer self-repetitions but more expansions on the second occasion. Also, the teacher switched from asking questions that required simple object identification to questions that invited some kind of comment. This study opens up the possibility that some interactional features may be more important at one stage of development and others at later stages.

4: Differences in the nature of interaction found in teacher – class lessons and small-group work A number of researchers have sought to establish whether small-group work results in more negotiation of meaning than teacher-directed lessons (Pica and Doughty, 1985a and 1985b; Doughty and Pica, 1986; Duff, 1986; Rulon and Creary, 1986; Porter, 1986; Fillmore, 1985; Ellis and Rathbone, 1987). The results obtained from these studies are complex and difficult to interpret. For example, group work does not always result in more modified interaction than lockstep teaching. Two-way information-gap tasks are much more likely to result in differences than one-way tasks as in the latter many of the learners opt out, irrespective of the mode of participation. Another mediating variable is the proficiency level of the learners. There are also differing positions regarding the value of interlanguage talk. Long and Porter (1985) argue that group work is potentially beneficial because there is more negotiation of meaning. However, these claims are not based on any research showing that interlanguage talk promotes acquisition. The only two studies that have attempted to relate participation type to learning outcomes (Fillmore, 1982 and 1985; Ellis and Rathbone, 1987) conclude that group work is not necessarily beneficial. The results of these studies certainly do not constitute definitive support for interlanguage talk, although it should be noted that there is a strong educational rationale for group work (Brumfit, 1984).

5: Differences in the amount of interactional adjustments undertaken by experienced and inexperienced teachers It is generally acknowledged that native speakers vary in the extent to which they modify their speech interactionally in conversations with non-native speakers. Long (1983c) suggests that one factor might be the previous experience native speakers have of foreigner-talk. Pica and Long (1986) in the study referred to above set out to investigate whether there were any classroom interactional differences between experienced and inexperienced elementary ESL teachers. The experienced teachers did use more other-repetitions and WH questions (as opposed to Yes/No questions), but in general the similarities outweighed the differences. Pica and Long suggest that this was because the interaction in all the classrooms reflected a one-way flow of information from teacher to learner. The absence of any negotiation of meaning was the 'natural' pattern of discourse in all the classrooms.

6:   *The extent to which teachers can be trained to adjust the way they interact in classrooms*   If there is little negotiation of meaning irrespective of experience, it is worth finding out whether training can induce teachers to change the 'natural' pattern. Long et al. (1984) provided six teachers with training designed to encourage them to ask fewer display questions and more referential questions and to extend the time they allowed for students to respond to their questions. They found that the training had an immediate effect and also that this effect carried over into later lessons.[9] In a similar study, Brock (1986) found that two teachers who received training in the use of referential questions asked significantly more of these questions during a reading and vocabulary lesson than two control-group teachers. It would be interesting to find out if the kind of strategies and tactics which Long considers important for acquisition are equally amenable to training.

All this research has been descriptive in nature. It differs from much of the other process research reviewed in chapter 4 in that it has been based on a theory of L2 acquisition which makes claims about what kind of input promotes acquisition. Because of this, researchers have felt able to make statements about what effect the processes they uncover have on acquisition. Such statements are, of course, worth no more than the theory on which they are based.

Evaluation

The evidence cited by Long (1983a) – like that provided by Krashen in support of the input hypothesis – is essentially indirect. I know of no L2 acquisition study that has succeeded in demonstrating that interlanguage changes are brought about by interactional modifications. This is not to say, however, that such modifications are not important – indeed the weight of the indirect evidence suggests that they do facilitate rapid language learning. It does warrant caution. There are sound reasons for believing that the negotiation of meaning is less central to the process of acquisition than advocates of the interactional hypothesis would have us believe.

First, some research giving counter-evidence. One of the few studies to have investigated the direct relationship between interaction and acquisition has produced results that do not support the interaction hypothesis. Slimani (1987) studied the effects of conversational adjustments on the acquisition of English by thirteen highly motivated learners of L2 English in an Algerian technical institution. She focused in particular on the learners' own requests for clarification. She concludes (1987:314): 'The use of conversational adjustments does not often reveal itself to have a direct beneficial effect on those who employ them.' In other words, those students who sought clarification did not gain from the 'negotiation' that ensued. It should be noted, however, that the data for the study came from form-focused, teacher-centred language lessons. Also Slimani's measure of acquisition was unusual. She measured **uptake** – the linguistic items which individual learners reported learning on charts they were asked to complete after each lesson. Slimani's study is interesting because it provides a methodology for investigating the relationship between various aspects of classroom interaction and acquisition. Such a methodology has been conspicuously missing. The results she obtained, however, must be treated with circumspection given the novelty of the way she measured acquisition.

Other doubts regarding the centrality of the negotiation for meaning have been theoretical in nature. A number of these are considered below:

1   Conversational interaction may facilitate communicative performance without facilitating acquisition of new linguistic features. Sato (1986), for example, points out that because of the interactional support the learner receives she may not experience any need to learn new features. In other words, the negotiation of meaning may have the opposite effect from that claimed by the interaction hypothesis; it may inhibit learning. A corollary of this argument, however, is that, although linguistic competence is not developed, strategic competence (i.e. the ability to deal with communication problems) may be enhanced. Thus, even if negotiation does not benefit acquisition of the L2 code it may help the learner to make better use of existing resources.

2   Negotiation of meaning may only be apparent and may not result in comprehension. Hawkins (1985) carried out a study to determine whether apparently appropriate responses made by learners actually signalled comprehension. She collected retrospective data from learners in order to determine whether what appeared appropriate responses in context did in fact represent comprehension. She found that in 50 per cent of the responses for which retrospective data from the learners were available comprehension had not taken place. Learners, in fact, often feign comprehension for social reasons, as Fillmore (1979) has pointed out. This is potentially very damaging for the interaction hypothesis as it suggests that negotiation results in far less comprehensible input than has been claimed.

3   The conversational adjustments which have been associated with the negotiation of meaning are also used for other purposes (cf. Aston, 1986). Varonis and Gass (1985) admit to difficulties in distinguishing exchanges involving the negotiation of meaning from exchanges involving understanding.

Similar interactional acts are involved in 'keeping the conversation going' as in the negotiation of meaning.

4 Negotiation of meaning only results in acquisition if there is a low **affective filter** (i.e. the affective state of the learner which controls whether the input becomes intake). Aston (1986) argues that difficult interactive classroom tasks designed to promote plenty of negotiation may in fact fail to do so because they produce tension in the learner.

The interaction hypothesis is part of a psychological theory of language acquisition. However, interaction in classroom settings, as elsewhere, is essentially a social phenomenon. Aston (1986:139) makes this point clear by suggesting that 'trouble shooting routines' often occur in order to allow the participants 'to perform a ritual of understanding or agreement'. They go through the motions of agreeing so that they can display solidarity. There is no reason why such social/negotiation should contribute to L2 acquisition.

Review

In this section we have taken a critical look at three hypotheses which share the view that acquisition is the result of the reception rather than the production of L2 samples. The weakest of the three hypotheses is the frequency hypothesis, as this merely claims that the frequency of items in the input determines the order in which they are acquired but does not specify why this should be so. The results of classroom research which has investigated this hypothesis are mixed. It is possible that input frequency has a delayed rather than an immediate effect on acquisition.

The other two hypotheses aim to be explanatory. Both the input and the interaction hypotheses emphasize the importance of meaning-focused communication as a source of comprehensible input, which is seen as the necessary condition for acquisition to take place. The input hypothesis considers comprehensible input from any source valuable. The interactional hypothesis emphasizes the importance of conversational adjustments which occur in attempts to negotiate meaning when there is a communication problem. As yet, there is very little direct evidence for either hypothesis. The strong claim that comprehensible input is *necessary* for acquisition is difficult to maintain. However, the weaker claim that comprehensible input *facilitates* acquisition is tenable, although it still remains to be shown exactly how this happens. It is still not clear how comprehensible input, obtained by whatever means, results in the acquisition of linguistic knowledge.

Production-based Theories

According to reception-based theories production plays no direct part in the process of L2 acquisition. Such theories do allow for an indirect role, however.

The interaction hypothesis, for example, acknowledges that certain types of learner utterance help to negotiate input which contains L2 features the learner is likely to attend to. In this section we will consider a number of hypotheses which claim production contributes directly to acquisition.

The output hypothesis considers learner production in isolation from input. The discourse hypothesis and the collaborative discourse hypothesis treat output as an integral part of classroom interaction. The topicalization hypothesis concerns the kind of learner participation which best promotes acquisition. It should be noted that all these theories address how production contributes to rapid and successful L2 learning rather than how new linguistic knowledge is internalized.

The Output Hypothesis

The output hypothesis (Swain, 1985) was not proposed as an alternative to the input/interaction hypotheses but as an addition. Swain argues that comprehensible input may well be important for L2 learning, but is insufficient to ensure that native-speaker levels of grammatical accuracy are attained. The learner needs the opportunity for meaningful use of her linguistic resources to achieve this. Swain (1985:248−9) attributes three roles to output:

1   The need to produce output in the process of negotiating meaning that is precise, coherent and appropriate encourages the learner to develop the necessary grammatical resources. Swain refers to this as 'pushed language use'.
2   Output provides the learner with the opportunity to try out hypotheses to see if they work.
3   Production, as opposed to comprehension, may help to force the learner to move from semantic to syntactic processing. It is possible to comprehend a message without any syntactic analysis of the input it contains. Production is the trigger that forces learners to pay attention to the means of expression.

The main evidence for the output hypothesis comes from research carried out as part of the Development of Bilingual Proficiency Project (cf. Swain et al., 1989). One part of this project examined the nature of the language proficiency achieved by 175 Grade 6 immersion students learning French as an L2 in the Ottawa region of Canada. Proficiency was investigated using the modular model of communicative competence developed by Canale and Swain (1980). According to this model communicative competence consists of three separate traits: grammar, discourse and sociolinguistic components. The subjects were administered separate tests for each trait. The results indicated that whereas they had achieved a level of discourse competence similar to that of native speakers of French, they had failed to achieve native-speaker levels for the grammar and sociolinguistic traits, despite several years' exposure to French in subject lessons. For example, in an oral interview they evidenced a low level of accuracy in verb forms. Swain (1985) argues that the students' failure to achieve native-speaker grammatical competence was not because they lacked comprehensible input as there was plenty of this available in the immersion classrooms (cf. Krashen, 1985). She speculates that the real reason was because they had limited opportunities for speaking in the classroom and were not 'pushed' in the output they did produce. Swain et al. (1989) report that student talk in teacher-fronted activities was indeed severely restricted. Teacher-initiated talk dominated, allowing little opportunity for extended student talk of a clause or more (less than 15 per cent of total student turns). Swain (1985) suggests that in such an environment the students develop strategies for getting their meaning across and consequently experience little need to develop their interlanguages.[10]

It is important to recognize that the output hypothesis predicts that production will aid acquisition *only when the learner is pushed*. Opportunities to speak may not in themselves be sufficient. Schmidt's (1983) study of Wes, a Japanese painter, acquiring English in first Japan and then naturalistically in Hawaii testifies to this. Wes had plenty of opportunity to speak English. His discourse and sociolinguistic skills developed substantially but his grammatical competence progressed very little. One reason for this could be that he was able to achieve his communicative goals without the need for grammatical accuracy. In other words, he was not 'pushed'.

One way of investigating 'pushed output' is to study those learner productions that occur in response to a native speaker's signals of comprehension difficulty. Pica (1988) examined the interactions between a native speaker and ten non-native speakers of English in order to discover whether the latter would resort to more target-like use of the L2 when the native speaker indicated difficulty in understanding what they had said. She did find some evidence to support the view that 'pushed output' of this kind became more grammatical, but she also found that it did so in less than half of the total learner responses. She suggested that, on the whole, the negotiated interaction offered the learners models of what the comprehensible output could have been like, rather than opportunities for producing comprehensible output themselves. In other words, the study gave greater support to the role of comprehensible input rather than comprehensible output.

A subsequent study by Pica et al. (1989), however, found that 'comprehensible output was alive and well and very much an outcome of linguistic demands placed on the NNS by the NS in the name of negotiated interaction'. The crucial factor uncovered by this study was the nature of the native speaker's signals of comprehension difficulty. The learners (in this case ten Japanese adults) proved much more likely to produce output modifications in response to clarification requests than to confirmation requests. Clarification requests such as 'Huh?' leave it up to the learner to resolve comprehension problems, whereas confirmation requests, which model what the native speaker thought the learner meant, obviate the need for improved output. The same study also showed that many of the modifications which learners made in their pushed output were morphosyntactic, as opposed to semantic.

These studies lend some credence to the output hypothesis. But they need to be treated with caution. Evidence that learners improve the grammaticality of their utterances when pushed does not demonstrate that they *acquire* knowledge of new L2 items. As with the input and interactional hypotheses, there is, as yet, no direct evidence to support the claim that pushed output promotes learning.

Research which has investigated the effectiveness of listening methods on learning (e.g. Asher, 1977; Winitz, 1978) indicate that the beginning stage of language learning does not require production on the part of the learner. However, this does not constitute evidence against the output hypothesis, which claims that pushed output is necessary in order to achieve *advanced* levels of grammatical proficiency. The real contribution of pushed output may be to encourage learners to make use of those variants in their current interlanguage systems which are more target-like. It may enable them to resolve variability in favour of target language norms. It is in this sense, perhaps, that it contributes to acquisition.

The Discourse Hypothesis

The discourse hypothesis derives from work on the variability of language use in general and of interlanguage systems in particular. Givon (1979) argues that syntax is inextricably linked to discourse. He sees it as 'a dependent, functionally motivated entity' with formal properties which reflect its communicative uses. Givon distinguishes two types of language: loose, paratactic pragmatic discourse structures and tight, 'grammaticalized' syntactic structures. This distinction is evident in the differences between informal/unplanned and formal/planned speech. Table 5.4 details the main differences between the two types of discourse.

Givon goes on to identify the communicative conditions which give rise to the two types of language use. Informal communication takes place under relaxed conditions where planning is not necessary and also when there is no time for planned speech. Planning takes place 'as you go'. Informal speech is accompanied by constant face-to-face monitoring which affords the speaker the opportunity for constant repair so that careful planning is not necessary. It occurs in contexts where there is a shared pragmatic background involving here-and-now topics, which obviate the need for a high level of explicitness. In contrast, formal language use is characterized by careful planning involving corrections and reformulations. There is often a lack of communicative stress in the actual performance of formal discourse because it comes already prepared. There is an absence of face-to-face monitoring and of shared pragmatic background. Topics regularly derive from displaced activity or abstract ideas. As a result meaning has to be encoded explicitly in the discourse. The distinction between the two types of discourse reflects a continuum rather than a dichotomy.[11]

A number of researchers have studied the variability inherent in learner language (see Tarone, 1988 for a review of the research). Tarone (1983)

Table 5.4   Informal/planned discourse and formal/planned discourse contrasted

Informal/unplanned discourse	*Formal/planned discourse*
Topicalized constructions (e.g. My father, he's sick)	Grammatical constructions (e.g. It's my father who is sick)
Loose coordination	Tight subordination
Plentiful repetition and slow delivery	Little repetition and fast delivery
Reduction and simplification of grammatical morphology	Full grammatical morphology
Short verbal clauses with few noun phrases per verb	Long verbal clauses with several noun phrases per verb
Prominent topic-comment structure	Use of grammatical subjects

Source: Based on Givon (1979)

argues that interlanguage is best viewed as a **capability continuum**. That is, the learner's competence consists of variable rules which account for the systematic way in which certain variants of a rule are used in formal/careful language use and other variants in informal/vernacular language use. For example, Ellis (1987a) found that L2 learners were more accurate in their use of the regular past tense in a written narrative when they had ample time to plan than in an oral narrative which they were required to perform spontaneously.

The discourse hypothesis states that learners will acquire those structures associated with the type of language use in which they typically participate. Thus, if a learner only has experience of informal/unplanned language use she will only develop the capability of performing in this kind of discourse; she will, therefore, develop what Givon refers to as the *pragmatic mode*. Conversely, if a learner only has experience of formal/planned language use she will only be able to take part in this kind of discourse and will develop the **syntactic mode**. Ellis (1984c) comments: 'Because different kinds of knowledge and different processes of language use are involved in different discourse types, it cannot be expected that the acquisition of one style will facilitate the use of another style.' The term **style** here refers to the learner's internalized linguistic competence.

There is an important corollary of the discourse hypothesis: in order to acquire a full linguistic repertoire the learner needs exposure to formal/ planned language use. It is through participation in this type of language use that the learner comes to 'grammaticalize' her language i.e. acquire the full range of morphological and syntactic devices provided by the grammar of the target language. The process of 'grammaticalization' requires both exposure to formal language and also the opportunity to produce it. Learners who experience only informal/unplanned language use will not be able to develop the full range of grammatical features of the target language, both because they will receive insufficient exposure to them and also because they will have no communicative need to produce them.

Applied to the classroom, the discourse hypothesis predicts that different learning outcomes will occur according to the type of language use the learners experience (Ellis, 1987b). Formal classroom teaching with its emphasis on linguistic accuracy will engage the learner in planned discourse and develop the corresponding type of competence. Informal teaching will provide opportunities for unplanned discourse and result in the learner developing the kind of competence that enables her to perform in this kind of language use. Relevant teaching is teaching that gives the learner access to the type of language use which she needs to master. The discourse hypothesis, then, leads to pedagogic proposals radically different to those based on the input or interaction hypothesis.

There has been no controlled study to test the discourse hypothesis. The hypothesis is, however, compatible with the results of a number of studies. Swain (1985), in the study referred to earlier, reports that immersion students' scores on literacy-based tasks were not strongly related to their performance on oral tests. In general, the students did better on written tasks requiring planned language use. For example, their scores on a written discourse task closely matched those achieved by native speakers (in contrast to their grammar scores in the oral interview). Swain suggests that such results reflect the students' familiarity with similar tasks in school. Pavesi (1986) found significant differences in the level of acquisition of relative pronoun functions in two groups of Italian learners of L2 English.[12] The formal, classroom learners outstripped the informal, naturalistic learners. Whereas the former provided evidence of having acquired the more marked pronoun functions (e.g. genitive 'whose'), the latter were generally restricted to the unmarked functions (e.g. subject and object). Also the informal learners displayed more pronoun copies (e.g. * 'The girl who John kissed *her* . . .'). Pavesi draws on the discourse hypothesis to explain the difference. She suggests that difference discourse modes (planned vs. unplanned) have different 'indexes of markedness' which affect the degree of elaboration achieved by different learners. Thus the unplanned mode provides less exposure to and fewer opportunities for using the more marked relative pronoun functions.

The discourse hypothesis should be considered nothing more than an interesting idea until further evidence is forthcoming. Long (1988a) argues that the hypothesis is unlikely on the grounds that although planned discourse may provide greater exposure to complex, marked linguistic features, these will not be *perceptually salient* to the learner. This argument, however, does not refute the hypothesis, which claims only that learners will master that type of discourse (and related linguistic features) in which they participate. It does not claim that participation is the sole causative factor of acquisition. The discourse hypothesis needs to be viewed as *part* of a complete theory, which will also need to account for how internal factors enable the learners to attend to certain linguistic features when they are ready and not before.

The Collaborative Discourse Hypothesis

A number of researchers have documented how the process of constructing discourse in two-way interaction enables learners to produce new grammatical structures. Wagner-Gough (1975) studied conversational data between native speakers and Homer, a six-year-old Iranian boy learning L2 English in a naturalistic setting. She gives instances of what she calls the use of an **incorporation strategy** by Homer. This involves 'borrowing' a chunk from the preceding discourse and then extending it by affixing some element to the beginning or end, for example (1975:165):

Mark: Come here:
Homer: No come here.

Jufy: Where's Mark?
Homer: Where's Mark is school. [= Mark is at school.]

Ellis (1985a) points out that the incorporation strategy provides an explanation for the ubiquitous 'no + V' construction in L2 acquisition. In this sense then 'conversation is the crucible for language acquisition' (Long and Sato, 1984).

Another form of assistance provided by discourse is that found in **vertical constructions**. Here the learner produces an utterance over several turns, as in this example from naturalistic acquisition in Hatch (1978b:407):

P: Oh-oh!
J: What?
P: this (points at an ant)
J: It's an ant.
P: ant

According to Scollon (1976) these vertical constructions function as the precursors of horizontal structures (e.g. 'Oh-oh, this ant') in L1 acquisition. That is, what the child can at first only do across turns and across speakers she is later able to do within a single utterance. Researchers such as Hatch have suggested that the same process occurs in L2 acquisition.

Collaborative discourse of the kind described above is fairly common in naturalistic conversations involving L2 learners, but is less well documented in classroom contexts. Ellis (1985c) gives examples of such discourse in conversations between a teacher and two pupils and demonstrates how it helped them to produce 'new' structures. However, Ellis's study involved withdrawing the learners from the normal classroom setting. Faerch (1985:186) provides a number of examples from teacher-controlled classroom discourse:

T: what does it mean when she says she wore thick bull's eye glasses
S: her glasses were thick
T: like

S: the glasses
T: the eyes of a
S: bull

Both teacher and student contribute to the building of this syntagm. There seems every reason to believe that such collaboration is not uncommon in classrooms.[13]

The question that arises is what role collaborative discourse plays in acquisition. Long and Sato (1984) point out that conversational assistance could be seen as facilitating communication rather than acquisition. Faerch (1985) takes up this point, suggesting that where the classroom is concerned scaffolded structures serve the function of helping the learner to take part in the discourse and nothing else. Faerch and Kasper (1986) suggest that it is unlikely that learners preserve a mental representation of a vertical structure, as it evolves over several turns. This objection, however, does not apply to utterances resulting from the use of an incorporation strategy. Both Faerch and Sato (1986) make the point that even if collaborative discourse is credited with making a positive contribution to syntactic structures, it is doubtful whether it plays any part in the acquisition of morphological features (such as regular past). It is possible that collaborative discourse plays a significant part in *early* acquisition, but it is doubtful whether all interlanguage rules can emerge in this way. Collaborative discourse may help the learner to develop the resources required in the *pragmatic mode* but not those needed in the *syntactic mode*.

The Topicalization Hypothesis

The role played by the learner in nominating and controlling the topic of the discourse in language acquisition has been commented on by both first and second-language researchers. Wells (1985) contrasts the interactional styles of mothers who are 'supportive' and those who are 'tutorial'. The former allow their children the opportunity to initiate topics which they help along by means of continuing moves. The latter cast their children in the role of respondents while the adult controls the discourse through the use of closed questions and evaluations of the child's contributions. Wells argues that the supportive style results in speedier acquisition. Hatch (1978b) finds that in naturalistic interactions between native speakers and child L2 learners the latter are generally allowed to nominate topics and that this provides a basis for building conversations. Long (1983c) includes at the top of his list of potentially facilitative foreigner-talk strategies 'Relinquish Topic Control'. He notes that native speakers often pass control of current and subsequent conversational topics to the native speaker and that 'implicit willingness to talk about whatever the non-native speaker feels comfortable with is pervasive' (1983c:132). Ellis (1984a) argues that topic control by the learner facilitates classroom acquisition. He also claims that fluency-work in the classroom (i.e.

activities designed to allow the learners to use their existing resources in natural communication) is enhanced by handing topic control over to the learner (Ellis, 1986).

The topicalization hypothesis, then, claims that acquisition is facilitated if the learner is able to nominate and control the topic of a conversation. Evidence in support of the hypothesis is available in Slimani's (1987) study referred to earlier. She found that 'whatever is topicalized by the learners, rather than the teacher, has a better chance of being claimed to have been learned' (p. 321). A learner would benefit from a topic initiated by another student to a much greater extent than from a topic initiated by the teacher. A learner also gained greater benefit if the topic was initiated by another student rather than by himself. Slimani suggests that when a student topicalized he offered learning opportunities to his classmates. She also suggests that learners may benefit more from listening to exchanges in which other students are involved than in participating in exchanges themselves. Her study was carried out in a classroom characterized principally by formal language teaching. There is a need for similar research to be carried out in classrooms providing more meaning-focused communication.

Most classrooms provide very little opportunity for student topic control. In Slimani's study, for instance, the teacher tended to monopolize the discourse. Other studies reporting the directorial role exerted by the teacher and its effect on discourse have already been reviewed in chapter 4. The implications of the topicalization hypothesis for pedagogy are clear. Opportunity has to found for the learner to initiate discourse by topic selection.

The topicalization hypothesis emphasizes the importance of a particular kind of learner output — that which occurs when the learner is given the opportunity to nominate and control the topic of conversation. Slimani's research suggests, however, that learner output may be of less benefit to the learner who produces it than to other learners.[14] In this respect, the topicalization hypothesis is as much a reception-based as a production-based theory. Learners advance by attending to input and they are more likely to attend closely if the input derives from another learner. It has been classified as a production-based theory here, because it claims that learner production in the classroom is important for acquisition — in contrast to reception-based theories.

Review

In this section, a number of theories which emphasize the role of learner production in classroom interaction have been described and evaluated. The output hypotheses emphasizes the gain to acquisition that accrues from the learner being 'pushed' to produce utterances that are precise and appropriate. Such pushing may encourage the learner to select those variable forms in her interlanguage that are closest to target-language norms. The discourse hypothesis claims that the type of language use the learner participates in functions as a determinant of acquisition. Participation in the planned mode is required to achieve higher levels of grammatical competence because only in this type of language use is there full grammaticalization. According to the collaborative discourse hypothesis, learners are able to produce syntactical structures beyond their competence with the help of 'scaffolding' provided by an interlocutor. This hypothesis helps to explain the occurrence of certain transitional constructions in the initial stages of language acquisition. Finally, the topicalization hypothesis suggests that learner production is important when learners have the chance to nominate topics and to control their development. This kind of output can serve as valuable input for other learners.

To conclude this section, two points need to be emphasized. First, although the theoretical positions which have been outlined emphasize the importance of learner output, they do so in the context of *interaction*. That is, production is seen as valuable not only in itself, but because it contributes to *discourse*. Interaction is a joint venture and ultimately it is not possible to isolate the separate contributions of the speakers or, perhaps, of production and comprehension. Second, the four hypotheses are not in competition with each other and no one hypothesis can claim to provide a complete explanation of classroom L2 learning.

Conclusion

The purpose of this chapter has been to examine a number of theoretical positions concerning the relationship between instruction and L2 learning. In doing so, 'instruction' has been defined as 'the interaction that takes place inside the classroom'. It is important to emphasize that this perspective has not excluded formal language teaching. The kinds of discourse that result from form-focused language work have been treated as constituting a particular kind of interaction. All classroom discourse, irrespective of whether it derives from form or meaning-focused instruction can be considered as interaction of one kind or another. This perspective has been informed by Allwright's (1984a:158) claim that 'it is through the joint management of interaction in the classroom that language learning itself is jointly managed.'

The theories described in this chapter have outstripped empirical research. There has been very little research which has attempted to establish a direct relationship between interaction and L2 acquisition. Indeed there are major difficulties in designing such research. More promising is research designed to investigate whether certain kinds of interaction promote comprehension. However, this still leaves the problem that comprehension and acquisition are not the same thing (see discussion on p. 105). Production-based hypotheses such as the output and discourse hypotheses also lack a firm empirical base. In addition, it should be noted that not all the research reported in this chapter has taken place inside the classroom. Much of it has been experimental in nature, although it has typically involved classroom learners.

What conclusions are possible? In answering this question it is useful to distinguish three possible roles for classroom interaction: a strong role, a weak role and a zero role. According to the strong role, interaction in some way *determines* the way learners acquire a L2. Ellis (1984a; 1985c), for instance, claims that syntactic structures develop out of learning how to do conversations and draws on the evidence provided by studies of collaborative discourse. Swain suggests that pushing learners to be precise and appropriate in some way induces them to acquire complex structures which they would otherwise ignore. According to the weak role, interaction *facilitates* but does not determine interlanguage development. This is the position taken up by proponents of the input and interaction hypotheses. The learner is responsible for selecting features from the input as intake (e.g. by means of the language-acquisition device). However, certain types of communication (i.e. those that ensure comprehensible input) make the learner's task easier by providing her with sufficient samples of just those features she is ready to acquire. According to the zero role, interaction only triggers learning, while some learning can take place without any interaction (cf. White, 1987). The position that I lean towards is that all three roles are possible. Some structures probably are learnt through the process of constructing discourse and some structures are consolidated by being 'pushed'. Certain kinds of interaction are especially helpful in enabling the learner to obtain intake. Many linguistic rules are acquired with little or no help from input or output. This position is motivated by my recognition of the many-faceted nature of language acquisition and my conviction that different grammatical properties can be acquired in different ways.

From the point of view of language pedagogy it is more important to consider how interaction can be organized in the classroom in order to promote acquisition than to argue about the precise role of communication. What kind of communication is 'optimal'? The answer to this question will need to draw on the insights provided by both reception and production-based theories.

An optimal communicative environment for classroom language learning can be considered one where:

1   There is clear separation of the student's L1 and the target language (Fillmore, 1985). This is required so that the students feel the need to communicate in the L2.
2   The students are involved and interested in what is being talked about. In order to achieve this it will be necessary to ensure that the students are given opportunities to control the topic of conversation. Students need to be allowed more initiative than is common in most language classrooms.
3   Both the teacher and the students make efforts to be understood. This calls for the use of effective interactional strategies on the part of all the participants to ensure that comprehension is achieved. Some strategies which have been found to work are the repeated use of patterns and

routines by the teacher and repetitive lesson formats (Fillmore, 1976). The interactional strategies found in the negotiation of meaning may also help, as may input rich in directives in the early stages (Ellis, 1984a).

4   The students are encouraged to produce utterances which tax their linguistic resources − at least some of the time. In order to achieve this it will be necessary for the teacher to vary the type of question asked to suit the students' level of proficiency (i.e. not to ask only simple display questions). It will also be necessary for the students to be able to initiate discourse so that they have the opportunity to perform a range of speech acts, requiring varied linguistic resources. Teachers should also encourage learners to reformulate their own utterances that cause comprehension problems. This can be effectively achieved by means of clarification requests.

5   The students have the opportunity to participate in the kind(s) of discourse (planned and/or unplanned) which correspond to their communicative needs outside the classroom.

6   In the initial stages the teacher helps to provide scaffolding for the production of structures which are too complex for learners to produce by themselves.

7   In the later stages, learners have adequate access to planned discourse rich in marked linguistic features.

8   Learner production is not forced. Learners need to be free to choose when to produce.

Optimal interaction of this kind is most likely to occur in meaning-focused instruction, although some features of it can also be found in form-focused instruction. It certainly does not follow that formal instruction is entirely without value, even if this is treated as 'interaction'.

NOTES

1   Krashen recognizes that comprehending input is not the same as acquisition. If the learner is not 'open' to input because of negative attitudes, it will not reach those parts of the brain responsible for acquisition. In this sense, then, comprehensible input is not 'sufficient'.

2   I am indebted to White (1987) for the reasoning behind this example.

3   Krashen provides no evidence to show that the methods he believes facilitative of acquisition provide more comprehensible input than those he does not consider effective. His argument is circular, in fact.

4   An account of Krashen's theory of how the skill of writing is developed can be found in Krashen (1984).

5   Two kinds of models have been used to explain the process of L2 acquisition; sequence models and growth models. Early L2 acquisition research (such as the morpheme studies) was based on a sequence model; learning progressed one

step at a time. Later research, in particular that associated with the study of learner variability (e.g. Huebner, 1979) has emphasized the holistic nature of interlanguage systems and the dynamic nature of interlanguage change.

6   There are relatively few studies of the L2 comprehension process. Exceptions are Carrell (1983) and Wolff (1987). These researchers disagree, however, over something as basic as whether L2 learners, like L1 users, are adept at top—down processing.

7   To claim that learners acquire past tense interrogatives from such exchanges is an example of the kind of 'leaps' that Hatch (1983b) warns about.

8   Clarification requests and confirmation checks are used to deal with communication problems. Teachers who dominate the classroom discourse may leave little room for learners to negotiate in this way. However, comprehension checks can be executed by the teacher without any loss of discourse control.

9   Nunan (1987) reports on a similar study to that of Long et al. (1984). A teacher was encouraged to focus on the use of referential questions in a communicative language lesson in order to relate the content of the lesson to the students' own lives. Nunan reports that 'the effect was immediately apparent'. Whereas an earlier lesson had resulted in little genuine communication, the lesson following the 'training' was characterized by such features as content-based topic nominations from the learners, student/student interactions, an increase in the length and complexity of student turns, the negotiation of meaning between teacher and learners and even an example of a student disagreeing with the teacher.

10   Further evidence in support of the output hypothesis can be found in a study carried out by Mitchell, Parkinson and Johnstone (1981). They correlated various teaching behaviours in 16 French as a foreign language classrooms in Scotland with pupils' scores on comprehension, narration and structure tests. Significant relationships between the test scores and the amount of pupil talk (as opposed to listening or reading) were found. Seliger (1977) also found a positive correlation between learners' participation in classroom interaction and learning outcomes. However, not all studies have produced similar results; amount of production does not always correlate significantly or even positively with acquisition. It should be noted that these studies have not examined 'pushed output' and, therefore, do not speak directly to the output hypothesis as formulated by Swain.

11   The distinction between informal/unplanned and formal/planned discourse has been made by a number of commentators. Olson (1977) distinguishes the notions of **utterance** and **text**. The former occurs in oral communication where language is typically inexplicit and unformalized because the participants are able to make use of nonverbal cues. Text refers to written language; it is decontextualized and formally explicit. Olson argues that language development proceeds from the ability to produce utterances to the ability to produce texts and that one of the main functions of schooling is to facilitate this development. Callfee and Freedman (1980) distinguish *natural* and *formal* language, which correspond closely to utterance and text, except that they consider the distinction to be independent of speech and writing. Cummins (1981:11) talks of 'a continuum of contextual support available for expressing or receiving meaning'. For Cummins, therefore, the distinction between **context-embedded communication** and **context-reduced communication** represents a continuum rather than a dichotomy. The general distinction represented by these various terms is clearly widely supported in the theoretical literature. This literature tends to assume that language users

progress from informal/unplanned language use to formal/planned language use. This is certainly true for L1 acquisition and perhaps also for the kinds of *second* language learners that Cummins describes (i.e. bilingual learners in Canada). However, it need not to be the case. It is possible for learners who have already acquired formal/planned language use in their L1 to start with this in L2 acquisition. Such learners will find context-reduced communication easier to handle than context-embedded communication. This is the position advanced by the discourse hypothesis.

12   Pavesi's study was based on the Accessibility Hierarchy for relative pronouns (Comrie and Keenan, 1978). This was derived from a study of relative clauses in a large number of different languages. An implicational scale for relative pronoun functions was established:

Subject > Direct object > Indirect object > Object of preposition >
Genitive > Object of comparative

According to this scale the most likely function of a relative pronoun is that of Subject and the least likely Object of comparative. Furthermore, the scale predicts that if a language permits relative pronouns with a given relative function (e.g. Direct object) then it will also permit relative clauses with pronoun functions higher in the hierarchy (i.e. Subject) but not with pronoun functions lower down (i.e. those to the right of Direct object).

13   It should be noted, however, that collaborative discourse can only occur if the learner has the opportunity to participate in an exchange involving several turns. Discourse that is rigidly controlled by the teacher so that learners are allocated only one move (i.e. responding) may prohibit collaboration. This may be one of the effects of a teaching style that makes extensive use of display questions.

14   Slimani's conclusion flies in the face of the output hypothesis, as it suggests that acquisition occurs when the learner is involved in listening rather than in production. It should be noted, however, that Slimani's study focused chiefly on vocabulary acquisition (her learners' reported uptake consisted almost entirely of lexical items). It is possible that different aspects of communication are responsible for different aspects of acquisition. The interactions which Slimani investigated occurred in the context of form-focused instruction. The results Slimani obtained, therefore, may not generalize to interaction in meaning-focused instruction.

6 Formal Instruction and Language Learning

Introduction

Teaching can be viewed in two different ways: (1) as interaction and (2) as formal instruction. In the last chapter we investigated the teaching–learning relationship by considering teaching as interaction. In this chapter, we will look at the relationship between formal instruction and learning. We will be concerned with direct pedagogic intervention – attempts to influence the way interlanguage develops through formal instruction which (1) focuses on some specific property of the target language and (2) tries to make the learner aware of what the correct grammatical use of the form is. The central question we will consider is whether formal instruction facilitates acquisition and, if it does, in what way. We will review research that has examined the effect of instruction on both the rate/success of acquisition and on the process/sequence of acquisition.

The Effect of Formal Instruction on the Rate and Level of L2 Acquisition

Long (1983b) reviewed a total of eleven studies that examined the effect of formal instruction on the rate/success of L2 acquisition. Six of these studies showed that instruction helped, two produced ambiguous results,[10] and three indicated that instruction did not help. All the studies used designs involving comparisons between learners receiving instruction and those experiencing exposure with or without instruction. In other words, they attempted to find an answer to the question 'Does L2 instruction make a difference?' by asking whether instruction or exposure produced the more rapid or higher levels of learning.

On the basis of this review Long claimed that 'there is considerable evidence to indicate that SL instruction does make a difference' (1983b:374). He also claimed that instruction was beneficial (1) for children as well as adults, (2) for intermediate and advanced students, (3) irrespective of whether acquisition was measured by means of an integrative or discrete-point test, and (4) in acquisition-rich as well as acquisition-poor environments.[2] Instruction was more effective than exposure in promoting L2 acquisition.

As an example of the studies that Long reviewed we will consider one (Krashen, Jones, Zelinski and Usprich, 1978) in some detail. The subjects were 116 ESL students who had experienced different amounts of instruction and exposure. The students were given three tests: the Michigan Test of English Proficiency, a free composition (which was graded by dividing the total number of words each learner wrote by the number of errors she made), and a cloze test. The test scores were correlated with both the number of years each student reported having spent in an English-speaking country and the number of years of formal English study. The correlations between the test scores and the measures of amounts of exposure and instruction were all statistically significant. However, the effect of formal language study was much stronger than that of informal contact. For example, 25 per cent of the total variance on the Michigan test was accounted for by instruction but only 3.2 per cent by exposure. The authors concluded that 'formal instruction is a more efficient way of learning English for adults than trying to learn it in the streets' (1978:260).

Since Long's review article there have been a number of other studies. We will consider three. Weslander and Stephany (1983) examined the effects of instruction on 577 children with limited English proficiency in Grades 2 to 10 in public schools in Iowa. Students who received more instruction did better on the Bilingual Syntax Measure, a test devised by Burt, Dulay and Hernandez (1973) to elicit natural speech. The effects were strongest at lower levels of proficiency in the first year of schooling and diminished in subsequent years. These results contrast with those obtained by Hale and Budar (1970). This study (which Long included in his review[3]) found that learners who spent two to three periods each day in special Teaching English as a Second or Other Language (TESOL) classes 'were being more harmed than helped'.

Similar results were obtained by Ellis and Rathbone (1987). They examined the effects of class attendance on the levels of learning achieved by 39 adult learners of L2 German. The setting was a foreign-language classroom in this case, so there was limited opportunity for naturalistic exposure. The instruction was very formal, consisting largely of controlled practice of grammatical items. Overall attendance during a six-month period was found to correlate significantly with a number of measures of grammatical learning,[4] including those based on elicited natural speech. This suggests a positive effect for instruction. However, no relationship was found between attendance and achievement in the first three months of the study. Ellis and Rathbone speculate that this may be because the instruction had a delayed rather than immediate effect, a point that will be taken up later.

The third study, Spada (1986), provides new insights which are of considerable importance. Whereas the studies that Long examined in his review sought to compare the effects of instruction with the effects of exposure,

Spada set out to establish whether there was any interaction between type of contact and type of instruction. She examined the effects of instruction and exposure in 48 adult learners enrolled in an intensive six-week ESL course in Canada. Spada found that although type and amount of contact appeared to account for variation in some aspects of the learners' proficiency before the effects of instruction were considered, it did not account for differences in the learners' improvement during the course. She concludes that contact is a less powerful predictor of differences in learners' L2 abilities than instruction. However, Spada also found that the type of instruction interacted with the amount of contact individual learners experienced: 'contact positively accounted for differences in learners' improvement on the grammar and writing tests when the instruction was more form-focused, and negatively accounted for differences on these measures when the instruction was less form-focused.' (1986:97). In other words, instruction based on direct intervention worked better than instruction based on indirect intervention where grammar and literacy were concerned when the learners had opportunity for plentiful informal contact outside the classroom. The implication of this study is that learners require both formal instruction and informal exposure and that the two together work better than either on its own.

Long's (1983b) review has been widely cited as demonstrating that formal instruction has a positive effect on L2 acquisition. There are, however, a number of reasons for exercising caution. We will examine some of the major ones.

1   As Long admits, many of the studies failed to control for overall amount of combined contact and instruction. That is, the results obtained by some studies showing that instruction was more important for learning than contact might reflect greater overall opportunity for acquisition inside and outside of the classroom. To counter this objection, Long points to studies (e.g. Krashen and Seliger, 1976) which showed that more exposure did not result in higher proficiency in learners who had been matched for the amount of instruction they had received. The results of these studies contrasted with those that showed that differences in the amount of instruction were positively related to differences in proficiency in learners who had received the same overall amount of exposure. Long argues that these contrasting results enable us to be more confident in finding a positive effect for instruction in studies which failed to control for overall acquisition opportunities. However, if such studies are excluded on the grounds of this design flaw, the number of studies in Long's original review which unambiguously show that instruction helps is reduced to two.

2   An intervening variable – which Long does not consider, but which Krashen, Jones, Zelinksi and Usprich (1978) do – is that of the learners' motivation. Students who are highly motivated to learn are likely to enrol in classes. Those who are less strongly motivated will keep away. Therefore, the

positive effect found for instruction may simply reflect stronger motivation on the part of the classroom learners.

3   Another serious problem concerns the assumption made by the authors of all the studies Long reviewed that the amount of formal instruction experienced by learners can be equated with the number of years spent in the classroom. None of the studies obtained any data about the nature of the classroom processes which took place in the name of instruction. We do not know for certain, therefore, that the instruction was form-focused. But even if we accept that this was likely for at least a large proportion of the total teaching time, there is still a problem. As we have seen, formal instruction can be viewed as 'interaction' rather than as an attempt to intervene directly in interlanguage development. It is possible, therefore, that the positive effects of instruction derived not from the fact that learners were focusing on form but from the communicative properties of the interactions which occurred. Long is aware of this problem and seeks to immunize against it by arguing that there is evidence to suggest that instruction is beneficial even in settings where the learners have plenty of opportunity for negotiation of meaning outside the classroom (i.e. 'acquisition-rich environments'). According to Long, this indicates that the instruction worked, not because it provided *comprehensible input* but because it required learners to focus on form. However, it is possible to find counter-arguments. Long admits one possibility – namely, that the so-called acquisition-rich environments were not so rich after all. Another is that learners were able to 'let in' more input in a classroom context because they felt more secure and more relaxed than in face-to-face interactions with native speakers in naturalistic settings. The main problem is that, given the design of the studies Long examined, there is no evidence to enable us to make an informed decision between these various arguments.

Despite these misgivings, it seems reasonable to assume that formal instruction is of value in promoting rapid and higher levels of acquisition. Long's review and the subsequent studies can be seen as providing tentative support to this claim. There is also the experience of countless successful language learners, which testifies to the value of form-focused study (e.g. Pickett, 1978). Spada's study is salutary in that it encourages us to recognize that comparing the differential effects of informal contact and instruction is, in fact, simplistic and potentially misleading. Clearly learners need both. Furthermore, formal instruction may work best when there are also opportunities for informal language use. In other words, the effects of instruction may not be absolute – as Long's review suggests – but contingent upon certain conditions being met.

The research which has been considered in this section is summarized in table 6.1. It provides no information about the process of classroom language learning. In the next section, we examine research which has investigated this issue.

Table 6.1 Empirical studies of the effects of instruction on the rate/success of L2 acquisition

Study	Type of classroom	Subjects	Proficiency	Data	Results
Carroll (1967)	Foreign language learning in United States (exposure abroad)	Adults – first language English	All proficiency levels	Integrative test	Both instruction and exposure help, but exposure helps most.
Chihara and Oller (1978)	EFL in Japan	Adults – first language Japanese	All proficiency levels	1 Discrete point test 2 Integrative test	Instruction helps, but exposure does not.
Krashen, Seliger and Hartnett (1974)	ESL in United States	Adults – mixed first languages	All proficiency levels	Discrete point test	Instruction helps, but exposure does not.
Briere (1978)	Spanish as a second language in Mexico	Children – local Indian language is first language	Beginners	Discrete point test	Both instruction and exposure help, but instruction helps most.
Krashen and Seliger (1976)	ESL in United States	Adults – mixed first languages	Intermediate and advanced	Integrative test	Instruction helps, but exposure does not.
Krashen et al. (1978)	ESL in United States	Adults – mixed first languages	All proficiency levels	1 Discrete point test 2 Integrative test	Both instruction and exposure help, but instruction helps most.
Hale and Budar (1970)	ESL in United States	Adolescents – mixed first languages	All proficiency levels	1 Discrete point test 2 Integrative test	Exposure helps but instruction does not – results doubtful, however.
Fathman (1976)	ESL in United States	Children – mixed first languages	All proficiency levels	Integrative test	Exposure helps but instruction does not – results doubtful, however.
Upshur (1968)	ESL in United States	Adults – mixed first languages	Intermediate and advanced	Discrete point test	Instruction does not help.

Study	Context	Learners	Proficiency	Measure	Findings
Mason (1971)	ESL in United States	Adults – mixed first languages	Intermediate and advanced	1 Discrete point test 2 Integrative test	Instruction does not help.
Fathman (1975)	ESL in United States	Children – mixed first languages	All proficiency levels	Integrative test	Instruction does not help.
Ellis (1984c)	ESL in Britain	Children – mixed first languages	Post-beginner level	Spontaneous speech from picture task	Instruction had no overall effect on production of WH questions – individual development not related to instructional opportunities.
Weslander and Stephany (1983)	ESL in United States	Mixed children and adolescents – Grades 2 to 10	Mixed levels of proficiency	Bilingual Syntax Measure	Instruction helps – particularly at lower proficiency levels
Ellis and Rathbone (1987)	German as FL in UK	Adults in higher education	Complete and false beginners	1 Spontaneous speech task 2 Discrete point test	Learners who attended most showed greatest gains on 1 and 2.
Spada (1986)	ESL in Canada	Adults in short intensive course	Intermediate	Various tests of communicative competence	Positive effect for instruction, but this worked best in learners who also had plenty of exposure.

The Effect of Instruction on the Process of L2 Acquisition

There have been a number of studies that have investigated whether instruction influences the process of L2 acquisition. These studies have sought to establish the effects of instruction in two ways: (1) by comparing classroom and naturalistic acquisition and (2) by means of classroom experiments designed to ascertain whether teaching specific items results in their acquisition.

Comparisons between Classroom and Naturalistic L2 Acquisition

Research that falls into this category has studied a number of 'process' features; L2 errors, the sequence of acquisition of grammatical morphemes and the sequence of development of syntactical structures such as relative clauses and word order.

Error Analysis

Errors provide evidence of the processes involved in interlanguage development (cf. chapter 3). Comparisons of the errors found in naturalistic and classroom L2 acquisition, therefore, help to show whether the processes involved in the two kinds of acquisition are the same or different. There are three possibilities:

1 the errors are the same;
2 instruction enables learners to avoid errors commonly found in naturalistic acquisition;
3 instruction results in different kinds of errors.

If (1) is true it can be concluded that the process of interlanguage development is immune to instruction; (2) provides evidence that instruction *facilitates* acquisition; (3) is more difficult to interpret; it suggests that instruction does affect the process of acquisition, but not necessarily in a positive way.

The available evidence indicates that instruction is powerless to prevent developmental errors occurring. Felix (1981) reports on a study involving thirty-four children studying L2 English in their first year in a German high school. He examined errors relating to negation, interrogation, sentence types and pronouns. Here we will consider the results he obtained for negation. Naturalistic learners typically go through an early stage in which negative utterances have the form of 'no' + verb — for example:

No you playing there.
Mariana no coming today.

Felix found a few examples of this kind of negative in the children's spontaneous classroom speech:

It's no my comb.

but they were rare, perhaps because there was little opportunity for spontaneous language use in the classroom. However, Felix found that even in drill situations, the students failed to produce correct negative sentences 45 per cent of the time. On these occasions they produced sentences of the kind:

Doesn't she eat apples.

instead of the correct negative:

She doesn't eat apples.

The use of 'doesn't' in this way is not found in naturalistic acquisition. However, Felix suggests it provides evidence of similar processes at work, as 'doesn't' was monomorphemic for the learners and appeared in sentence-initial position. In other words, these classroom learners were using 'doesn't' in the same way as naturalistic learners use 'no'. On the basis of the results obtained for negation (and similar results for the other structures), Felix concluded that the parallels between tutored and naturalistic learners were striking.

In a similar study, Felix and Simmet (1981) concluded that the processes of acquisition of the English pronoun system were also unaffected by instruction. The subjects were seventy students in a classical language high school and a modern language high school in Germany. During the course of a school year, they received instruction in the use of English pronouns. This instruction took the form of explanations and practice of each separate pronoun form in an incremental fashion. However, learner data obtained from classroom recordings indicated that the students did not master pronouns as whole forms, but as bundles of semantic features, with one feature being acquired at a time. Thus, gender was acquired first, followed in turn by person, number and case. Felix and Simmet provided evidence to show that this feature-oriented approach was typical of both L1 and naturalistic L2 acquisition. They argued that the students made use of 'instruction-independent learning strategies'.

Whereas these two studies indicate that the process of acquisition cannot be manipulated by instruction, the third error-analysis study we will examine suggests that instruction can have an effect. However, the effect is not the desired one; instruction does not prevent 'natural' errors but can interfere with natural processing. Lightbown (1983), in a study referred to in the previous chapter, reports on the acquisition of a number of grammatical features by seventy-six ESL students in a Canadian high school. In this study, learner data were obtained outside the classroom by means of a communication game. We will consider the results for V-ing. Lightbown found that the frequency and accuracy of V-ing declined from Grade 6 to Grade 7. At the earlier time the learners produced V-ing correctly as in:

He's taking a cake

while at the later time they substituted the uninflected verb form:

He take a cake.

V-ing is acquired early in naturalistic L2 acquisition without any evidence of the kind of subsequent decline observed in these classroom learners. Lightbown suggests that the explanation for the unusual reversion is to be found in the formal instruction the learners experienced. 'Over-learning' of V-ing occurred as a result of intensive instruction in this feature towards the end of Grade 5. This led to frequent and accurate use of the form during Grade 6. However, instruction in V-ing was discontinued in this year, while instruction in the use of the present simple tense was stepped up. This resulted in the learners dropping V-ing in favour of simple forms in Grade 7. Lightbown contrasts the 'rote learning' of V-ing with the natural process by which V-ing is learnt in meaning-focused language use. She comments: 'By forcing learners to repeat and overlearn forms which have no associated meaning to contrast them with any other form(s), we may be setting up barriers which have to be broken down before the learners can begin to build up their own interlanguage systems,' (1983:239). In other words, formal instruction can temporarily interfere with the natural process of language learning.

To sum up, the evidence provided by these error analysis studies suggests:

1   In some structures such as English negation and the pronominal system, instruction is unable to circumvent the natural processes of acquisition.
2   Instruction can result in some structures such as V-ing being 'overlearnt'.
3   'Over-learning' has to be overcome before real interlanguage development can take place.

The evidence, then, suggests that formal instruction either has no effect or a deleterious effect on L2 acquisition.

Morpheme Acquisition Studies

The 1970s saw a number of cross-sectional studies of English morpheme acquisition by naturalistic or mixed L2 learners (e.g. Dulay and Burt, 1974b; Bailey, Madden and Krashen, 1974; Larsen-Freeman, 1976b). The procedure followed by these studies has been described in chapter 3 (see section on

performance analysis). The results obtained were used to make claims that there was a more or less standard of 'natural' order of accuracy/acquisition;[5] this was not influenced by the learners' L1, age or whether the medium of production was speech or writing.

Performance analysis has provided a convenient basis for investigating a number of interrelated questions:

1 Is there any difference between the order of instruction and the order of acquisition?
2 Is it possible to alter the 'natural' order of acquisition by means of instruction?
3 Do instructed learners follow the same order of acquisition as untutored learners or a different order?

We will examine some of the research which has sought answers to these questions.

The available research indicates that the order of acquisition of English grammatical morphemes does not follow the order in which these items are taught. Turner (1979) investigated three eighteen-year-old Spanish learners of L2 English who were enrolled on an intensive English programme at the University of Texas. The order of acquisition they manifested in both natural speech and elicited data was not strongly related to the order of instruction as stated in their teachers' lesson plans. Turner notes that the instruction might have been expected to have influenced the acquisition of simple structures such as plural -s and past tense -ed. However, the learners failed to show any acquisition of these forms. Turner also administered the Michigan Diagnostic Grammar Test and found that the learners scored correctly on items testing knowledge of the past tense. Drawing on Krashen's distinction, Turner concluded that instruction has little effect on 'acquisition' but has a considerable effect on 'learning'. Makino (1980) obtained very similar results. He used written data based on picture stimuli from a total of 777 learners of L2 English in Grades 8 and 9 in rural and urban high schools in Japan. No relationship between the teaching order of morphemes in the two textbooks that were used and the observed acquisition order was found.

A number of other studies have investigated whether instruction in the accurate production of specific morphemes results in a disturbance of the 'natural' acquisition order. For example, Perkins and Larsen-Freeman (1975) examined the effects of one month's intensive instruction in articles, past irregular and possessive -s on twelve Venezuelan students recently arrived in the United States. They found that the instruction did not result in any change in the accuracy order of five morphemes in the spontanenous speech of the learners from the beginning to end of the period of study. They concluded that the instruction did not influence the route of acquisition.[6]

Comparative studies of the acquisition orders found in tutored and untutored learners have produced mixed results. Krashen, Sferlazza, Feldman and

Fathman (1976) found similar orders for the two kinds of learners. So too did Makino in the study referred to above. However, Sajavaara (1981) found a disturbed 'natural' order among Finnish students, while Fathman (1978) found both similarities and differences between adolescents acquiring English informally in the United States and those studying English in formal classrooms in Germany. It is difficult to interpret these findings as the studies used different types of data (e.g. written vs. spoken) and also some of the so-called untutored learners may have received formal instruction.

Lightbown's study (1983; 1987), however, does suggest that instruction can affect the order of acquisition of grammaticäl morphemes. She found that the order evident in school students' spontaneous speech differed from Krashen's (1977) 'natural' order. The auxiliary was performed more accurately and V-ing less accurately by the classroom learners. Lightbown argues that these differences were the result of the 'distorted' input derived from instruction. However, she found that the effect was only temporary. Natural processing took over once the structures were no longer the object of instructional attention.

The most important comparative study which has been carried out to date is that by Pica (1983; 1985a). Pica studied the acquisition orders of three groups of six learners: (1) instruction only, (2) purely naturalistic and (3) mixed (i.e. learners who received formal instruction and had opportunity for informal contacts). The data consisted of hour-long audiotaped conversations between each subject and the researcher. Pica calculated the rank orders for eight morphemes using the standard method (i.e. based on suppliance of morphemes in their obligatory contexts). She also obtained accuracy scores that took into account over- as well as under-suppliance of each morpheme in order to build up a picture of the learners' abilities to perform in a completely target-like manner.

Pica found no evidence that the accuracy order of the instructed group was disturbed. The morpheme rank order of this group was significantly correlated with the orders obtained for both the naturalistic and mixed groups. It also correlated strongly with Krashen's (1977) 'natural' order. Pica comments: 'all groups of subjects, across all language contexts, exhibited a highly similar overall rank order or morpheme suppliance in obligatory contexts' (1983:479).

However, when Pica investigated over-suppliance of grammatical morphemes (i.e. overgeneralizations such as 'teached' and the use of morphemes in non-obligatory occasions as in 'He lived in London now'), she found considerably more instances in the instructed than in naturalistic group. For example, the instructed group overused V-ing to a much greater extent, a result that replicates Lightbown's finding. Also when Pica investigated the accuracy levels of individual morphemes, group differences were apparent. In the case of the plural -s inflection, suppliance was greater in the instructed group than in the mixed or naturalistic groups. The naturalistic learners tended to omit plural -s on nouns premodified by quantifiers (e.g. 'three boy') − a pattern of language use frequently noted in pidgins. Differences were also evident on third person -s. The percentage accuracy of this morpheme in the instructed group was 63 per cent, but only 22 per cent and 25 per cent respectively in the mixed and naturalistic groups.

Pica is cautious in making claims for instruction. She points out that the sample (only eighteen subjects, six per group) was very small and that the study was restricted to adult native speakers of Spanish. She also emphasizes that any claim must be restricted to interlanguage *production* and that no conclusions can be drawn about *acquisition* or *ultimate attainment*.[7] But Pica suggests that the results support the prevailing view that learners contribute a great deal of 'natural ability' to their acquisition of a second language. Instruction does have some effects, however; it can inhibit the use of non-standard forms and it can, in certain circumstances, have a positive effect on levels of accuracy. Pica (1983) suggests that instruction can help learners to outgrow the use of pidgin-like constructions that are communicatively effective but ungrammatical. Pica (1985a) argues that the impact of instruction is related to the linguistic complexity of different features:

1 Production of simple morphemes like plural and third person -s is improved by instruction.
2 Instruction can result in over-production of forms like V-ing (i.e. learners attach -ing to base verbs where its use is not required). Such forms are less simple than -s forms because they perform a range of functions.
3 Instruction has no impact on complex structures such as article *a*. This is because the rules for form—function relationships in such structures are not readily transparent.

Pica's work, therefore, introduces the interesting possibility that instruction has a direct effect on acquisition, but that this impact is selective — a point to be returned to later.

It is difficult to come to any firm conclusions regarding the effect instruction has on the process of acquisition on the basis of the morpheme studies reviewed above. The bulk of the studies found that the rank accuracy order of tutored learners did not differ from that of naturalistic learners. Morpheme studies are methodologically flawed, however (see chapter 3). The assumption that accuracy order is the same as acquisition order is almost certainly unjustified. Also, the 'accumulated entities' view of L2 acquisition (Rutherford, 1987) is misplaced. This view is inadequate for a number of reasons. The learner does not work on one structure at a time but on the whole system or sub-system. Morpheme studies had their heyday in the 1970s. Pica's classroom study was one of the last to be published. Their value to our understanding of L2 acquisition is extremely doubtful.

The detailed study of individual morphemes — of the kind illustrated in Pica's research — is informative, however, as it throws light on those linguistic factors that mediate between instruction and learning. Such research needs to be complemented by studies of *syntactical* features.

The Acquisition of Syntactical Features

Most modern linguists would consider the syntax of a language of greater theoretical interest than its morphology. Arguably, the same holds for L2 acquisition studies. There has been a general shift in focus from morphemes to syntax. This shift is reflected in studies of naturalistic and classroom acquisition.

There are two kinds of syntactical structures which have attracted interest. The first are **transitional structures**. These are structures like negatives and interrogatives that are learnt in a series of stages with the target-language structure as the final stage. Each stage constitutes a necessary stepping-stone to the next stage. The second type are the syntactical structures that make up a **structural group**. In this case, the structures conform to target-language norms. Examples are relative-clause structures in English and word-order rules in German.

There has been a substantial amount of research which has investigated the L2 acquisition of English negatives and interrogatives in naturalistic settings. The available research (cf. Ellis, 1984a; ch. 2) suggests that there is predictable series of stages through which learners pass. Such structures present an interesting test for the efficacy of instruction, as their interim stages involve the production of deviant syntactical patterns such as:

No play baseball
Britta no have this
This is flag?
What they are picking?

The key question is whether instruction can help the learner to avoid such transitional forms and lead her directly to the target structures. We have already considered evidence from error-analysis studies that suggests this unlikely (see p. 136). We will now consider a number of longitudinal studies.

Ellis (1982; 1984a) carried out a one-year study of three children aged between ten and thirteen in a London language unit. Ellis collected samples of speech that the learners produced in meaning-focused classroom interactions. He found that the developmental profile for both negatives and interrogatives was more or less identical to that reported for naturalistic L2 acquisition. For example, early negatives consisted of anaphoric negation (i.e. 'no' by itself or 'no' + a separate statement), followed by external negation (e.g. 'no sir finish') and then internal negation (e.g. 'somebody not driving with this'). The children failed to reach the next stage, where the negative particle is realized with a full range of auxiliary verbs. Ellis claims that the children appeared to rely on exactly the same processes that characterize the acquisition of negatives in a natural setting, despite the fact that standard negative structures were formally taught at various points during the year.

Ellis's learners were not pure classroom learners, so caution needs to be exercised in claiming that instruction has no effect on the acquisition of transitional structures on the basis of his study. It is possible that exposure to natural language use overrode the instruction they received.

Weinert's (1987) study, however, is not subject to the same caveat. She carried out a four-year study of the acquisition of German negation by Scottish secondary school children. Data for the study consisted of both the utterances the learners produced in class and speech elicited by means of a meaning-focused task performed outside the classroom. Weinert found that the negative utterances produced by first-year students consisted mainly of routines and patterns of the kind:

Das ist kein _____.
Ich spiele nicht gern _____.

This gave the appearance of relatively well-formed negative sentences. However, the first year data also included examples of non-standard negative structures of the kind found in naturalistic acquisition. In the second year the learners used external negation more frequently:

Nein, ich lerne Karate.

The learners gradually switched from external to internal negation between the second and fourth years, first producing utterances with pre-verbal negation:

Zola Budd nicht spiele Fussball.

and later the standard post-verbal negation:

Ich kann nicht spiele Gitarre.

Weinert argues that the learners constructed their interlanguage systems in the same way as naturalistic learners. She speculates that instruction might actually hold learners back by interfering with the organic processes of acquisition. For example, external negation might have appeared productively in the first year of acquisition but for the formulaic learning that resulted from extensive drilling of negative patterns.

One study (Ewbank, 1987), however, does suggest that instructed learners follow a different route to that of naturalistic learners. Ewbank investigated the acquisition of L2 German negatives by six university students. She found that all the learners placed the negator sentence final at one stage of development (e.g. Es ist Wanduhr nicht). This has not been reported in naturalistic L2 acquisition. Ewbank speculates that it was the result of students' attempts to speak in 'complete sentences' — a requirement of the instructional method. If this explanation is accepted, it constitutes further evidence that instruction can interfere with the natural processes of acquisition, resulting in deviations from both target language and interlanguage norms.

Comparative studies of group structures also indicate that instruction has little effect on acquisition. We will consider the results of two studies — one of English relative clauses and the other of German word-order rules.

A number of researchers have claimed that the acquisition of relative clauses conforms to general principles of linguistic markedness. Studies of naturalistic or mixed learners (e.g. Gass, 1979) have shown that Comrie and Keenan's Accessibility Hierarchy (see n 12 to ch. 5) is able to predict the order in which the grammatical functions of relative pronouns are acquired. Pavesi (1984 and 1986) reports on a cross-sectional study designed to establish whether markedness principles applied equally to the formal and informal acquisition of relative pronouns. Her formal learners were forty-eight EFL students in an Italian high school; her informal learners were thirty-eight Italian workers in Edinburgh. She elicited sentences requiring relativization in different syntactical positions by means of picture cues. Using implicational scaling, she was able to show that (1) the acquisition of relative pronouns progressed from unmarked to marked functions and (2) both groups of learners manifested the same implicational ordering. In other words, there was no difference in the acquisitional sequence. There were other differences, however. The formal learners demonstrated greater quantitative development, i.e. they produced a larger number of the more marked features. Also, the informal learners produced errors consisting of *noun* copies, while the formal learners produced *pronoun* copies:

The man who my father was talking to *the man* .... (= noun copy)

The man who my father was talking to *him* .... (= pronoun copy)

However, Pavesi does not consider formal instruction *per se* the source of these differences. Instead she argues that the higher levels of acquisition shown by the formal learners was the result of exposure to the planned discourse found in classroom communication (see discussion on p. 121).

The second study investigated the classroom acquisition of German word-order rules. Ellis (1989b) based his research on the findings of studies of naturalistic L2 acquisition (e.g. Meisel, 1983; Clahsen, 1985) which show that learners acquire German word-order rules in a predictable sequence:

1: Adverb preposing This rule states that, optionally, adverbs can be moved into sentence initial position, e.g.

Da spielen Kinder.
(There play children.)

The rule requires inversion (see below), but naturalistic learners typically acquire the rule in the first place without inversion,[8] e.g.

Da Kinder spielen.

2: *Particle* This rule states that non-finite verbal elements are moved to clause final position, e.g.

Ich möchte heute Abend ins Kino gehen.
(I would this evening into the cinema go.)

3: *Inversion* This rule states that a finite verb form precedes the subject of its clause in certain linguistic contexts, e.g.

Wann gehen wir ins Kino?
(When go we into the cinema?)

4: *Verb-end* This rule states that the finite verb is placed in final position in subordinate clauses, e.g.

Er fragte mich, warum ich traurig war.
(He asked me why I sad was.)

In order to explain this acquisitional sequence, Meisel (1983) and Clahsen (1984) have suggested that development proceeds in accordance with the cognitive complexity of the different operations involved in the production of each structure. Psycholinguistic restrictions govern acquisition, such that one operation serves as the prerequisite for another, more complex operation. These processing operations are discussed in some detail later (see table 6.3).

Ellis set out to investigate whether a group of thirty-nine learners of German as a foreign language in beginner courses manifested the same route of acquisition for the obligatory word-order rules (i.e. particle, inversion and verb-end). He used data collected by means of a communication task which the learners performed in pairs on two separate occasions. The results revealed the same order of acquisition for both the learners individually and as a group, i.e.

Verb-end > Inversion > Particle

This order did not correspond to either the order in which the three rules were first introduced or to the order of emphasis placed on the three rules in the classroom instruction the learners received in the six months' duration of the study. Ellis concluded that the learners followed their own internal 'syllabus' in the same way as untutored learners. This syllabus proved immune to instruction, despite the fact that the learners (college undergraduates) were well equipped in terms of experience and cognitive skills to benefit from direct intervention. Ellis noted, however, that the learners were in general *successful* in acquiring some knowledge of verb-end, the most advanced of the word-order rules – in contrast to naturalistic learners who in many cases failed to acquire inversion or verb-end in the studies carried out by Meisel and Clahsen.[9] German word-order rules have attracted considerable interest from classroom researchers. We will consider a number of other studies in a later section of this review.

These comparative studies of L2 syntax lend further support to the claim that the effects of instruction are extremely limited. The pervasive finding is that the overall *sequence* of acquisition is the same in classroom and naturalistic settings. There is some evidence to suggest that instruction may help to push the learner further along the sequence, but there is also some evidence to suggest that it may inhibit progress by encouraging the use of alternative strategies of production.

Review

We have now looked at a number of studies which have investigated the effect of instruction on interlanguage development by means of comparisons between classroom and naturalistic acquisition. Table 6.2 provides a summary of these studies.

Comparative studies of the effects of instruction afford a number of insights, but are difficult to interpret. This is because there is no way of deciding whether any difference between classroom and naturalistic L2 acquisition is the result of formal instruction *per se* or of the special communicative properties of classroom interaction. Comparative studies provide no information about the impact of instruction on the acquisition of specific linguistic features. In Long's (1983b) terms they shed light on the *relative utility* of instruction but not on its *absolute value*. Experimental studies, however, are not subject to this limitation, although they do have other problems.

Experimental Studies of the Effect of Instruction

Experimental studies enable us to examine whether explicit instruction directed at feature x results in x being acquired. The design of these studies follows a similar pattern. The learners' existing L2 knowledge is measured by means of a pre-test. The 'treatment' follows in the form of instruction focusing on one or more specific linguistic features. This usually takes place in the learners' normal classroom setting. A post-test is then administered in order to determine what gains in knowledge have taken place. In some studies, a further post-test is administered some time later in order to establish whether any gains identified by the first post-test are durable.

Experimental studies fall into three groups: (1) accuracy studies, (2) acquisition-sequence studies and (3) 'projection' studies (i.e. studies that seek

Table 6.2 Comparative studies of instructed and naturalistic L2 acquisition

Study	Type of classroom	Subjects	Proficiency	Data	Results
Felix (1981)	German as a FL in secondary schools	11-year-old children	Complete beginners	Recordings of classroom speech	Similar errors in negatives, interrogatives word order and pronouns as found in naturalistic learners.
Felix and Simmet (1981)	German as a FL in secondary schools	11-year-old children	Complete beginners	Recordings of classroom speech	Analysis of pronoun errors indicates same processes as in naturalistic acquisition.
Lightbown (1983; 1987)	English as a SL in schools in Canada	Children in grades 6, 7 and 8	Mainly lower intermediate	Spontaneous speech on picture task	V-ing overused by grade 6 children; replaced by V simple form in grade 7. Progressive aux, followed a similar pattern of development. Forms 'overlearnt' but natural processing takes over later. Impact of instruction evident some time after instruction given.
Turner (1979)	Intensive ESL course in USA	3 × 18-yr-olds	Beginners	Spontaneous speech and grammar test	Order of morpheme acquisition same as naturalistic order and different from order of instruction. Effect of instruction evident in grammar test.

Table 6.2 (Cont.)

Study	Type of classroom	Subjects	Proficiency	Data	Results
Makino (1980)	EFL in Japanese high school	Students in grades 8 and 9	Lower intermediate	Written data based on picture stimuli	Order of morpheme acquisition same as naturalistic order and different from teaching order in text books.
Perkins and Larsen-Freeman (1975)	ESL in university in USA	12 Venezuelan students recently arrived in USA	Intermediate	Translation test and spontaneous speech on picture task	Morpheme order in spontaneous data same as natural order and did not change as result of instruction. Order on translation task did change, however.
Fathman (1978)	EFL in Germany	Adolescents in high schools	Mixed levels of ability	Oral production test	Morpheme order correlated with order obtained from uninstructed ESL learners in United States.
Sajavaara (1981)	EFL in Finland	Adolescents in high school		Elicited speech	Morpheme order differed from natural order – articles ranked lower.
Pica (1983)	EFL in Mexico/ ESL in USA	6 adult EFL learners/6 adult ESL/and 6 adult natural learners	Mixed levels of ability	Audiotaped conversations with researcher	Morpheme order same as natural order – but instructed learners overused V-ing and supplied plural and 3rd person -s more frequently.

Study	Context	Subjects	Level	Data type	Findings
Ellis (1984a)	ESL in Britain	3 children aged 10–13 yrs	Complete beginners	Communicative classroom speech (i.e. focus on meaning)	Overall developmental route for negatives and interrogatives the same as in naturalistic acquisition – some features (e.g. past -ed) delayed.
Weinert (1987)	German as a FL in Scotland	Students in forms 1 to 4 in secondary school	Complete beginners to intermediate	Non-communicative classroom speech and spontaneous speech in communication game	Same pattern of development for negatives as in naturalistic learners – form 1 learners acquired formulas from language drills.
Ewbank (1987)	German as a FL in USA	6 adult learners at university	Beginners	Oral description of pictures	Some differences in stages of acquisition of negatives but these are not caused directly by the instructional sequence, but reflected the requirement to compose whole sentences.
Pavesi (1984; 1986)	EFL in Italy; ESL in Scotland	48 adolescents in high school; 38 Italian workers	Mixed ability levels	Oral data on relative clauses elicited by picture cues	Same order of acquisition of relative pronoun functions in instructed and naturalistic learners – instructed learners showed greater quantitative development.
Ellis (1989b)	German as a FL in Britain	39 adult learners in higher education	Beginners	Spontaneous speech in communication activity	Order of development of German word order rules same as in naturalistic learners and different from order of instruction.

to establish whether instruction in feature x not only results in the acquisition of x but also triggers the acquisition of features $y \ldots n$).

Accuracy Studies

In accuracy studies the effects of instruction are measured by investigating whether there are any gains in the accuracy with which specific structures are performed after the 'treatment'. We will consider four such studies. First, Schumann (1978) attempted to improve the accuracy with which Alberto, a Spanish-speaking learner of English in the United States, produced negatives. His reason for giving instruction was to discover whether the apparent 'pidginization' of Alberto's English could be overcome. Prior to the instructional experiment, Alberto's negatives were mainly of the 'no + V' type. The instruction covered a seven-month period, during which both elicited and spontaneous negative utterances were collected. There was a marked improvement in the accuracy of elicited negatives (64 per cent correct as opposed to 24 per cent before the instruction). However, the accuracy of the spontaneous utterances showed no significant change (20 per cent correct as opposed to 22 per cent before instruction). Schumann concluded that the instruction influenced production only in test-like situations, while normal communication remained unaffected.

Second, Lightbown, Spada and Wallace (1980) studied the effects of instruction on the accuracy with which three different structures were produced: (1) the -s morpheme, used to perform five functions (plural, possessive, third person singular, copula and auxiliary); (2) 'be' in sentences like 'He is sixteen years old'; and (3) locative prepositions indicating motion toward a goal (e.g. 'to'). The subjects were French-speaking children and adolescents learning English principally in a classroom setting in Canada. Data were collected by means of a grammaticality-judgement test that required the learners to identify which sentences were correct and which ones were incorrect and then to correct the incorrect ones. This test was administered on three occasions -- immediately before the instruction, immediately after and five months later. The instruction took place over a two-day period and consisted of a review of the target structures using a list of twenty-five correct and incorrect sentences. Overall scores immediately after the instruction showed an average of almost 11 per cent improvement for the secondary school students. A control group showed only a 3 per cent improvement. The Grade 6 students improved about 7 per cent. The researchers comment: 'the improvement was clearly attributable to the period of review instruction' (1980:164). However, the scores on the second post-test fell back to a level between those of the first and second administration. The suggested reason for this is that 'improvements ... were based on the application of knowledge temporarily retained at a conscious level, but not fully acquired' (p. 166). This study, then, suggests that instruction can result in increased accuracy in production but that the gains may not be long-lasting.

Third, Ellis (1984b) investigated the effects of instruction on the production of four semantically appropriate WH pronouns ('who', 'what', 'where'
and 'when') and of inversion in interrogatives. The subjects in this study were
thirteen children aged between ten and thirteen learning English full-time in a
London language unit. The instruction consisted of three one-hour lessons
involving contextualized practice in both teacher-led and group work. Inter-
rogative data were collected by means of an elicitation game that required the
subjects to ask questions about a picture. This resulted in relatively spontaneous speech. The game was played by the learners in pairs immediately
before and after the instruction. There was no significant improvement in the
accuracy with which either semantically appropriate WH pronouns or interrogatives with inversion were produced for the group as a whole. However, a
number of children showed a marked improvement. Ellis speculates that the
within-group differences may have been the result of individual learner factors
or of the way in which opportunities for practice were distributed. To test the
latter possibility he calculated the number of opportunities for practising
'when' interrogatives experienced by each child in one of the lessons. Somewhat surprisingly, children with the fewest opportunities were the ones who
showed the largest gains in accuracy in 'when' interrogatives.[10]

Fourth, Kadia (1988) studied whether formal instruction was successful in
enabling a Chinese student at the University of Toronto to avoid errors in the
placement of pronominal direct objects, as in:

Last time I show Beth it.
He told me that he will call up me this evening.

The pre-test consisted of a substitution task and a grammaticality-judgement
task. Forty minutes of formal instruction consisting of formal explanation and
drill was provided. The subject was observed in informal contexts for nine
weeks following the instruction and a post-test, similar to the pre-test, was
administered two months after the instruction. Kadia found that the instruction
had no real effect on the subject's spontaneous language production, but there
was some evidence that it aided her controlled production (i.e. in the substitution
task). This study, then, produced similar results to that of Schumann.

Taken together these studies suggest that there are constraints on the
effects that instruction can have on acquisition. The studies by Schumann,
Ellis and Kadia indicate that spontaneous speech production may be impervious
to instruction. Three of the studies (Schumann, Lightbown et al, and Kadia)
lend support to the claim that instruction can improve accuracy in careful,
planned speech production. However, this improvement may disappear over
time, as more 'natural' processes take over. Ellis's study also raises an important
question – how does formal instruction actually contribute to acquisition?
The results he obtained do not support the common-sense assumption that it
is practice that counts. This is a salutary finding as it reminds us of the need
to find out *how* instruction works as well as *whether* it works.

Sequence of Acquisition Studies

The sequence of acquisition studies which we will consider have been based on the substantial body of research into the naturalistic acquisition of L2 German word-order rules by adult migrant workers and their children and, more recently, of the L2 acquisition of English by members of ethnic minority communities in Australia (cf. Pienemann and Johnston, 1987). This research indicates that there is a natural sequence for the acquisition of these rules (see p. 144 above), which holds for adults and children and which applies irrespective of the learners' L1. The classroom research carried out by Pienemann and his associates (Pienemann, 1984, 1985 and 1986; Johnston 1987a and 1987b; Pienemann and Johnston, 1987; Nicholas, 1985; Jansen, 1987) has been designed to discover whether formal instruction is sufficiently powerful to disrupt the sequence of acquisition. The results provide us with the most powerful evidence collected so far that under certain conditions formal instruction can influence L2 acquisition. These conditions govern both the nature of the linguistic feature which is being taught and the timing of the instruction.

The major strength of Pienemann's research is that it is based on a well-defined theory of L2 acquisition which has enabled him and fellow researchers to test specific hypotheses. Pienemann emphasizes that the theory is *predictive*, not merely explanatory. We will begin by outlining the theory.

The Multidimensional Model (Meisel, Clahsen and Pienemann, 1981) distinguishes two sets of linguistic features; **developmental** and **variational**. Developmental features are those that are constrained by developing speech-processing mechanisms. Variational features are those that are not so constrained. In other words, the model predicts that certain features will be acquired in sequence because of the mental operations involved in processing them, while other features are 'free'. Variational features, however, are not entirely random, as their acquisition is dependent upon certain psychosociological factors such as the learner's mental make-up and her position and prospects in the host society (Johnston, 1987b). German and English word-order rules are examples of developmental features, while copula 'be' is an example of a variational feature.

The processing operations responsible for the acquisition of developmental features involve the learner's ability to manipulate syntactic elements in grammatical strings. Pienemann (1986) and Johnston (1987b) characterize the developmental stages through which a learner must pass in terms of the different processing operations involved. These are summarized in table 6.3, with examples from L2 English. It is important to recognize that each operation makes possible the production of not just one but a number of structures. The operations are sequential: the learner's capacity to perform the operations involved in one stage entails her already being able to perform those of the immediately preceding stage. Acquisition, however, does not proceed by means of sudden jumps from one stage to another; rather it is a continuous process. That is, the learner continues to work on the processing operations involved

Table 6.3 Processing operations involved in the acquisition of grammatical rules

Stage	Processing operation	Linguistic realization
1	Production relies on non-linguistic processing devices. Learner has no knowledge of syntactic categories.	Undifferentiated lexical items; formulas such as 'I don't know' and 'I can't'.
2	Production of simple strings of elements based on meaning or information focus. Learner still has no knowledge of syntactic categories.	Canonical word order; intonation questions (e.g. 'You playing football?')
3	Learner is able to identify the beginning and end of a string and to perform operations on an element in these positions e.g. learner can shift an element from beginning to end of string and vice versa. These operations are still pre-syntactic.	Adverb-preposing (e.g. 'Today I play football'); do-fronting (e.g. 'Do you play football?'); neg. + V (e.g. 'No play football').
4	Learner is able to identify an element within a string and to move this element from the middle of the string to either the beginning or the end. This operation is again characterized as pre-syntactic.	Yes/No questions (e.g. Can you swim?); pseudo-inversion (e.g. 'Where is my purse?').
5	Learner is now able to identify elements in a string as belonging to different syntactic categories. She is able to shift elements around inside the string.	WH inversion (e.g. 'Where are you playing football?'); Internal neg. (e.g. 'He did not understand?').
6	Learner is now able to move elements out of one sub-string and attach it to another element. This stage is characterized by the ability of the learner to process across as well as inside strings.	Q-tags (e.g. 'You're playing football today, aren't you?'); V-complements (e.g. 'He asked me to play football?')

Source: Based on Johnston (1976); Pienemann, Johnston and Brindley (1988)

in one stage while beginning to acquire those involved in the next. For this reason it is possible for gaps to appear in the grammatical rules associated with the processing operations of a particular stage. Although a learner has mastered a processing operation, she may not apply this to all the grammatical structures that it is now possible to produce. Pienemann suggests that the frequency of gaps correlates with the learner's overall orientation to the learning task. That is, if a learner is concerned with accuracy, few gaps will appear, but if she is more concerned with communicative effectiveness some gaps are likely to occur (see discussion of this distinction with reference to variational features below). However, the model does claim that it is impossible for the learner to skip over a stage. Both Pienemann and Johnston make a very strong claim for this sequence — namely, that it is 'strictly implicational' and not just 'statistical' (Johnston, 1987b). In other words, they maintain that the sequence does not allow any exceptions. All learners follow it.

The developmental features identified by the initial research into naturalistic L2 acquisition were all word-order rules. However, in subsequent research it has been shown that the general processing operations can also be applied to English and German morphology. Pienemann (1987) distinguishes local and non-local morphemes. Local morphemes require Stage 4 processing operations i.e. the ability to transfer information to the perceptually salient beginning and final positions of a string. An example in German is the ge- prefix in developmental past participles (e.g. ge-denkt; ge-kommt). Non-local morphemes are those that require the sentence-internal transfer of grammatical information (i.e. Stage 5 processing operations). An example is English 3rd person -s, where information has to be transferred from the grammatical subject to the verb in order to determine whether -s should be added. Extending developmental features to include morphemes has greatly increased the power of the model.

The factors that determine whether a variational feature is or is not acquired are of a very different kind. Learners differ in the extent to which they orient towards communicative effectiveness or towards correctness and standardness. Those learners who give primacy to the instrumental function of language are likely to make use of simplified and restricted forms. In this way they can reduce the amount of processing time spent on linguistic features and so allocate more to the conveyance of meaning-content. Other learners give greater importance to the integrative function. This involves using language in such a way as to identify with native speakers of the host community. These learners are more· likely to pay attention to target-language norms. Thus, whereas the first kind of learner might say 'I Spanish', the second kind is more likely to say 'I am Spanish' (Johnston, 1987b:13). The learner is credited with limited processing resources and needs to make a decision about how to put these to best use. Variation between learners is a result of the different decisions they make.

The acquisition of an L2, then, proceeds on two dimensions, as shown in figure 6.1. Development on one dimension is independent of development on the other. Thus a learner like C can progress a long way along the developmental dimension while remaining oriented towards the instrumental function of language and, as a result, continuing to manifest simplification and restriction of variational features. A learner like B, on the other hand, displays development on both dimensions, i.e. progresses along both the developmental and variational axes. Learner A is the opposite, showing little development on either axis.

A number of general hypotheses relating to the effect of instruction on L2 acquisition have been based on this model. These are:

1 Instruction will not enable learners to acquire any developmental feature out of sequence.
2 Instruction will enable learners to acquire a developmental feature providing that the processing operations required to produce those

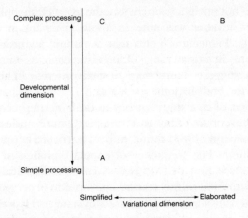

Figure 6.1 The Multidimensional Model of L2 acquisition
      Source: Based on Johnston (1987b)

features that precede it in the acquisitional sequence have already been
mastered.
3   Instruction directed at developmental features for which the learner is
    not ready may interfere with the natural process of acquisition.
4   Instruction will help learners to acquire variational features.

Hypotheses relating to the acquisition of specific grammatical features have
been tested in a number of studies, which we will now examine.

An experimental study set up to investigate these hypotheses was carried
out by Pienemann (1984). The subjects were ten children aged between seven
and nine years who had been learning L2 German naturalistically. Data were
collected on two occasions − before and after the period of instruction − by
means of interviews between pairs of subjects and between each learner and a
student interviewer. Additional data were also collected by means of hidden
recordings in the children's playing environment. The instructional targets
were *inversion*, one of the German word-order rules linked to Stage 5 processing
operations and copula, a variational feature. Pienemann does not provide a
detailed account of the instruction used, but it appeared to involve the use of
dialogues and fairly intensive drilling.

For inversion, the results for only two of the children are given. Teresa
failed to acquire inversion. Pienemann provides evidence to show that prior to
the instruction she had not acquired *particle*, the word-order rule associated
with the processing operations of the previous developmental stage (Stage 4).
Following the instruction, some of Teresa's utterances did manifest inversion,
but Pienemann claims that these were all rote-memorized patterns. Whenever
Teresa deviated from the classroom dialogues, she failed to apply inversion.
She provided no evidence of being able to use the rule productively. In
contrast, Giovanni did acquire inversion. He showed that he had already

acquired particle (but not inversion) before the instruction took place. Following the instruction, Giovanni was able to apply inversion in a wide range of linguistic contexts. Pienemann notes that in natural acquisition a new rule is applied initially only in a small range of linguistic contexts. Giovanni's advanced use of inversion suggests more than normal progress. These results, then, provide support for both hypotheses 1 and 2.

The second part of this study set out to examine the effects of instruction on the use of the copula. This is a variable feature and one that Clahsen, Meisel and Pienemann (1983) found to be a particularly reliable index of the learner's orientation. The frequency of copula omission in the five subjects for whom results are provided decreased considerably after the instruction. Furthermore, acquisition of this feature appeared to proceed independently of acquisition of the developmental feature (inversion). Hypothesis 4 was supported, therefore. However, data obtained from one of these subjects some nine months later indicated that the rate of copula omission had risen markedly. It is possible, therefore, that the effects of instruction on the acquisition of variable features is short-lived, at least for some learners (cf. the results reported for Lightbown, Spada and Wallace, 1980).

Hypothesis 3 claims that premature learning of a developmental feature may be counterproductive. Pienemann's study lends support to this hypothesis. The results show that for two of the learners the use of the *adverb-preposing* rule actually fell away as a result of the instruction on the use of inversion. Adverb preposing is an example of a rule with Stage 3 processing operations. One of the consequences of this rule in German is that inversion is also required:

Jetzt bin ich müde.
(Now am I tired.)

When learners first acquire adverb-preposing, however, they do so without inversion:

* Jetzt ich bin müde.
(Now I am tired.)

Pienemann suggests that as a result of the instruction these two learners discovered that when they used adverb preposing they should also apply inversion. However, they were not able to do this, because they were not developmentally ready. They knew, therefore, that their utterances containing a preposed adverb were incorrect. This led them to *withdraw* the use of this rule in order to avoid producing incorrect sentences. Pienemann notes that this resulted in the loss of an effective means of attention-focusing.

In addition to this important study — which gives support to all four of the general hypotheses listed above — a number of cross-sectional and longitudinal studies of the classroom acquisition of L2 German give support to the

Multidimensional Model. Daniel (1983) carried out a cross-sectional study of adult beginners of German as a L2 at a university in Australia. Her results revealed the same implicational order of acquisition of word-order rules. Westmoreland's (1983) study was also cross-sectional and involved similar kinds of learners. The implicational order followed the same developmental sequence as in the other studies.

We have already referred to the longitudinal study carried out by Ellis (1989b). Pienemann (1987) carried out a similar study. The subjects were three adult classroom learners of L2 German. Once again these were complete beginners at the start of the study. He documents when specific word-order rules were introduced in the instruction and was able to show that in the case of developmental features the instruction had no effect unless a learner was ready to acquire a new rule. For example, the particle rule was explicitly taught in week 7 of the course but was not acquired until week 17 by Steven, until week 15 by Guy and not at all by Vivien (who was studied for only nine weeks). A similar contrast between the instructional input and the learners' output was evident for inversion and verb-end. Pienemann draws two major conclusions from this study: (1) formal learners progress step by step irrespective of the teaching schedule and (2) the sequence of acquisition is the same in classroom as in naturalistic acquisition.

This longitudinal study also provides further evidence of avoidance behaviour induced by premature instruction. Pienemann found that the three classroom learners differed from naturalistic learners in the way they handled the German perfect tense. He argues that this structure belongs to Stage 5 (i.e. co-occurs with the acquisition of inversion). Naturalistic learners tend to make use of lexical markers of pastness (e.g. temporal adverbials) and a simplified version of the standard perfect verb structure, e.g.:

* Er hat sprechen.
(He has speak.)

instead of

Er hat gesprochen.
(He has spoken.)

The classroom learners were taught the complexities of the perfect verb structure at an early stage. However, because they were unable to handle the necessary processing operations, they tended to avoid using the form altogether, substituting modal + verb structures. Their chances of conforming to the norms of correctness were greater with these because the main verb consisted of the unmodified infinitive.

As a result of this research, Pienemann has put forward the **teachability hypothesis**. This states (1985:37): 'instruction can only promote language acquisition if the interlanguage is close to the point when the structure to be taught is acquired in the natural setting (so that sufficient processing requisites are developed).' The hypothesis rules out the possibility that instruction can help the learner to beat the natural order of developmental features. However, it does allow a clear role for instruction. First, instruction can facilitate natural language-acquisition processes if it coincides with when the learner is ready. This facilitation is evident in three different ways: (1) increased speed of acquisition, (2) increased frequency in rule-application and (3) application of the rule in a wider range of linguistic contexts. Also the teachability hypothesis allows for the positive effect that instruction can have on the acquisition of variational features. Instruction may serve a particularly important function here as it may help communicative-oriented learners to avoid early fossilization.

A corollary of the teachability hypothesis is that premature instruction can actually be harmful. Johnston (1987a) distinguishes three kinds of response to premature instruction. First, there are learners who attempt to perform structures that are beyond them by adapting them to the processing operations they have acquired. This results in erroneous versions of these structures. Second, there are learners who substitute developmentally less complex substitutes for rules that they know they cannot perform. Johnston suggests that this strategy is common among university students. Thirdly, learners who are very norm-oriented (i.e. obsessed by correctness) may avoid difficult structures entirely when instruction draws attention to the errors they make. It is this last response that is likely to result in interference with the normal progress of acquisition.

The teachability hypothesis is the most powerful account we have of how formal instruction relates to learning. As we shall see later, it can explain the conflicting results found in other studies of classroom L2 acquisition. It is important, however, to recognize the limitations of the model and the research that supports it. The theoretical basis of the model has been criticized on a number of counts. Hulstijn (1987), for instance, has pointed out that Pienemann does not set quantitative or qualitative criteria by which to judge whether a specific processing operation has been acquired, nor is it entirely clear whether the notion of processing operation applies to acquisition or production or both. The empirical research upon which the hypothesis has been based is still very limited. Given all the variables involved in teaching–learning, it cannot yet be concluded that instruction has no impact on developmentally advanced features. Pienemann and his associates provide very little information about the kind of instruction their subjects experienced. It is possible that their failure to find any effect was not because instruction *per se* was incompatible with learning such features but because the particular type of instruction they provided was wrong. It must be said, however, that the strength of the theoretical framework that underpins the hypothesis – the implicationally ordered set of processing operations – gives grounds for claiming that instruction is powerless to affect at least some aspects of L2 acquisition.

We now turn to research based on a totally different theoretical framework. This has produced results that cannot be easily be explained by the teachability hypothesis.

'Projection' Studies

The final group of studies in this review of the experimental research is based on predictions derived from the study of linguistic universals. Two types of universals can be distinguished: typological universals and universals based on Chomsky's theory of Universal Grammar (cf. Ellis, 1985a: ch. 8). The former have been identified by examining a representative sample of natural languages. The latter have been identified by studying individual languages in depth in order to establish the set of principles or parameters which govern the way any grammar is constructed. Both approaches allow for the existence of **implicational universals**. These relate the presence of one linguistic property to the presence of one or more other properties. For example the Accessibility Hierarchy for relative clauses (see ch. 5, n. 12) predicts that if a language allows for relativization in the object of comparative position, it will also allow relativization in all positions higher up the hierarchy. Similarly, Universal Grammar predicts that the pro-drop parameter determines whether a whole cluster of features (including optional omission of subjects and free inversion in simple sentences) is or is not present in a language.

Implicational universals allow predictions to be made about the acquisition of sets of linguistic features. The learner is credited with a **projection device** (Zobl, 1983) that enables the acquisition of one rule to trigger the acquisition of all the other rules that cluster with it. This device explains why learners are able to acquire a language quickly despite the immense complexity of the task and the relative poverty of the input they experience.[11] One of the interesting questions that can be asked is whether instruction can activate the projection device. Specifically, researchers have asked whether instruction directed at feature x is powerful enough to trigger acquisition of features $y, z \ldots n$, which are implicationally linked to x. They have investigated whether instruction aimed at **marked** linguistic features (i.e. features that are difficult to acquire because they are not universal) can facilitate the automatic acquisition of **unmarked** features (i.e. features which are universal and, therefore, easy to learn).

Gass (1979) based her study on the Accessibility Hierarchy. She investigated the effects of instruction on adult ESL learners' acquisition of relativization. The experimental group were given instruction in recognizing and producing sentences in which the object of preposition was relativized (i.e. a position low down in the Accessibility Hierarchy). A control group was given similar instruction involving sentences in which the subject and object were relativized (i.e. positions high up in the hierarchy). The results of a sentence-combining task (administered before and after the period of instruction) showed that the learners in the experimental group not only succeeded in improving their scores on object of preposition but also on all the positions higher in the hierarchy. In contrast, the control group improved their scores on the subject and object positions but failed to demonstrate any improvement on the lower positions. Gass's study, therefore, lends support to the projection hypothesis. It has been replicated with similar results by Eckman et al. (1988).

Zobl's (1985) study also supports the hypothesis. This investigated the effects of fifteen minutes of instruction on the acquisition of English possessive adjectives by approximately forty French-speaking university students in Canada who were assigned randomly to two groups. Both groups received intensive oral practice consisting of question and answer and teacher-correction. The first group received practice directed at the use of possessive adjectives with non-human entities (e.g. 'his/her car'); the second group's instruction involved examples of human-possessed entities (e.g. 'his/her sister'). Zobl claimed that these two features are implicationally ordered, such that acquisition of the latter (the marked form) would result automatically in the acquisition of the former (the unmarked form). The experiment bore this out. The second group of learners showed gains in both features, while the first group showed gains in neither. Zobl also reports a replication of this study one year later. The results were the same except that the first group did this time show some gains in the use of possessive adjectives with non-human entities. However, these gains (the target of instruction) were still smaller than those demonstrated by the second group, which received no instruction at all in this feature. Zobl also examined the errors made by both groups. The first group tended to overgeneralize 'his' and to substitute the developmentally simpler 'the'. The second group overgeneralized 'her' but were less likely to substitute 'the'.

The third study (Henry, 1986), investigated whether fifteen adult English learners of L2 Chinese were able to predict the positioning of relative clauses with regard to the head noun on the basis of general exposure to word-order phenomena but without any specific instruction in the use of relative clauses. The word order of Chinese is basically head-final (i.e. modification generally precedes the head noun). English is basically head-initial (i.e. modification in general follows the head noun). The students were asked to translate ten sentences, some of which contained relative clauses, into Chinese. Those students who attempted to translate the relative clauses invariably positioned them before the head-noun. When asked why they thought Chinese had pre-nominal relative clauses they gave answers like the following:

Well, if you want to say 'the door of the house' you have to say 'frangzi de menkour', 'house of door', and you put adjectives before the noun, so it just sounded right that way.

Henry concludes that these students were able to access parameters of word order and that this enabled them to 'know' features that they had not actually been taught.[12]

These three studies indicate that the relationship between instruction and acquisition is much more complex than is generally assumed. We may draw the following tentative conclusions:

1   Instruction can result in learners acquiring not only those features that have been taught but also other features that are implicationally associated with them.

2   Instruction in marked features can facilitate the acquisition of unmarked features, but not vice versa.

3   Instruction in unmarked features may result in learners' simplifying their interlanguages, whereas instruction in marked features aids the process of complexification.

The notion of 'projection' is an extremely powerful one. Of course, instruction is not necessary for projection to take place; unfocused input will suffice. However, instruction may be particularly helpful for the simple reason that it can supply the learner with plentiful examples of those marked features that will serve to trigger the acquisition of unmarked features. Also, as Zobl (1985:342) suggests, marked data may be necessary if interlanguage construction is to progress beyond a certain stage of complexity, and the best way to ensure the learner receives such data in sufficient quantity and attends to it is through formal instruction.

Review

Table 6.4 provides a summary of the experimental studies which have been discussed in this section. In contrast to many of the comparative studies, this research provides convincing evidence that instruction can have a direct effect on the acquisition of specific linguistic features. It also suggests both the conditions that have to be met in order for the instruction to work and the conditions under which instruction will prove most effective. The research is not entirely comforting to supporters of instruction, however. There is evidence to indicate that the effects can wear off over time. This suggests that although instruction may bypass natural processing mechanisms in the short term, these will eventually reassert themselves. Also, there is an apparent contradiction in the results obtained from the sequence of acquisition studies carried out by Pienemann and his associates and those obtained from the projection studies based on the study of linguistic universals. Whereas the former support the claim that instruction will only work if it is directed just one step ahead of the learner's current level of acquisition, the latter support the claim that instruction will be more effective if it is directed several steps beyond the learner's current level. These claims derive from very different underlying theories. If we are to make overall sense of the relationship between formal instruction and learning we will need to develop a comprehensive theory that will explain and reconcile the two sets of results.

This review of the research has covered (1) studies which have examined the effect of instruction on the rate and level of success of acquisition and (2) studies which have investigated whether instruction influences the process of acquisition. The available research is now quite extensive, although it is also limited in a number of ways (e.g. the size of the sample, the nature of the instruction provided and the choice of target structures). Also it is not easy to interpret. We turn now to consider what answers can be given to the central question with which we began the review.

Table 6.4 Experimental studies of the effect of instruction on L2 acquisition

Study	Type of classroom	Subjects	Proficiency level	Data	Results
Schumann (1978)	ESL in United States (one-to-one instruction)	One adult learner	'Fossilized', i.e. no development taking place	Spontaneous speech + imitation test	Instruction had no effect on negatives in spontaneous speech, but improvement in imitation scores occurred.
Kadia (1988)	ESL in Canadian university	One adult learner	'Fossilized', i.e. no development taking place	Spontaneous speech, substitution test + grammaticality judgement test	Instruction had no effect on spontaneous language use Performance on grammaticality-judgement test declined but performance in substitution test improved after instruction.
Lightbown et al. (1980)	ESL in Canadian schools	Children and adolescents (Grades 6, 8 and 10)	Mixed ability levels	Grammaticality-judgement test	Instruction resulted in increased accuracy in use of -s morphemes, 'be' and locative prepositions, but accuracy deteriorated in test administered 5 mths later.
Ellis (1984b)	ESL in Britain	13 children and adolescents (10 to 15 yrs).	Mixed ability levels	Game designed to elicit unmonitored interrogatives	Instruction had no significant effect on accuracy of production of interrogatives for group as a whole, but individual learners showed marked gains.

Pienemann (1984)	German as a L2	10 children (aged 7 to 9 yrs)	Mixed ability levels	Oral interviews and hidden recordings	Inversion rule acquired by one learner who was developmentally ready, but not acquired by another learner who was not developmentally ready; accuracy in use of copula increased, but had decreased some 9 mths later; instruction in inversion led to one learner abandoning already acquired rule.
Gass (1979)	ESL in the USA – intensive university course	Adults	Intermediate	Grammaticality-judgements and sentence joining tasks	Group that received instruction on marked relative pronoun function showed improvement on this function and on unmarked functions; group that received instruction on unmarked relative pronoun function showed improvement only on this function.
Eckman et al. (1988)	ESL in the USA – intensive university course	Adults	Low intermediate and intermediate	Sentence-joining task	Generalization of learning occurred from marked to unmarked structures rather than vice versa (i.e. results as those obtained by Gass).

Table 6.4 (Cont.)

Study	Type of classroom	Subjects	Proficiency level	Data	Results
Zobl (1985)	ESL by French speakers in Canada	Adults	Low level	Oral questions based on pictures designed to elicit noun phrases with possessive adjectives	Group that received practice in marked feature (human-possessed entities) showed gains in this feature and in unmarked feature; group that received practice in unmarked feature (nonhuman-possessed entities) showed no greater gains in this feature and no gains in marked feature. Type of errors made by two groups also differed.
Henry (1986)	Chinese as a L2	Adults	Low level	Translation of sentences into Chinese	Students avoided positioning relative clauses after head noun even though they had no instruction in this feature.

Does Formal Instruction Work?

The answer suggested by this review of the research to the question 'Does formal instruction work?' is a tentative 'yes'. The evidence is of three kinds. First, instructed learners appear to outperform naturalistic learners. Second, there is evidence that instruction aids the acquisition of useful formulas. Third, instruction can result in the acquisition of some new linguistic rules and can improve control over existing knowledge.

Rate of Acquisition

In general, classroom learners learn more rapidly and progress further than naturalistic learners. This provides weak evidence in favour of the claim that instruction affects acquisition. The evidence is weak because we cannot be sure that it is the focus on the linguistic code that is responsible for the advantage. Other factors might be the cause. Classroom learners may be more motivated to learn. It may be classroom *input* rather than instruction that is responsible. Classroom learners may obtain more comprehensible input or they may benefit from access to marked linguistic forms in planned discourse. There is, however, a line of argument that supports the view that it is the focus on form that is responsible. Studies of naturalistic acquisition (e.g. Schmidt, 1983) have shown that learners sometimes do not develop high levels of linguistic accuracy even though they do become communicatively effective. Grammatical competence appears to be partially independent of other components of communicative competence and to develop it successfully may require more than successful interaction. Schmidt points out that there are no well-documented studies of adults who have successfully learnt the grammar of a L2 solely through interaction. If Schmidt is right and some degree of conscious attention to form is needed for adults to acquire high levels of linguistic competence, this would suggest that instructed learners do better than naturalistic learners precisely because they are encouraged to focus on form.

Instruction and the Acquisition of Formulas

Instruction seems to facilitate the acquisition of formulas. A number of the studies in the review bear testimony to this. Weinert (1987) and Pienemann (1984), for example, both draw attention to the routines and patterns that learners memorize during the course of instruction and then reproduce later in their free speech. It is possible that much of what commonly passes for formal instruction (e.g. pattern drills and dialogues) actually results in the acquisition of unanalysed units. In other words, although the aim is to help the learners acquire a *rule*, the product the learner takes away is a useful formula or two. In this case, the effect of instruction is not what was intended.

However, there are also cases when teachers have set out to teach a formula. Ellis (1984a) documents how one teacher successfully taught a group of ESL beginners 'I don't know'. Instruction based on notional/functional materials might also be seen as an attempt to teach ready-made phrases — what Hatch (1983b) calls 'canned speech'. Formulas can be taught in much the same way as vocabulary. They require little processing effort and, therefore, can be learnt easily.[13] However, if the efficacy of instruction goes no further than formulas, it must indeed be considered limited. A *strong* case for instruction must show that it is capable of influencing the acquisition of productive rules.

Instruction and the Acquisition of Rules

A number of studies in the review show that instruction has no effect on the acquisition of linguistic rules. Felix (1981:109) represents the conclusion that many researchers have reached when he says: 'the possibility of manipulating and controlling the students' behaviour in the classroom is in fact quite limited.' Other research (e.g. Lightbown's) has shown that instruction may appear to work initially, only for its effects to wear off after time. This is how Lightbown (1985c:102) summarizes her findings:

> the learners heard and practised certain language items ... In class, and for a period of time outside of class, they appeared to 'know' these forms in the sense that they used them correctly in appropriate contexts. Later, however, some of these 'correct' forms disappeared from the learners' language and were replaced by simpler or developmentally 'earlier' forms.

These studies have been used to claim that L2 acquisition involves certain natural processes that cannot be bypassed. As a result learners follow a sequence of development which instruction is powerless to change.

On the basis of much of the research, therefore, it would be possible to argue that instruction has no major impact on the acquisition of linguistic rules. There is also evidence, however, for two alternative positions. First, a number of studies indicate that instruction can have an immediate effect. Second, there is some evidence to suggest that instruction can have a delayed effect.

Instruction can have an immediate effect providing that certain conditions are met. These conditions concern the nature of the linguistic structure itself and the timing of the instruction.

Linguistic Conditions

Linguistic structures need to conform to two criteria to be amenable to instruction:

1 They must be formally simple, i.e. they must not involve any psycho-linguistically complex processing operation.

2 Form—function relationships must be transparent. A truly simple feature will be one that performs a single function. A complex feature will be one that is linked to a number of different functions.

Figure 6.2 gives examples of linguistic features from English that conform to these criteria. Only features that meet both criteria are teachable (i.e. those features listed in cell A). Features that meet one criterion but not the other will be resistent to instruction (i.e. features in cells B, C and D). It is interesting to speculate that the most difficult structures will be those that are *both* formally complex *and* that display opaque form—function relationships (i.e. features in cell D), but there is no clear evidence for this as yet.

Attempts to teach structures which are not learnable can produce a number of different results. The instruction may be simply ignored with the result that the learner falls back on developmentally easier rules or substitutes randomly from her available repertoire. This is likely if the structures require complex processing operations. It is also possible that premature instruction aimed at unlearnable structures can interfere with acquisition — by encouraging the learner to avoid what she finds psycholinguistically difficult. Premature instruction can also result in the learner abandoning a transitional construction which serves as a necessary stepping-stone to the acquisition of the target structure because she is made aware of its incorrectness. In this way, instruction may actually impede acquisition. If the structure can be easily processed, but the form—function relationships are opaque (as with V-ing) the learner is likely to acquire the form but to make unique use of it by establishing her own system of form—function relationships. The overt manifestation of this is overuse and overgeneralization.

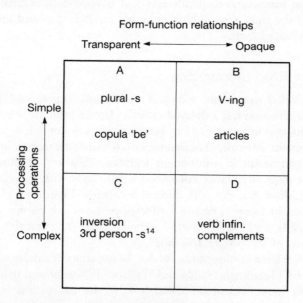

Figure 6.2 The teachability of different linguistic structures

Instruction directed at structures that require complex processing operations can prove successful if it is timed to occur when the learner is developmentally ready to acquire the new feature. The evidence for this comes from the research into the acquisition of German word-order rules (e.g. Pienemann, 1984). Each word-order rule involves certain processing operations. These operations are psycholinguistically ordered such that one serves as a prerequisite for another. Instruction cannot beat the order, but it can help the learner to progress more rapidly and improve control over each operation, providing that the teaching proceeds in conformity with the natural sequence of development.

The capacity of instruction to produce an immediate effect on the acquisition of new linguistic material must be considered very limited, however. Only some features — very few, in fact — are teachable at any one time and the effects of instruction on the acquisition of these features may only be temporary. Otherwise instruction can only work if the learner is at the right stage of development. One way of enhancing the effects of instruction would be to make efforts to ensure that the instruction conforms with what is teachable. Pienemann (1985:163) has put forward arguments in support of what he calls 'natural grading'. This requires that the instruction proceed in line with what the learner is able to process. Pienemann's proposal has met with the obvious criticism that teachers are generally not in a position to know when individual learners are ready to acquire the next rule (Long, 1985b; Lightbown, 1985c). Pienemann, Johnston and Brindley (1988) have responded to this criticism by developing 'an acquisition based procedure for second language assessment' — an instrument which teachers can use to profile individual learners' stage of acquisition. However, by their own admission this instrument is not yet sufficiently accurate. Also, practical problems would remain regarding how to ensure that learners at disparate levels of development received the right instruction at the right time. This would call for individualized teaching of a highly sophisticated kind.

The Delayed Effect of Instruction

Given the limited immediate effect of instruction, the second position — namely that instruction has a delayed effect — becomes an attractive one. The empirical evidence in support of it, however, is very limited — as might be expected, given the difficulty of designing a study to investigate how instruction at one time might result in subsequent learning. Ellis and Rathbone (1987) reported that class attendance correlated significantly with measures of subsequent acquisition but not with current measures. Lightbown (1983) noted that instruction in V-ing in Grade 5 affected performance on this structure in Grade 6. Lightbown (1987) reported a similar delay in instructional effect on the acquisition of the progressive auxiliary.

Some studies have produced results that do not support a delayed hypothesis — the study by Lightbown, Spada and Wallace (1980) showed that the effects of instruction were evident immediately after the instruction but wore off later. Harley (1987) found that the gains which an instructed group of Grade 6 immersion learners experienced in the use of French *imparfait* and *passe compose* in comparison to a control group were not evident three months later, although in this case it was because the uninstructed group eventually caught up with the instructed group.

There is a strong logical argument to support the delayed-effect position. We have seen that the review of the research indicates that instruction accelerates acquisition and that it is associated with higher levels of ultimate proficiency. We have also seen that instruction does not seem to result in the immediate acquisition of new features, except in rather exceptional circumstances. The question that arises is how instruction facilitates learning when it is, in general, powerless to intervene in the natural processes of interlanguage development. One explanation is that instruction in some way primes the learner so that acquisition becomes *easier* when she is finally ready to assimilate the new material. As Lightbown (1985c:108) puts it, 'formal instruction may provide 'hooks', points of access for the learner.' According to this view, then, we should see instruction as an 'acquisition facilitator' (Seliger, 1979). It speeds up learning *in the long term* and helps to prevent the kind of grammatical fossilization found in adult naturalistic learners.

How does this happen? We can only speculate. One possibility is that instruction raises the learner's consciousness about the existence of linguistic features which she would otherwise ignore. For example, instruction can help the learner to 'know' − in some declarative sense − that the third person singular verb requires -s. Initially, however, she is unable to process this form. But because she 'knows' about -s, she is better equipped to perceive it in the input. When the prerequisite processing operations for -s have been developed, it is acquired. In this way, declarative knowledge serves as a platform for the acquisition of subsequent procedural knowledge. Conscious awareness of forms that contribute little to communicative effectiveness may be necessary to ensure that they are eventually acquired − at least where adults are concerned.

This explanation is also compatible with one set of results that are otherwise difficult to explain. We saw that 'projection' studies such as that carried out by Zobl (1985) indicate that instruction directed at marked features can trigger the acquisition of implicated unmarked features. These findings, it was noted, appeared to contradict other findings that developmental structures cannot be learnt out of sequence. Now, in the projection studies the instruments used to measure the effects of the instruction (typically grammaticality-judgement tasks) have encouraged the use of conscious grammatical knowledge. If this is so, the results they have produced may not be so incompatible with the results of other studies which have measured acquisition using instruments that tap more spontaneous language use. These latter studies provide information about the effects of instruction on procedural knowledge. We arrive at the intriguing possibility that whereas instruction is limited in the effect it can have on procedural knowledge, it can have a considerable effect on the acquisition of declarative knowledge, as this is not subject to processing constraints. The projection studies provide us with an important clue as to how teaching directed at conscious knowledge should be organized: it should focus on marked forms.

This conclusion is partly compatible with the results obtained by Schumann (1978) and Kadia (1988), which showed that instruction did have an immediate effect on monitored language use, but none on spontaneous use. However, Schumann's and Kadia's learners failed to show any improvement in spontaneous language use later as well. It may be that these learners needed more time for the benefits of instruction to show or it is possible that certain social and psychological conditions have to be met for instruction to have the delayed effect that is being proposed.

One objection to the delayed-effect hypothesis is Pienemann's finding that instruction can have a deleterious effect on the learner's current interlanguage (see above). This objection arises, however, only if the instruction entails practice aimed at developing the procedural knowledge needed in *production*, as the processing operations which determine the sequence of acquisition of developmental features relate only to production. The objection disappears if the goal of the instruction becomes declarative knowledge and if the instructional activities are directed at consciousness-raising. This argument, then, constitutes additional support for an instructional approach involving consciousness-raising rather than drill.[15]

Summary

To sum up, there are grounds for believing that form-focused instruction does help the acquisition of linguistic competence. Instruction can work *directly*; that is, it can have an immediate effect on the learner's ability to perform the target structures in natural communication. However, not all structures are teachable. Also teachable structures have to be taught at the right time. It is likely, therefore, that instruction works *indirectly* in the main; that is, it has a delayed effect. According to this interpretation, instruction contributes to declarative rather than procedural knowledge. Declarative knowledge serves as a facilitator of ultimate procedural knowledge by helping to make forms salient that would otherwise be ignored by the learner. Conscious knowledge of marked forms may help to accelerate learning and may also be necessary to prevent fossilization.

Conclusion

In this chapter we have considered whether and under what conditions attempts to intervene directly in the process of L2 acquisition by means of form-focused instruction are successful. We have reviewed a number of studies which have addressed this issue and examined different theoretical positions. The conclusion reached was that formal instruction does contribute to L2 acquisition. In some cases, depending on the nature of the target structure and when the intervention takes place, instruction can have an immediate effect. In other cases formal instruction may have a delayed effect, by providing the learner with more or less explicit grammatical concepts, which will later help her to attend to these features in the input and so acquire them procedurally. Learners who receive formal instruction outperform those who do not; that is, they learn more rapidly and they reach higher levels of ultimate achievement.

The research which we have studied has been psycholinguistic in nature. It has been quantitative and, in many instances, experimental. The focus has been on measuring the learning that results from instruction and, on the basis of this, inferring to what extent and in what ways the instruction affected L2 acquisition. Such research contrasts with the research which we considered in chapter 4, which focused on the classroom behaviours which arise as part of the teaching–learning process, usually without reference to whether any learning took place. Studies of the effects of formal instruction have been product- rather than process-oriented.

One of the difficulties of this product-orientation is that 'formal instruction' is treated as an undifferentiated phenomenon. As defined in the introduction to this chapter, it is instruction that (1) focuses on some specific property of the target language and (2) tries to make the learner aware of what the correct form or use of the form is. But such a definition raises a number of problems:

1   It is not clear what unit the definition should be applied to (e.g. 'course', 'lesson' or 'sequence'). Most of the research has been based on the assumption that a whole course or a whole lesson can be classified as 'formal instruction'. However, as Bialystok (1981:65) has pointed out, 'a formal learning situation encompasses many more features than those which are explicitly designated as the goal of the lesson.' Any lesson will be made up of both form and meaning-focused exchanges. It is difficult to imagine a lesson which is entirely form-focused, let alone a complete course. It should also be noted that instruction that is primarily meaning-focused can involve form-focused exchanges, as when the teacher side-tracks to explain the meaning of a lexical item or deal with a grammatical problem.

2   The definition also ignores the fact that what is form-focused instruction to the researcher or the teacher may not be so for the learner. Teachers and learners do not always share the same goals. There is evidence to show that when teachers operate in a form-focused way, learners sometimes respond meaningfully (McTear, 1975).

3   A 'focus' on form can be achieved in different ways. There are different kinds of practice drill. The teacher may or may not provide an explanation of a grammatical point. It is possible that some kinds of form-focused instruction

work while others do not. If a researcher finds that the learners have failed to acquire a particular linguistic feature, this may reflect a failure in the *kind* of instruction offered rather than in formal instruction *per se*.

4   Learners may vary individually in the extent to which they are able to benefit from formal instruction or from different kinds of formal instruction. The studies reported in this chapter give no or little recognition to the role of individual differences in learning style among learners.

These problems arise out of the asocial nature of the research. They can only be overcome by incorporating a process element into research designs in order to examine how 'formal instruction' is negotiated by the classroom participants. Very few studies have done so to date. It is a characteristic of much of the research that 'formal instruction' is either treated as a given or as something that can be defined without reference to actual classroom events (e.g. in terms of a syllabus, textbook content or the aim of a lesson plan).

For this reason, it is wise to treat the results which have been obtained with some caution. It is not possible to ignore them, however. In order to build a theory of L2 classroom learning it is essential to consider what learning (if any) results from formal instruction. The study of learning as a product of instruction is still in its infancy but already it is an important component of second-language classroom research. Until we have better studies, which are truly process—product in design, we will have to proceed with the material to hand.

NOTES

1   The two studies that produced 'ambiguous results' showed, in fact, that instruction did not promote acquisition i.e. that naturalistic exposure was more effective. However, Long subjected both studies to careful scrutiny and demonstrated that the results could be interpreted as lending support to instruction.

2   An 'acquisition-rich' environment is one where the learner receives plenty of comprehensible input outside the classroom. An 'acquisition-poor' environment is one where the learner receives little 'comprehensible input' in natural settings.

3   Hale and Budar's (1970) study was one of the two studies that Long claimed produced 'ambiguous results'.

4   There are considerable difficulties in interpreting such a correlation. It cannot be claimed that attendance *caused* acquisition to take place. One possible interpretation is that more regular attendance resulted in greater contact with instruction which in turn enhanced acquisition. Another interpretation is that learners who were more strongly motivated attended more. It is not possible to decide whether attendance is functioning as a measure of motivation or of the direct effects of instruction.

5   Not all researchers were happy to equate 'order of accuracy' with 'order of acquisition'. Larsen-Freeman, for instance, preferred to talk only about accuracy.

6   Perkins and Larsen-Freeman also collected data from a translation task. The results obtained from these data did show some effect for instruction, as the

Consciousness
Raising

...eased considerably and was reflected
...er with that carried out by Schumann
...struction can have an effect on careful,
...informal, unplanned language use.
...*quisition* is an important one. However,
...estigate anything other than production,
...1at has been acquired is by studying what
...lly) or writing. If all researchers followed
...anything to say about acquisition. It is more
...rly what *kind of production* has been studied.
...ing to whether the production is unplanned or
...n instructed and naturalistic L2 acquisition should
...ta (i.e. spontaneous speech). Pica's study does, in fact,
...nis requirement.

8 ... ..s, therefore, an example of a transitional structure, as the utterances that result are non-standard in form. The other word-order rules, however, reflect target-language norms. Adverb preposing is an *optional* rule, whereas the other three rules are obligatory.

9 The learners studied by Meisel and Clahsen were migrant workers in Germany. Obviously, it is difficult to compare rates of acquisition in such disparate groups as migrant workers and educationally successful classroom learners. Differences may have as much to do with their social and educational backgrounds as with the presence or absence of formal instruction.

10 Ellis's (1984b) finding that learners who participated the least frequently in practice showed the biggest gains runs contrary to received opinion that 'practice makes perfect'. It suggests that formal instruction consisting of formal practice may not be the best way to promote L2 acquisition. It does not show that instruction *per se* has no effect; instruction that involves consciousness-raising without practice may still work.

11 The claim that input is impoverished is central to the arguments put forward by researchers who work within the Universal Grammar paradigm. It should be noted, however, that researchers operating in different paradigms dispute the claim.

12 Of course, it is not necessary to invoke a theory of Universal Grammar to explain Henry's results. Learners may simply be generalizing existing 'rules'. They have discovered that possessed nouns go before the noun (unlike in English), so they extend this rule to cover relative clauses.

13 It is also possible that teaching formulas (intentionally or unintentionally) can inhibit the acquisition of linguistic rules – as Weinert (1987) suggests.

14 Not all researchers would agree that 3rd person -s involves complex processing operations. However, Pienemann argues that it is an example of non-local morphemes, as the learner has to transfer information from the grammatical subject to the verb. This would account for its late acquisition. So would other explanations, however. 3rd person -s is not perceptually salient and has little communicative value.

15 It should be noted that Pienemann (1985) himself makes it clear that the teachability hypothesis applies only to L2 *production*. He does not object to learners being exposed to a rule beyond their immediate processing capacity in the input. One might expect, therefore, that he would not object to consciousness-raising of the same rule.

7   An Integrated Theory of Instructed Second Language Learning

Introduction

The aim of this chapter is to develop a theory of instructed second language acquisition. The intention is not to develop a radically new account of how language learning is influenced by teaching but rather to provide an economical explanation which is consistent with the theoretical positions and research discussed in previous chapters.

All theories are purposeful − that is, they are constructed with a particular goal in mind. The theory presented here has two primary purposes. The first is to provide a set of statements or hypotheses about classroom L2 learning which are testable and, therefore, falsifiable. In this sense, the theory aims to be **scientific**, as defined by Popper (1976). The second purpose is to provide an account of classroom L2 learning that is relevant and accessible to teachers. In this sense, the theory aims to be **appropriate** to the needs of a particular set of users.[1]

There are plenty of theories of L2 acquisition already in existence. McLaughlin (1987) provides a detailed examination of five of the most prominent. Ellis (1985a) considers seven. These theories seek to account for the interaction of those sets of factors which affect the process and success of L2 learning. In other words, they describe the conditions under which efficient L2 learning can take place. Spolsky (1988) suggests that a theory should take account of four sets of factors: (1) the knowledge and skills which the learner possesses at any given moment in the learning process, (2) various components of ability, (3) various affective factors such as personality and motivation and (4) the opportunities for learning. A theory of instructed language learning must ultimately account for the same set of factors. The difference between such a theory and a theory of naturalistic L2 learning will rest not on its basic components but rather on the contents of each component and the way they interact.

A theory of classroom L2 learning should be clear about *what* it is seeking to explain. In particular, it should specify whether it intends to account for **competence** or for **proficiency**. Taylor (1988) argues that there has been considerable terminological confusion in the use of 'competence'. He draws attention to the fact that Chomsky in his initial and more recent uses of the term explicitly distinguishes the idea of 'knowledge', which is static, from the idea of 'ability to use knowledge', which is dynamic. Taylor suggests that the term **competence** be restricted to the former and **proficiency** be used to label the latter.[2] This is an important and useful distinction as it contributes to conceptual clarity and helps us to decide precisely what a theory of classroom L2 learning which seeks to be relevant to teachers should address. Teachers are concerned with both how knowledge is acquired and, crucially, with the learner's ability to make use of this knowledge. Any theory that seeks to be relevant to the needs of teachers, therefore, must address both competence and proficiency. Arguably teachers have little to gain from a theory of competence by itself (a point that Chomsky has himself acknowledged).[3] They need a theory that helps them to understand and plan for how new knowledge is formed on the one hand and how learners learn how to use this knowledge correctly and appropriately on the other. The theory presented in the following pages is an attempt to build an integrated theory of this kind.

This chapter will begin with an account of cognitive learning theory. Currently, considerable attention is being paid to cognitive accounts of how learning takes place and the extent to which they can be applied to L2 learning (McLaughlin, 1987; O'Malley, Chamot and Walker, 1987; Bialystok, 1988). A cognitive theory views language learning as a complex skill which, like other such skills, involves the use of various information-processing techniques to overcome limitations in mental capacity which inhibit performance. Learning takes place when the learner is able to carry out operations automatically as a result of practice. In chapter 2 we saw the dangers of extrapolating from a general theory of learning; language learning cannot be assumed to be a 'skill' of the same kind as playing a piano or playing tennis. However, cognitive theory, as formulated in the work of Shiffrin and Schneider (1977) and Anderson (1980; 1983; 1985) provides a much more powerful account of many of the phenomena of instructed L2 learning than did structuralist-behaviourist theories.

Cognitive learning theory is a powerful explanation of how learners develop the ability to use their L2 knowledge (i.e. proficiency) and, therefore, is particularly relevant to the aim of this chapter, but it is unable to provide an adequate explanation of how this knowledge is acquired in the first place. This is because it fails to recognize that L2 acquisition is determined, in part, by linguistic as well as cognitive factors. However, the theory serves as a platform for developing an integrated theory of instructed L2 learning, which attempts to account for both proficiency and competence.

Cognitive Theory and Instructed Language Learning

Cognitive theory is the result of extensive research into the role that mental processing plays in learning. It has benefited in particular from research into information processing i.e. how information is stored and retrieved. Cognitive theory seeks to explain three principal aspects of learning: (1) how knowledge is initially represented, (2) how the ability to use this knowledge develops and (3) how new knowledge is integrated into the learner's existing cognitive system.

The Representation of New Knowledge

New knowledge is acquired in two stages (Weinstein and Mayer, 1986). First, the learner selects which features in the environment to pay attention to and transfers this information into short-term memory. Second, the learner acquires some or all of these features by transferring the information into long-term memory for permanent storage. New information can be comprehended by means of **inferencing**, i.e. using existing knowledge and the context in which the new information occurs. However, the learner will tend to ignore new information that does not accord with her existing knowledge-system. Ausabel (1971) refers to this as **obliterative subsumption**.[4] It can be overcome if the learner receives corrective feedback which enables her to compare her own performance with that of some external model and if she notices the difference.

Developing the Ability to Use Knowledge

Information which has been transferred into long-term memory is not initially available for use in all performance conditions. Two accounts of how learners achieve control over new information have attracted the attention of L2 researchers. The first concerns the distinction between **controlled** and **automatic processing** and the second that between **declarative** and **procedural knowledge**.

A number of researchers (e.g. Posner and Snyder, 1975; Schneider and Shiffrin, 1977) distinguish the mental operations that a person is able to perform effortlessly and automatically from those that can only be performed with considerable difficulty and relatively slowly. Learning involves the automatization of memory nodes, so that information which was initially only available for use through controlled processing can be handled spontaneously. Automatization is necessary because the learner has limited processing capability and needs to free capacity to deal with new information and to form higher-level plans. For example, a learner who is struggling with the effort of pronouncing words correctly will have little time to pay attention to grammar. Once pronunciation becomes automatic, however, she is free to attend to higher-level skills.

This processing model of learning also accounts for why learners vary in the way they perform different tasks. Tasks vary in the amount of attention they require and also in where attention needs to be focused. Thus, a tennis player may be able to perform a copy-book backhand if allowed to focus exclusively on how to execute this particular stroke, but may fail to achieve backhand returns during the course of an actual game. A practice-session and a competitive match constitute different kinds of tasks.

The distinction between declarative and procedural knowledge comes from the work of J. Anderson (1980; 1983; 1985). Declarative knowledge involves 'knowing that'. It consists of such information as the definitions of words, facts, rules and memory for images and sequences of events. Procedural knowledge is 'knowing how'. It is represented in memory in terms of 'production systems' consisting of a condition and an action as in this example from O'Malley, Chamot and Walker (1987): 'IF the goal is to generate a plural of a noun and the noun ends in a hard consonant, THEN generate the noun + /s/.'

Anderson identifies three stages in the learning process:

1   In the **cognitive stage** the learner makes use of conscious activity. The knowledge acquired is typically declarative in nature and can often be described verbally by the learner.
2   In the **associative** stage, errors in the original declarative knowledge are detected and corrected and the knowledge is also proceduralized. During this stage condition−action pairs which are initially represented in declarative form are gradually converted into production sets. The initial declarative representation is never lost, however.
3   Finally, in the **autonomous** stage performance becomes more or less totally automatic and errors disappear. The learner relies less on working memory and performance takes place below the threshold of consciousness.

These two accounts of how new knowledge becomes automatic have much in common. It is clear that there is a loose correspondence between controlled processing and declarative knowledge and between automatic processing and procedural knowledge. Both models are based on the notion that human beings have limited information-processing abilities and, therefore, need to activate certain kinds of knowledge rapidly and easily.

There is, however, one important difference, which can be encapsulated in the distinction between 'attention' and 'consciousness'. It is possible for a learner to pay attention without doing so consciously. Controlled processing − in Shiffrin and Schneider's terms − can take place with or without any conscious awareness on the part of the learner. Also the learner may or may not be able to articulate what she has done. In contrast, declarative knowledge − in Anderson's terms − involves the learner's conscious attention and can be explicitly formulated. Only when this knowledge is subsequently proceduralized does consciousness disappear. This distinction is of considerable importance when it comes to applying the theory to language learning, as it concerns the central question of whether L2 knowledge starts out as conscious and explicit or whether it is subconscious and implicit.

Integrating Knowledge

The third aspect of learning involves the way in which the acquisition of new information leads to a restructuring of the learner's knowledge system. As learning takes place, the existing system is modified in order to take account of the new information. Karmiloff-Smith (1986) (cited in Mclaughlin, 1987) describes how the process of restructuring takes place. In the first place adults and children master components of a new task but do not impose any overall organization on the information they obtain. Later, however, organization is created as learners attempt to simplify, unify and gain control over the internal representation of their knowledge. Whereas in the first stage learners are unduly influenced by input data and are responsive to corrective feedback, in the second stage they are more strongly influenced by their own mental schemas and under-utilize external feedback. There is a third stage, however, when the learner is able to balance environmental and mentalistic influences without threatening the stability of the knowledge system. It should be noted that according to this view of learning the manner in which knowledge is represented varies at different stages of development.

Cognitive Theory and L2 Acquisition

There have been a number of attempts to apply cognitive learning theory to L2 acquisition. These have been based on the assumption that L2 learning is no different in kind from any other kind of complex skill learning. O'Malley, Chamot and Walker (1987:288), for instance, comment: 'The theory suggests that language-related codes and structures are stored and retrieved from memory much like other information, and that language acquisition follows the same principles of learning as do other complex cognitive skills.' J. Anderson (1983:398) writes: 'little direct evidence exists to support the view that language is a unique system.' Language is, therefore, deprived of the unique status attributed to it by generative linguists in the Chomskyan tradition and by those researchers who seek to explain L2 learning with reference to the principles of Universal Grammar (cf. Cook, 1985; 1988). The extent to which cognitive theory can account for L2 learning depends crucially on the extent to which language constitutes a general skill or a specific faculty of the human mind.

Strategic Competence

One aspect of cognitive learning theory which has received considerable attention in L2 acquisition research is procedural knowledge.[5] Faerch and Kasper (1983) identify a number of sub-components of procedural knowledge. Reception procedures involve such strategies as bottom−up and top−down processing and inferencing. Production procedures consist of the various strategies which learners use both to plan and to monitor their output. Conversational procedures concern the devices needed to communicate appropriately and to construct coherent discourse. Communication strategies are used to solve problems which the learner experiences in the planning and execution of speech as a result of inadequate resources. It is by these means that the learner is able to automatize L2 knowledge for both comprehension and production. Knowledge can only become 'procedural' when it can be manipulated in the various ways described by Faerch and Kasper. Learners need to develop **strategic competence** (Canale and Swain, 1980).

Bialystok's Model

The most fully worked out cognitive theory of L2 learning is that developed by Bialystok (Bialystok, 1979; 1981; 1982; 1983; 1988; Bialystok and Sharwood-Smith, 1985). The theory has subtly changed over the years (with concomitant changes in terminology),[6] but the central premises have remained intact, reflecting the general distinctions discussed above. The following account of Bialystok's theory is based on her later publications.

Like other cognitive psychologists who have addressed L2 learning, Bialystok explicitly affirms the principle that language is processed by the human mind in the same way as other kinds of information (Bialystok, 1988:32). Language proficiency is described with reference to two dimensions: an analysed factor and an automatic factor. The analysed factor concerns the extent to which the language learner is aware of the structure of her linguistic knowledge. In unanalysed knowledge, which is characteristic of the early stages of L2 learning, the learner is not aware of the structure and organization of knowledge. As learning takes place awareness increases, enabling the learner to identify the formal structure. Awareness takes the form of 'a propositional mental representation' of linguistic knowledge which may or may not be conscious to the learner. Bialystok is emphatic that the degree of analyticity is not linked to consciousness and is not explicitly represented in the mind of the learner: 'it is erroneous to equate analyzed knowledge with articulated knowledge, or knowledge of rules' (Bialystok, 1988:40).

However, analysed knowledge does make 'articulated knowledge' and metalingual knowledge possible. Its real significance lies in the fact that it can be operated on by the learner and so is available for language uses of the kind required in formal education (e.g. academic essay writing). Learners who only have access to unanalysed L2 knowledge will be restricted to the kinds of language use for which this is appropriate (e.g. everyday conversation). The process by which knowledge gradually becomes analysed during the course of L2 acquisition corresponds to the general process of cognitive restructuring described above.

The automatic factor concerns the relative access which the learner has to

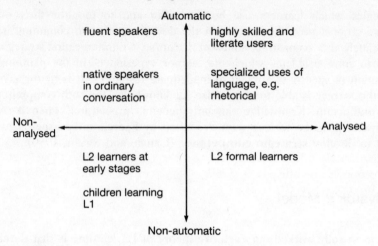

Figure 7.1   Bialystok's two dimensions of language proficiency
        Source: Bialystok (1988:37)

knowledge. Knowledge gains in automaticity as learning takes place. It is reflected in easier access and more fluent performance. Automaticity is achieved through practice.

These two factors are independent of each other. Thus development on the analysed dimension occurs independently of development on the automatic dimension. Learners begin with unmarked knowledge, i.e. knowledge that is non-automatic and unanalysed. The simultaneous development of both dimensions is difficult, so learners are likely to concentrate on one factor or the other. Some learners will choose to go for automaticity, others will concentrate on analysing their knowledge by breaking down formulaic expressions acquired as unanalysed chunks. The learning context will also influence what kind of acquisition takes place. Informal L2 learners are more likely to emphasize automaticity, formal learners will stress analyticity. Figure 7.1 illustrates the different kinds of learners and language uses predicted by the model.

Cognitive Theory and Instructed L2 Learning

There has been no attempt to develop a specific cognitive theory of *instructed* L2 learning. However, both general cognitive theory and Bialystok's bi-dimensional model have been applied to the classroom. Key issues which have been addressed are the relationships between (1) practice and automaticity, (2) classroom interaction and procedural knowledge and (3) formal instruction and analysed knowledge.

One view holds that practice is the key to the development of automaticity.

McLaughlin (1987) adopts this position, claiming that considerable training is necessary before automatic processing can take place. Errors occur because the learner has not yet automatized performance and does not have the time to make use of controlled processing. Errors can also occur as a result of obliterative subsumption. Practice can help to activate mental nodes, strengthen connections, increase speed of access and thereby reduce errors. Corrective feedback – an essential component of practice – can help to overcome the effects of obliterative subsumption by helping the learner to preserve the essential attributes of the new linguistic forms (Seliger, 1977).

Johnson (1988) suggests that a number of criteria have to be met before correction can be effective in eliminating errors (or 'mistakes', as he prefers to call them):[7]

1   The learner must have a desire or need to eradicate the mistake.
2   She must be able to form an internal representation of what the correct behaviour looks like.
3   She must realize that her performance is flawed.
4   She must have the opportunity to perform in real conditions.

The latter point is particularly significant, as it constitutes the principal difference between a cognitive and a behaviourist view of practice. Whereas audiolingual learning theory emphasized the controlled practice of specific forms in specially contrived exercises, cognitive learning theory stresses the need for practice in real operating conditions. Only in this way will the learner succeed in achieving automatic control of her knowledge for use in authentic communication.

Cognitive theory also emphasizes the importance of ensuring that the classroom provides adequate opportunities for the proceduralization of knowledge. We saw in chapter 4, however, that many classrooms fail in this respect. Classroom process research has shown that interaction is qualitatively different in classroom and natural discourse and that this is reflected in the learning and communication strategies learners employ. It can be argued that in many cases language classes do not really prepare students for participation in ordinary face-to-face interaction because they do not provide the conditions needed to ensure that full automatization of L2 knowledge takes place.

According to cognitive theory, formal instruction can help to increase the learner's analysed knowledge. Focusing on specific linguistic forms and encouraging the learner to manipulate these with varying degrees of awareness facilitates restructuring and also builds propositional representations of L2 knowledge. This enables the learner to participate in the kinds of decontextualized language use which require analysed knowledge. The aim, then, is awareness-raising rather than automaticity via proceduralization. This is not so very different from the aim of cognitive code learning theory (see chapter 3), one of the main assumptions of which was that perception and awareness of second language rules are separate from their actual use. One of the legacies of audiolingualism is that the two functions of instruction – the development of automatic and analysed knowledge – have been conflated.

Problems with Cognitive Accounts of Classroom L2 Learning

Cognitive learning theory offers a powerful account of how L2 learning takes place. Nevertheless, it is inadequate in two important respects where instructed L2 learning is concerned. First, the theory cannot easily account for the presence of acquisitional sequences. Second, it is rather vague regarding the role of explicit knowledge.

The existence of acquisitional sequences that are immune to instruction is well attested (see chapter 6). The fact that instruction appears powerless to affect the order in which developmental structures are acquired cannot be accounted for by cognitive learning theory. Neither automatization nor re-structuring can explain why a word-order rule such as verb-end emerges at a particular stage of development in the interlanguage of L2 German learners. These processes are also inadequate to account for why instruction in a marked linguistic feature such as relative pronoun as object of preposition can trigger the acquisition of associated unmarked features such as subject and object relative pronouns (Gass, 1979; Eckman et al., 1988). According to Bialystok's theory learners begin with knowledge that is non-automatic and non-analysed. But this theory provides no means of specifying which non-automatic and non-analysed items of knowledge are developed first and which later. McLaughlin (1987) attempts to protect the theory against this criticism (which he fully acknowledges) by referring to Sajavaara's (1978) proposal that predictable acquisitional sequences reflect routines that are fully automatic at the very moment they emerge and, therefore, are not subject to the process of automatization that governs other knowledge. Such a suggestion is not very convincing, however, as it is not clear why this happens to some knowledge forms and not others and, more crucially, because the available empirical evidence suggests that developmental structures such as German word-order rules are not fully automatized at the point of emergence but, in fact, take time to become so. The basic assumption of cognitive learning theory – that language learning and use are not different in kind from other kinds of skill learning and use – is not fully justified.

This criticism does not constitute a total rejection of cognitive learning theory, however. It demonstrates the need for a comprehensive theory that incorporates both a cognitive explanation of how learners develop the ability to use their knowledge in different kinds of tasks (i.e. a **proficiency** theory) and a linguistic explanation of how learners acquire a knowledge of L2 rules (i.e. a **competence** theory).

Bialystok and Sharwood-Smith (1985) offer the outlines of such a theory. They distinguish two components of L2 acquisition: knowledge and control. Knowledge has both a quantitative and qualitative dimension. The former concerns how much the learner knows. The latter concerns the way in which the language system has been organized and represented in the learner's mind, which changes over time. Control refers to the processing system which is used during actual performance. An analogy with a library is used to make the distinction clear. The number of books corresponds to 'quantitative knowledge' and the system for arranging them on the shelves to 'qualitative knowledge'. The procedures involved in retrieving a given book from the library are analogous to 'control'. Bialystok and Sharwood-Smith emphasize that control involves both knowing the retrieval procedures and being able to operate them with speed and efficiency. A cognitive theory of language learning, then, will inform principally about control procedures and their application (i.e. procedural knowledge or what Bialystok calls the automatic factor). It also explains how learners develop the ability to use their knowledge in different kinds of language use (i.e. by means of analysing knowledge). A linguistic theory – which is accommodated in the model – is needed to explain how knowledge of L2 properties enters interlanguage. Cognitive and linguistic theories, as currently formulated, are not as complementary as Bialystok and Sharwood-Smith's model suggests, however. In particular, it is not clear what qualitative aspects of an L2 grammar are governed by linguistic or cognitive factors.

The second major problem of a cognitive account of L2 acquisition concerns the role of explicit knowledge. Explicit knowledge refers to knowledge which is consciously represented in the mind of the learner and which can be articulated on request. Any theory of *instructed* language learning, however, will need to provide a clear account of the relationship between explicit and implicit knowledge. Anderson does offer an account, but this is unsatisfactory, because it does not conform with the known facts of L2 acquisition. He claims that using declarative knowledge makes it automatic so that it can be used below the level of consciousness. Learning begins with conscious attention on the part of the learner, resulting in declarative knowledge. O'Malley, Chamot and Walker (1987) argue that this is true in both naturalistic and classroom learning. In the case of the former conscious attention will be focused on the functional uses of language, while in the latter attention is focused on formal aspects. In naturalistic learning learners will be conscious of routines and patterns, while in classroom learning they will conscious of 'rules'. The fact that learners – particularly adults – are conscious of some aspects of what and how they are learning is not in dispute, neither is the fact that there are differences both among individual learners and in acquisitional settings regarding what aspects of the L2 are initially dealt with consciously. The problem lies in conflating automaticity with consciousness. Anderson is, in fact, claiming that implicit knowledge of linguistic forms is dependent upon prior explicit knowledge, but the available evidence suggests otherwise and supports Krashen's claim that learners (including adults) can acquire an L2 subconsciously. However, it does not follow from this that explicit knowledge has no role to play in the development of this grammar.

Summary

This section has examined in some detail various cognitive learning theories in order to determine to what extent they can account for instructed L2 learning. The following conclusions have been reached:

1   In developing a theory of L2 learning it is necessary to distinguish 'knowledge' and 'control' and to take account of both linguistic and cognitive factors.
2   Cognitive learning theory provides an adequate account of how learner's obtain control over L2 knowledge; free practice enables controlled processing to become automatic. Learners need appropriate interactional opportunities to activate strategies for proceduralizing knowledge.
3   Cognitive theory can also provide some insights into how learners restructure their L2 knowledge in order to make it available for use in an increasing range of tasks, including those requiring decontextualized language use.
4   A cognitive theory is unable to explain the sequence of acquisition of grammatical structures.
5   A cognitive theory is unable to account for the part played by explicit knowledge and cannot, therefore, fully explain how formal instruction contributes to L2 acquisition.

A comprehensive theory of instructed L2 learning will need give recognition to the fact that some aspects of L2 acquisition (those that are associated with the ability to use L2 knowledge) are governed by general cognitive factors, while other aspects (those associated with how an L2 grammar is constructed) are governed by linguistic factors.

An Integrated Theory

The theory described in this section seeks to explain how instructional input (in its various forms) provides the learner with the data needed to construct her interlanguage. It recognizes that different aspects of L2 learning require different kinds of explanation and that neither a purely linguistic nor a purely cognitive framework will provide a complete explanation.

L2 Knowledge is Differentiated

An initial premise is that L2 knowledge is differentiated. **Explicit** and **implicit knowledge** are held to be different in kind and to be stored separately in the brain. Explicit knowledge is conscious and declarative. Implicit knowledge is subconscious and procedural, although not necessarily fully automatic. Neither kind of knowledge is developmentally primary — that is, the learner may acquire a particular 'rule' explicitly in the first instance and then proceed to acquire the same rule implicitly at a later point, or vice versa. Only implicit knowledge is developmental, however; it is manifested as acquisitional sequences.

The claim that implicit and explicit knowledge constitute discrete types of knowledge runs contrary to the views of other theorists (e.g. Faerch, Haastrup and Phillipson, 1984). According to the models proposed by these theorists knowledge is continuous rather than dichotomous. Explicit and implicit forms represent the two poles of a continuum. Explicit knowledge is defined as metalingual knowledge and implicit knowledge as knowledge that can be used without any reference to a formal rule. Intermediate levels of knowledge are reflected in the learner's ability to decide that speech is or is not in accordance with an L2 rule or her ability to describe a rule in her own (but not in metalingual) terms. Faerch et al's position, however, conflates the two processes of consciousness-raising and automatization. They state (1984:203), for instance:

> The process of developing more consciousness about implicit knowledge is part of the general process of consciousness-raising. A process in the opposite direction — the learner gradually developing an ability to use a certain rule for productive and receptive purposes without being aware of this — is usually referred to as an automatization process.

Such a model does not allow for the possibility that both explicit and implicit knowledge can be accessed with varying degrees of automaticity.

The claim that explicit and implicit knowledge are distinct is in accord with Krashen's Monitor Model; 'acquired' knowledge is implicit and 'learnt' knowledge is explicit. Krashen (1985) advances a number of arguments in favour of this position. Some learners — like 'P' (Krashen and Pon, 1975) — demonstrate explicit knowledge of some very simple rules without being able to perform these in everyday communication. Conversely, they demonstrate implicit knowledge of some very complex rules of which they have no conscious knowledge. A study by Hulstijn and Hulstijn (1984) showed that learners with no explicit knowledge of two Dutch word-order rules nevertheless demonstrated competence in the use of the rules. Seliger (1979) asked twenty-nine monolingual children, eleven bilingual children and fifteen adult ESL learners to state the rule for using 'a' and 'an' and then elicited samples of speech from the same subjects, allowing them time to focus on form if they wanted to. He found no relationship between the subjects' performance and conscious knowledge of the rule even though many subjects believed that the rule had guided their speech. Kadia (1988) reports that her subject (an adult Chinese learner of English in Canada) had 'a rich metalinguistic knowledge' but that the relationship between her ability to state the rules for transitive phrasal verbs and ditransitive verbs and her spontaneous production of these rules was very poor. There was a better relationship where written test performance was concerned. These studies lend support to the claim that the two types of knowledge are separate.

It is, however, not easy to decide between these two positions. As McLaughlin (1978b) has pointed out, it is very difficult to tell what kind of knowledge a learner is using in any single performance. We cannot distinguish very easily editing by 'feel' (which involves implicit knowledge) from editing with the 'monitor' (which involves explicit knowledge).[8] Whether the two knowledge types are perceived as dichotomous or continuous depends to a large extent on whether the theorist posits any interface between them (i.e. whether explicit knowledge can be converted into implicit and vice versa). The theory presented here, like Krashen's and unlike that of Faerch et al. adopts a non-interface position.

It is important to recognize (contrary to the position taken up by Faerch et al.) that explicit knowledge does not require metalingual expertise. It can be articulated with varying degrees of precision and varying degrees of technicality. It can also vary in the extent to which it is descriptively adequate, i.e. accounts for implicit knowledge. A linguist's description will be more adequate than a teacher's, which in turn is likely to be nearer the mark than the representation formed by the learner (Seliger, 1979). Explicit knowledge, then, can be differentiated according to how it is articulated and how elaborate it is (Sharwood-Smith, 1981).

Implicit knowledge can also be differentiated. It can consist of the rules by which utterances are constructed or it can consist of ready-made chunks of language (cf. Ellis, 1985a:167−75). Pawley and Syder (1983) argue that an important component of the native speaker's linguistic knowledge is the hundreds of thousands of 'lexicalized sentence stems' which every speaker has stored in her memory. These are defined as 'a unit of clause length or longer whose grammatical form and lexical content is wholly or largely fixed' (1983:190). Examples are such expressions as 'Need any help?' and 'I see what you mean.' Pawley and Syder suggest that there is a continuum between fully productive rules and lexicalized sentence stems. Because speakers are able to retrieve the latter as wholes they economize on processing effort and thereby gain in fluency. A number of researchers have noted the existence of formulaic expressions in the speech of L2 learners (e.g. Fillmore, 1976; Krashen and Scarcella, 1978; Ellis, 1984). This distinction between stereo-typical expressions and productive rules also seems to correspond in part to Bialystok's notion of unanalysed and analysed knowledge.

Productive implicit rules can also be differentiated. Research based on typlogical universals or Universal Grammar distinguishes marked and unmarked linguistic knowledge. For example, the Accessibility Hierarchy (see chapter 6) posits that a relative pronoun functioning as subject as in:

The footballer who scored the goal has been mobbed.

is less marked than a relative pronoun functioning as object of preposition as in:

The house that we moved into was built in the 1920s.

Similarly, a verb which takes two noun phrases as in:

They offered the hospital a donation.

can be considered more marked than one that takes a noun phrase followed by a preposition phrase as in:

They explained the problem to me.

(Mazurkewich, 1985). Functional models of language such as that developed by Givon (1979) also differentiate linguistic knowledge, in this case according to whether it is typical of unplanned/informal or planned/formal language use. The discourse hypothesis discussed in chapter 5 is based on this distinction.

The recognition that knowledge is differentiated is central for understanding the role played by instructional input in L2 learning, as different kinds of input result in different kinds of knowledge and, more significantly, different kinds of input are needed to achieve acquisition of different kinds of knowledge.

Control

As in the framework proposed by Bialystok and Sharwood-Smith, control is considered to be separate from knowledge. Control applies to both explicit and implicit knowledge. Thus the learner is able to access both conscious and subconscious linguistic rules with varying degrees of automaticity. Newly acquired knowledge is typically accessed only by means of controlled processing. With opportunities for free practice, however, it can be processed more rapidly and efficiently. The development of control is reflected in both increased accuracy in the performance of specific linguistic features and in increased fluency (e.g. fewer pauses and longer runs between pauses).

Instructional Input

A basic distinction has been drawn between meaning and form-focused instruction. In the case of the former the learner is engaged in communication where the primary effort involves the exchange of meaning and where there is no conscious effort to achieve grammatical correctness. In the case of the latter the learner is engaged in activities that have been specially designed to teach specific grammatical features. The input that derives from these two kinds of instruction differs with regard to its communicative properties (e.g.

meaning-focused instruction is likely to afford the learner an opportunity to listen to and to perform a greater range of language functions than will form-focused instruction) and also with regard to the kind of response it typically evokes in the learner (e.g. form-focused instruction encourages the learner to reflect on the formal features of the language while meaning-focused instruction encourages semantic processing).

As we saw in chapter 6, the instructional input in many lessons will be mixed, affording the learner the opportunity to attend to both meaning and form – to experience language or to study it. Teachers shift the focus as the lesson unravels – at one moment engaging the learners in meaningful communication and at another directing their attention to the linguistic code. It may also be possible, however, to distinguish whole lessons and even whole courses of instruction according to whether the emphasis is primarily on meaning or form (Spada, 1987). A form-focused lesson will always afford the learner input that goes far beyond the specific property which is the instructional target. Ultimately, of course, it is the learner and not the textbook or the teacher that determines in what way the input is attended to. An activity intended by the teacher to focus the learner's attention on form may be treated by her as an opportunity for meaningful communication, or vice versa. However, given that the *raison d'être* of the classroom is to learn the language, the learner may be predisposed to attend to form. The evidence obtained from many classrooms (even so-called communicative ones) is that the interactions that take place are far removed from those found in natural settings (see chapter 4).

Learning Style

Learning style – the learner's affective and cognitive orientation to learning – also plays an important part in instructed language learning, although there has not been space in this book to deal with this aspect. Not all learners are receptive to instructional input. Only learners with a positive affective orientation to learning the L2 are likely to benefit from the instruction. Tolerance of ambiguity and motivation govern the extent to which individual learners are open to input and also how frequently they participate in classroom activities, either actively or as 'silent speakers' (Reiss, 1983).

Even if a learner is receptive to input, she may not be cognitively suited to the type of instructional input provided. An experiential learner, whose natural learning style predisposes her to focus on communication, may be held back if she is faced with an input that is predominantly form-focused. Likewise, a studial learner who is required to participate extensively in meaning-focused instruction may be inhibited. In addition, learners who find that their learning style is incompatible with the instructional style may develop anxiety and so lose confidence and motivation, perhaps even to the point of abandoning instruction.

Instruction and the Acquisition of Explicit Knowledge

The theory claims that different kinds of instruction typically result in different kinds of L2 knowledge. In order to examine how this happens we will consider first the relationship between instruction and explicit knowledge and then go on to consider how instruction influences the acquisition of implicit knowledge. It needs to be stressed straight away, however, that there is no simple correlation between form-focused instruction and explicit knowledge or between meaning-focused input and implicit knowledge.

Classroom learners typically make use of their cognitive problem-solving skills in order to derive conscious rules about the form of the L2 grammar. They will do this whether the method of instruction invites them to or not. Arguably, however, form-focused instruction facilitates the acquisition of explicit knowledge, although very little is known about how effective instruction is in teaching explicit knowledge. Krashen (1982) argues that 'learning' is limited to linguistic forms that are simple in structure and transparent in function (see chapter 3). Seliger (1979) argues that the rules learners construct are typically anomolous — blurred reflections of the teacher's pedagogic rules, which in turn are imprecise versions of the linguist's rules. Seliger describes a number of characteristics of both conscious learner-formed rules and pedagogic rules. They go beyond the information given, they do not provide accurate descriptions of the speaker's internal knowledge and they do not correspond to actual language behaviour. The picture painted by Krashen and Seliger is overly pessimistic, however. Diary studies (e.g. Ellis and Rathbone, 1987) reveal that learners are able to acquire conscious representations of quite complex rules and that they actively seek to do so. Doubtless many of these representations lack precision and accuracy, at least in their original formulation, but they can be worked on, gradually refined and extended to account for new features which the learner observes in the input or new information obtained subsequently (cf. Kadia, 1988).

In chapter 6 the possibility was floated that linguistic theory explains how explicit rather than implicit knowledge is acquired. One of the hypotheses based on this theory that is receiving considerable attention at the moment is that unmarked properties of the L2 emerge in interlanguage before marked ones. Current models of generative grammar (e.g. Chomsky, 1981) provide a rich source of information from which to derive operational hypotheses regarding the role of markedness. One of the advantages of this approach in the study of L2 acquisition is that 'very specific claims' can be advanced and tested (Rutherford, 1987). Another hypothesis that is attracting attention is that instruction directed at marked linguistic features serves to trigger acquisition of associated unmarked features, i.e. learners are able to project their explicit knowledge beyond that which they have actually been taught. This is clearly speculative at the moment, but should it prove to be correct, it would indicate that there is a preferred order of presentation of explicit knowledge.

Instruction and the Acquisition of Implicit Knowledge

Instruction contributes to the acquisition of implicit knowledge in a number of ways. Both meaning-focused and form-focused instruction can facilitate learning.

The Role of Meaning-focused Instruction

Meaning-focused instruction supplies the learner with input for processing. One well-documented way in which this occurs is through 'scaffolding' (cf. chapter 5). Learners build structures vertically with the support provided by their own and others previous utterances. They then learn the structures they build in this way and subsequently produce them horizontally. This route to linguistic knowledge is of limited value, however, except perhaps for beginners.

Of greater importance is access to comprehensible input. Despite reservations regarding the role which this plays (see chapter 5), it is hard not to conclude that comprehensible input functions as the primary source of data in L2 acquisition. One way in which this occurs is by supplying the learner with ready-made chunks — lexicalized sentence stems — which can be memorized as wholes and used to perform communicative functions that are important to the learner. In this case, there may be a fairly direct relationship between input and acquisition, with the learner's innate language-learning mechanisms not involved. Research has shown that even in a classroom context certain chunks or formulas occur with considerable frequency (Ellis, 1984a). Input frequency together with communicative need probably act as the determinants of acquisition of this kind of implicit knowledge.

Input frequency is probably much less important where productive implicit rules are concerned. Two conditions govern whether input becomes intake:

1 the learner must attend subconsciously to the presence of a specific feature in the input (i.e. notice the feature without reflecting on it);
2 the learner must have reached a stage of development which makes it possible to incorporate this feature into her interlanguage system.

Both conditions are necessary for acquisition to take place. Neither attention nor readiness is sufficient by itself. Cognitive mechanisms govern which features learners attend to. For example, there is ample evidence in both L1 and L2 acquisition to show that elements that occur at the beginnings and ends of sentences are more salient than elements that occur sentence-medially (Slobin, 1973; Clahsen, 1984). Linguistic factors govern whether the feature attended to is learnable. For example, universal principles of grammar (see above) may guide the process of acquisition or there may be a hierarchy of linguistic processing operations (see p. 153) which determine when a specific feature is acquirable.

In emphasizing the role played by linguistic universals or linguistic processing operations, however, it is not necessary to discount the contribution of comprehensible input (chapter 5). From the point of view of a theory of *instructed* L2 learning, comprehensible input is of special importance because it enables us to address the question about how 'intervention' should take place. We can speculate that neither input which is entirely unproblematic nor input which is so problematic that it is entirely incomprehensible is likely to encourage the learner to attend to specific linguistic features. Long's (1983a) claim that negotiated input is best for learning may not have been empirically demonstrated but it is supported by the common-sense assumption that attention to 'new' features will be encouraged if a degree of problematicity occurs. It is worth noting that it is the problematicity of such exchanges not their successful resolution which is the crucial factor in determining whether or not the learner attends to the new features.

Meaning-focused instruction also provides opportunities for learner output and this, too, contributes to the acquisition of implicit knowledge. The output hypothesis (chapter 5) states that learners need to be 'pushed' into producing output that taxes their existing linguistic resources in order to develop a full grammatical competence. The discourse hypothesis claims that learners need the opportunity to participate in a variety of discourse modes (ranging from the planned to the unplanned). Linguistic knowledge is tied to the particular type of discourse in which it is learnt. Access to planned/formal discourse may be particularly important for acquiring implicit knowledge of the marked properties of the L2.

The Role of Form-focused Instruction

Implicit knowledge can also be acquired via form-focused instruction, although there are a number of constraints governing the teachability of linguistic structures (chapter 6). Successful instructional intervention in interlanguage development occurs in the case of:

1: Lexicalized sentence stems   Routines and patterns can be memorized as wholes. Some instructional methods (e.g. the notional/functional approach) are particularly well suited to ensuring that the learner is equipped with a supply of ready-made phrases. Beginner learners, in particular, need access to such phrases before they can begin interacting with native speakers.

2: Developmental structures that are 'learnable'   These are structures which are acquired in a fixed acquisitional sequence as a result of the processing operations they require of the learner (chapter 6). Direct instruction will only result in the acquisition of a structure that the learner is 'ready' for, i.e. the next one in the sequence from that which she has already acquired. Direct instruction aimed at structures which are more than one step ahead of the learner's current interlanguage will founder and may even interfere with the acquisitional process.

3   Variational Structures   Not all linguistic structures are subject to developmental processing. Some — like copula 'be' — are variational in the sense that they can be acquired at different stages of development and in the sense that they are acquired by some learners but not by others, in accordance with their sociopsychological attitudes.

The role of form-focused instruction is restricted where implicit knowledge is concerned. In practical terms, only instruction directed at formulaic phrases is likely to prove profitable. The principal source of implicit knowledge is meaning-focused instruction.

Instruction and the Acquisition of Control

A widely held view is that learners gain control over their L2 knowledge through practice. For example, Sharwood-Smith (1981:166) writes:

> it is quite clear and uncontroversial to say that most spontaneous performance is attained by dint of practice. In the course of actually performing in the target language, the learner gains the necessary control over its subjects such that he or she can use them quickly without reflection.

Sharwood-Smith's subsequent comments make it clear that by practice he means 'controlled practice'.[9] That is, he believes that by consciously rehearsing structures, the learner proceduralizes them. Sharwood-Smith cites no empirical evidence to support this position, nor in fact is there much. The available research suggests that controlled practice may result in spontaneous productive use only of those linguistic forms which the learner is 'ready' to handle (Ellis, 1988b). In the case of certain structures (variational features, for example) practice may lead to increased accuracy, but perhaps only temporarily (see chapter 6). Thus controlled practice appears to have little long-term effect on the accuracy with which new structures are performed. It also has little effect on fluency as measured by temporal variables. Ellis and Rathbone (1987), for instance, found no relationship between the amount of controlled practice *ab initio* learners of German took part in and speech rate.

How then do learners achieve control? The answer lies in meaning-focused instruction. This provides the conditions the learner needs to activate those procedures that are responsible for both automatizing knowledge and for compensating for lack of it. In order to develop control the learner needs to practise in 'real operating conditions'. Only in this way will the learner develop the strategic abilities needed to perform her competence accurately and fluently.

licit Knowledge in L2 Acquisition

ns that explicit knowledge does not turn into implicit
e). Given that implicit knowledge is the primary goal of
ing, this raises the question 'What is the role of explicit
a claims that its role is extremely limited. In the integrated
e, however, explicit knowledge is of major importance.
knowledge is hypothesized to work has already been
6. Briefly, it is claimed that conscious knowledge functions
acilitor, enabling the learner to 'notice' L2 features in
iput which would otherwise be ignored. The features
r, are acquired from this input in accordance with the
cognitive and linguistic processing faculties. Figure 7.2
ic representation of this process.

Schmidt and Frota (1986) lends support to this view. They
er they studied (called 'R') benefited from formal instruction
d information about the structure of the target language
h could have been derived only with great difficulty from
However, R did not learn everything he was taught in the
is able to use it spontaneously in subsequent interaction.
and used what he was taught if he subsequently heard it and
6:279). The diary study kept by R shows that he tended to
features in the input immediately after they had been taught
t that conscious awareness of what was present in the input was
to learning. Schmidt and Frota argue that R was able to notice
een his own output and the input as a result of the explicit
had acquired.

the gap' hypothesis helps to explain a number of aspects of
guage learning. For example, it provides a way of accounting for
e feedback might aid learning. Corrective feedback juxtaposes
uage form with the target-language form, putting the learner in
sition to notice the difference. Such feedback serves as a way of
learner's consciousness about the lack of correlation between the
uage and her own interlanguage.[10] It should be noted, however,
rrective feedback which Schmidt and Frota refer to occurs in the

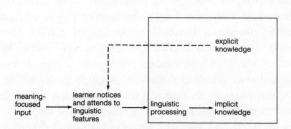

Figure 7.2 The role of explicit knowledge in the acquisition of implicit knowledge

overall context of natural (and, therefore, meaning-focused) interaction and not in the context of specially contrived language practice. The hypothesis also suggests why instructed learners do better than naturalistic learners – they know more 'facts' about the language. Schmidt and Frota speculate that those learners whose explicit knowledge is the most developed will learn the most.

The theory, therefore, allocates a significant role to explicit knowledge, while maintaining that there is no direct interface between the two types of knowledge. Two general points need to be emphasized. First, it follows from the theory that formal instruction directed at explicit knowledge can facilitate the process of acquiring implicit knowledge. The learner is not just a 'language-acquisition device' but can take conscious decisions, which will aid learning. Second, the effects of explicit knowledge will be indirect and delayed. One reason for this is that the explicit knowledge may be 'fuzzy' (see discussion on p. 189). The main reason is that noticing and attending to developmental linguistic features is no guarantee of their acquisition. The learner also has to be 'ready' to assimilate them into her interlanguage.

Output

Output can be generated in a number of ways. The learner can rely entirely on implicit knowledge. In doing so, the learner is likely to make extensive use of formulaic expressions and vertical constructions in the early stages so as to offset the processing difficulty that arises from trying to use non-automatic implicit knowledge productively. The learner can also 'borrow' from her L1 (Corder, 1978a) by translating using whatever implicit and explicit L2 knowledge comes to hand. Learners can also edit their output using either kind of knowledge (i.e. editing by 'feel' vs. editing by 'monitor'). Which means of generating output a learner chooses will depend, in part, on whether she is oriented towards correctness or towards fluency. If the former, she is more likely to resort to explicit knowledge to compensate for the lack of implicit knowledge. It will also depend on the nature of the communication task, in particular on whether there is a felt need to focus on form (Hulstijn and Hulstijn, 1984; Hulstijn, 1988).

The learner's output also contributes to acquisition. One way is by being pushed to produce sentences which stretch the limits of her competence (the output hypothesis). It also contributes in another way. The learner's output is part of the totality of input available for processing. Thus utterances generated in the ways described above feed into the learner's own acquisition device. This means that 'utterances initiated by means of explicit knowledge can provide feedback into implicit knowledge' (Sharwood-Smith, 1981:166), so providing a further way in which explicit knowledge can facilitate acquisition. As Schmidt and Frota observe, however, such 'auto-input' is not always beneficial, as, often enough, learner output is erroneous. Thus learners may learn their own, incorrect solution to a problem. This may account for why some errors are so persistent and why learners often feel that that their errors are not really errors. However, learners also learn their correct productions. Thus a linguistic form that has just entered the learner's interlanguage can be strengthened by means of her regular attempts to use it.

Summary

The integrated theory is summarized in diagrammatic form in Figure 7.3. The principal hypotheses of the model are:

1 Instructional input is 'filtered' by the learner in accordance with her learning style. The learner will be predisposed to attend to linguistic features in the input if she responds positively (cognitively and affectively) to the type of instruction.
2 Implicit and explicit knowledge constitute different kinds of knowledge and are stored separately.
3 Instructional intervention can take the form of meaning-focused and form-focused activities. Learners can respond to classroom input as 'interaction' or as 'formal instruction'.
4 Explicit knowledge is derived largely from form-focused instruction.
5 Implicit knowledge is derived largely from meaning-focused instruction. For acquisition to take place the learner must attend to specific linguistic features in the input and be ready to incorporate these into her interlanguage.
6 Implicit knowledge can also be taught directly if (a) the learner is developmentally 'ready' or (b) the target forms are not subject to developmental constraints.
7 Explicit knowledge serves to sensitize the learner to the existence of non-standard forms in her interlanguage and thus facilitates the acquisition of target-language forms in accordance with (5) above.
8 Control over linguistic knowledge is achieved by means of performing under real operating conditions in meaning-focused language activities.

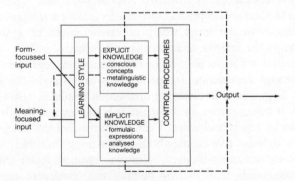

Figure 7.3 A model of instructed L2 acquisition

9   The learner's own output serves as input to the language-processing mechanisms. Deviant output that is subject to corrective feedback raises consciousness and facilitates acquisition of the correct forms.

Conclusion

This chapter began with an outline of cognitive learning theory, as this has been applied to language teaching. This theory is able to explain some of the known facts about the relationship between instruction and learning. In particular, it provides a convincing account of how learners obtain control over their L2 knowledge. However, cognitive learning theory is unable to explain the sequence of L2 acquisition nor does it convincingly elucidate the relationship between explicit and implicit knowledge and the role of instruction in this.

The integrated theory of instructed L2 acquisition builds on cognitive learning theory but also tries to incorporate those aspects of language learning that depend on linguistic and psycholinguistic factors and which, it is claimed, are responsible for the way in which linguistic knowledge enters the learner's interlanguage. Descriptions of some of the linguistic factors are to be found in current accounts of Universal Grammar (e.g. Cook, 1988). Some of the psycholinguistic factors are dealt with in discussions of how developmental features are acquired (e.g. Pienemann, 1986).

The theory proposed in this chapter rests, in part, on the hypothesis that explicit and implicit knowledge are distinct types of knowledge which are stored separately. This hypothesis is controversial; it is probably true to say that theorists are most divided on this issue. The main argument for claiming separation is that the available evidence indicates that instruction is often powerless to convert explicit into implicit knowledge. In other words, the relationship between the two types of knowledge is not one of automaticity.

Although the integrated theory adopts a non-interface position, it differs from other such theories (such as the Monitor Model) in allocating a major role to explicit knowledge. The theory hypothesizes that explicit knowledge functions as a facilitator of implicit knowledge by making the learner conscious of linguistic features in the input which otherwise might be ignored. Explicit knowledge helps the learner to *notice* marked forms.

The integrated theory is able to resolve the central paradox of instructed language learning. Instruction frequently fails to result in the direct acquisition of new linguistic structures, yet instruction results in faster learning and higher levels of achievement. In the main, it is the learner who is in charge of both what can be learnt and when it can be learnt, not the teacher.[11] But the teacher has a definite role to play both by ensuring that there are adequate opportunities for meaning-focused communication to foster the acquisition of implicit knowledge and also by helping the learner to develop explicit knowledge.

NOTES

1 The two goals − building a theory that is both **scientific** and **appropriate** − are in potential conflict. A scientific theory which formulates statements with the precision needed to ensure testability may not be accessible to many teachers. Equally, a theory which is appealing to teachers (e.g. the Monitor Model) may not be very scientific in Popper's sense. The dangers of trying to be both scientific and appropriate are not always recognized.

2 The distinction between 'knowledge' and 'ability' should not be confused with the distinction between 'linguistic' and 'sociolinguistic/pragmatic' aspects of language. The idea of 'knowledge' and 'ability to use' applies equally to both aspects. It follows, therefore, that 'proficiency' is concerned with both the ability to use linguistic knowledge (correctness) and the ability to use pragmatic rules (appropriateness). The focus of this book is on the linguistic rather than pragmatic aspects of language.

3 It is worth noting that whereas linguists have emphasized competence as knowledge, educationalists have emphasized competence as behaviour (cf. Taylor, 1988:160).

4 Overgeneralization errors can be seen as examples of obliterative subsumption. For example, the learner who says:

   * My father made me to go to bed.

   may do so because she has internalized a rule for infinitival complements which states that the infinitive occurs with 'to', as in:

   My father asked me to go to bed.

   and has ignored the fact that the verb 'make' does not conform to this rule in sentences in the active voice.

5 The term 'procedural knowledge' is used to refer to two different aspects of learning: (1) to knowledge which has been proceduralized and is, therefore, automatic; (2) to the strategies or procedures that are involved in the processing of knowledge for actual use. The two are interrelated, as knowledge becomes proceduralized as a result of the learner mastering the procedures required to process it.

6 In early accounts of the theory Bialystok referred to *explicit* and *implicit* knowledge. She abandoned these terms because she did not wish to suggest that *consciousness* was a factor and also because she wished to distinguish the automaticity and analysability of L2 knowledge. Her initial distinction tended to conflate these.

7 Errors are the result of a lack of competence; mistakes are the result of the learner's failure to perform her competence (cf. ch. 2). Arguably, mistake-correction has a better chance of succeeding because the learner already knows the linguistic structure. Error-correction can only work if new knowledge is created.

8 McLaughlin argues that the distinction between controlled and automatic processing is more tenable because it can be empirically tested by means of controlling the amount of time learners have to perform a particular task. In contrast, the explicit/implicit knowledge is not amenable to empirical study and, therefore, is not falsifiable. One response to this might be to argue that if a theory aims to provide a 'reasonable interpretation' rather than a 'scientific explanation' this

objection is irrelevant. However, it is possible to conceive of methods of testing the separation of implicit/explicit knowledge by using introspective research techniques which invite learners to comment on what kinds of knowledge they used in performing different tasks.

9 The term 'practice' is used with widely different meanings in language teaching. On the one hand it can refer to the kind of controlled practice associated with audiolingual pattern drills. On the other it can refer to the regular use of the L2 in real communication. Such usage of the term does not contribute to clear thinking and it might be better to restrict it to 'controlled practice'.

10 In contrast to the positive contribution of corrective feedback supplied by the learner's interlocutors (i.e. 'other-correction'), the learner's attempts to correct her own output appear to be of little value for acquisition. Schmidt and Frota (1986) claim that R's self-corrections had no discernable effect on his interlanguage development.

11 Corder (1980:11) concludes a perceptive review of what L2 acquisition research has to say about the teaching of grammar by arguing that 'teaching should be coordinated with learning and not learning with teaching'. However, this does not mean that no grammar teaching should take place. It means that the learner must be left to make use of grammar teaching in her own way. This is precisely the position adopted in this chapter.

8 Final Comments

Introduction

In the preceding chapters we have explored different ways of investigating how a second language (L2) is learnt through instruction. On the basis of the insights obtained from this survey I have proposed a theory of instructed language learning. It is now time to stand back and to identify what the main questions are for which answers are still needed and what kinds of research might help us to find these answers. First, though, I want to try to pinpoint some of the problems inherent in much of the research undertaken to date.

Problems of L2 Classroom Research

The L2 classroom researcher seeks to show how instructional events cause or impede the acquisition of a second language. In order to achieve this, it is necessary to (1) identify which instructional events are significant, (2) find valid and reliable measures of the L2 learning that takes place and (3) be able to demonstrate that the relationship between instructional events and learning is in some way causal. Researchers have faced a number of problems in carrying out each of these tasks.

There are different ways of identifying 'significant' instructional events. One way is to base selection on some explicit theory. This is the approach recommended by Long (1988b). He argues that classroom researchers should choose 'psycholinguistically relevant design features' as a basis for enquiry. The distinction between form-focused and meaning-focused learning activities — which Long proposes — is derived from Krashen's Monitor Model. Another way is to examine the methodological recommendations of language educationalists. Teacher training handbooks (e.g. Gower and Walters, 1983; Harmer, 1983) represent a rich source of information regarding those instructional events which experienced professionals in the field consider significant. Research which looks at the role of practice (e.g. Seliger, 1977) or of small-group work is a good example of this approach.

Both approaches are problematic, however. Constructs such as 'form vs. meaning-focused instruction' and 'practice' are notoriously difficult to operationalize in terms of actual social or cognitive behaviour in the classroom. The same problem faces researchers who have tried to investigate the 'method' construct (see chapter 1), though on a much larger scale. The problem is that a priori definitions of classroom events often turn out to be imprecise, incomplete and inaccurate. Allwright (1988b) argues: 'any *a priori* characterization of learning and teaching environments is bound to be suspect for fundamental research purposes.' Allwright believes that the characterization of instructional events should 'emerge from research' rather than be imposed upon it externally.

The difficulty of identifying potentially significant instructional events, then, confronts the researcher with a dilemma. Should she opt for theory-led research or should she concentrate on collecting data in order to arrive at accurate accounts of what actually happens in the classroom? Or is it possible to operate deductively (as Long wants), while making certain that the instructional events studied really do take place (as Allwright wants)?

The problems associated with the measurement of learning are no less tractable. There is no direct window through which the researcher can peer to discover how the learner is learning or what she has learnt. How, then, can the researcher discover what the effects of the learner's participation in instruction are? One solution, adopted by some researchers, is to try to tap the learners' intuitions about the L2. This is usually undertaken by means of some kind of grammaticality-judgement task (i.e. a task that requires the learner to state whether individual sentences are well-formed or not). Another solution is to collect samples of naturally occurring language use and analyse these to see if there is any evidence to show that the learner is able to employ target features correctly. Clearly the concept of 'learning' that underlies these two approaches to data collection is very different. Not surprisingly, the results obtained diverge considerably.

These two approaches to the measurement of learning in L2 acquisition research are supported by different theories of language and of language learning. The measurement of intuitions is undertaken by researchers who work within a theory based on the competence/performance distinction. Their aim is to establish what the learner 'knows' rather than what she 'does'. The analysis of actual language use is undertaken by researchers who base their study of L2 acquisition on cognitive theories of language processing. As long as there are competing theories of language and language learning, there will be differences in opinion regarding how learning should be measured.

The question remains, though, as to what constitutes valid data for the study of classroom L2 acquisition. In order to answer this question, it is surely important to consider the purpose of the research. In the case of classroom research, the aim is to investigate how learners develop the ability to use the L2 accurately, appropriately and fluently, as this is the goal of instruction. It is, therefore, surely more important to pay attention to research that addresses what learners can do in real-life situations than what they know but may be unable actually to use. In terms of the distinction developed in chapter 7, classroom research is directed at understanding how instruction contributes to **proficiency** rather than to **competence**. The measures of learning that are chosen should reflect this aim. Thus we ought to place greater confidence in measures of learning derived from natural language behaviour than in those obtained from artificial grammaticality-judgement tasks.

The most serious problem, however, is how to investigate the *relationship* between instructional events and learning outcomes. How can the researcher show that learners acquire new linguistic knowledge (or greater control over existing knowledge) as a result of taking part in specific instructional events? One possible way is to aim at explanation-through-description − that is, to build up a detailed understanding of how instructional events are enacted in the classroom and, by so doing, illuminate the factors that appear to influence whether learning takes place or not. This is the approach adopted by many classroom process researchers (see chapter 4). The problem, however, is that usually no evidence is collected to demonstrate whether any learning actually takes place. A second way is to try to establish a relationship between the occurrence of specific types of classroom behaviour (such as participation by the learner or the teacher's use of referential questions) and measures of learning. The problem here is that it is only possible to demonstrate that instruction and learning *correlate*; it is not possible to show that instruction *causes* learning. A third way is to carry out some kind of carefully designed experiment in order to examine whether a specific kind of 'treatment' results in predicted learning outcomes. Experiments do allow the researcher to make firmer statements about causation, but they have their own problems. For one thing, experiments can often result in an artificial teaching−learning environment. However, the experimental approach has led to some interesting results in the case of form-focused instruction (see chapter 6). The main problem lies in trying to set up experiments to show whether and to what extent different kinds of meaning-focused instruction facilitate learning. As we have seen, there is an absence of such studies.

It is important to recognize these problems. The research which this book has reported must be treated circumspectively because of them. We should not expect the research to produce clear-cut answers, if only because it begs the kinds of questions outlined above. We would do better to see the research − even the experimental studies − as contributing to understanding, rather than providing explanations.

Questions for Future Research

The questions which future research will need to address will be very similar to those which have informed research to date. They key questions are likely to be:

1 What kinds of instructional events are 'significant' for the study of L2 acquisition? How can these events be reliably identified?
2 To what extent is the distinction between form-focused and meaning-focused instruction a real one? Is it possible to identify specific classroom behaviours that are characteristic of each type of instruction?
3 How do learners acquire implicit knowledge of the L2 as a result of comprehending meaning-focused input in the classroom?
4 To what extent and what ways can form-focused instruction contribute to the acquisition of implicit knowledge of the L2?
5 What forms does explicit knowledge of the L2 take?
6 How can instruction contribute most effectively to the development of explicit knowledge?
7 To what extent and in what ways does explicit knowledge facilitate the acquisition of implicit knowledge?
8 How can learners increase their control over existing L2 knowledge (i.e. become more fluent) in a classroom setting?
9 What individual learner factors influence the way a learner responds to instruction?

These questions derive from the theory of instructed second language acquisition presented in chapter 7. Individual studies will need to focus on more narrowly formulated questions, based on these general issues. For example, research based on question 5 might try to investigate the nature of the learners' metalingual competence in specific domains of linguistic knowledge (e.g. verb tenses; word-order rules; overt discourse markers).

The Case for Hybrid Research

What kind of research is needed to seek answers to these questions? It is unlikely that any one type of research will succeed. Progress in understanding classroom language acquisition is most likely if researchers are prepared to adopt a variety of qualitative and quantitative methods. There is a continued need for ethnographic research directed at identifying significant classroom processes and also for experimental research to try to establish causative links between instructional variables and learning. There is also a case for the use of introspective methods to investigate how individual learners respond to instructional events. Above all, there is a need for hybrid research, i.e. research that combines the procedures of both hypothesis-forming and hypothesis-testing methods.

There has, in fact, been relatively little mixed research. Researchers have tended to fall into camps and to argue the case for their preferred approach. The old controversy between those who favour an experimental approach and those who favour ethnographic enquiry or the use of introspective methods is very much alive in L2 classroom research. But it is a sterile and unnecessary debate.

Let us look at an example of how hybrid research might help us to probe a difficult research question. We have seen that research which has sought to investigate how learners acquire new linguistic knowledge by comprehending input has made little progress. There are a number of reasons for this:

1 Qualitative research (e.g. discourse analysis) has been unable to demonstrate a causative relationship between input and acquisition.
2 Experimental studies have gone some way towards demonstrating how specific kinds of input promote comprehension, but have been unable to show that comprehension promotes acquisition.
3 It is difficult to manipulate the input in order to investigate how specific linguistic features affect acquisition without drawing the learner's conscious attention to the features, i.e. encouraging the learner to process the L2 as form rather than for meaning.
4 It is not clear how we can measure the acquisition that results from exposure to meaning-focused input.

Ellis (1989c) outlines a research proposal that might begin to overcome these problems. He suggests the use of partially artificial reading texts, which have had non-standard rules inserted into them. To encourage the students to attend to meaning rather than to form they are asked to do a faster reading exercise. To investigate what the subjects actually do as they read, a number of them are interrupted and asked to state what they have just been thinking about (cf. Cavalcanti, 1987). Or selected subjects are asked to read the text aloud and a careful study is made of how they 'read' the doctored sentences in the text. In this way, qualitative information about how learners process the text, including the artificial elements, can be undertaken. In addition, comprehension can be measured in order to obtain some summative measure of how much has been understood. Finally, without forewarning, the subjects can be asked to state in what ways the grammar of the artificial text differs from that of the standard language or, alternatively, can be asked to translate standard sentences into the artificial language, in order to measure what information about the 'new' linguistic features they have been able to internalize.

Hybrid research, such as this proposed study, incorporates both experimental and qualitative procedures. It seeks to establish cause and effect, but also to uncover the processes involved in language use and language learning. It aims to provide explanations, while at the same time increasing understanding.

The arguments in favour of hybrid research are well rehearsed. In chapter 1 we saw that the comparative method studies foundered because of the absence of any qualitative information regarding what actually took place in the classroom in the name of the different methods. In chapter 4 we saw that Long (1980) stressed the importance of a process element in classroom experiments in order to provide detailed information about the instructional 'treatment' under investigation. There is also research that shows that different learners respond differently to the same instructional events (e.g. Slimani,

1987) and which demonstrates the importance of eliciting information from learners about how they learn (e.g. Faerch and Kasper, 1987). But the lesson has not really been learnt. There are few L2 classroom studies that combine experimental design with ethnographic and/or introspective techniques designed to shed light on the underlying processes involved in both instruction and learning.

Conclusion

It is easy to be pessimistic about the results achieved to date. Chaudron (1988:180) concludes his own review of L2 classroom research as follows:

> Despite the obvious increase in the amount of classroom-oriented research in recent years, few of the suggestions offered here can be made with great confidence, for the existing research is difficult to synthesize.

It is not only a problem of synthesis. There are, as we have seen, problems with the research itself. One way forward is better research. Chaudron is confident that, as we learn how to do better research, we will be able to make more confident statements about how instruction contributes to acquisition.

It might be wise, though, not to place too much faith in better research. For a start, old problems tend to be ignored. This might not matter too much, however, if we do not look to research to provide *answers* and instead accept that it is only likely to provide *insights* or *clues* about what happens when teachers try to intervene in the process of language learning. We will always need to interpret the clues with the help of common sense based on our practical experience of what works and does not work in the classroom. In this way we can avoid becoming consumers of research and, instead, build our own theories of how learning takes place through instruction.

Bibliography

Adams, S. 1982, Scripts and the recognition of unfamiliar vocabulary: Enhancing second language reading skills. *Modern Language Journal*, 66:155–9.

Adjemian, C. 1976, On the nature of interlanguage systems, *Language Learning*, 26:297–320.

Allen, P., Fröhlich, M. and Spada, N. 1984, The communicative orientation of language teaching: An observation scheme. In Handscombe, J., Orem, R. and Taylor, B. (eds), *On TESOL '83: The Question of Control*, Washington, DC, TESOL.

Allwright, R. 1975, Problems in the study of the language teacher's treatment of learner error. In Burt, M. and Dulay, H. (eds), *On TESOL '75*, Washington, DC, TESOL.

Allwright, R. 1980, Topics, turns and tasks: Patterns of participation in language learning. In Larsen-Freeman (1980).

Allwright, R. 1983, Classroom-centred research on language teaching and learning: a brief historical overview. *TESOL Quarterly*, 17:191–204.

Allwright, R. 1984a, The importance of interaction in classroom language learning, *Applied Linguistics*, 5:156–71.

Allwright, R. 1984b, Why don't learners learn what teachers teach? – The interaction hypothesis. In Singleton, D. and Little, D. (eds) *Language Learning in Formal and Informal Contexts*, Dublin, IRAAL.

Allwright, R. 1988a, *Observation in the Language Classroom*, London, Longman.

Allwright, R. 1988b, The characterization of teaching and learning environments: Problems and perspectives. Paper given at Conference on Empirical Research into Foreign Language Teaching Methods, Bellagio, Italy.

Anderson, J. 1980, *Cognitive Psychology and its Implications*, San Francisco, Freeman.

Anderson, J. 1983, *The Architecture of Cognition*, Cambridge, Mass.; Harvard University Press.

Anderson, J. 1985, *Cognitive Psychology and its Implications* (2nd ed.), New York, Freeman.

Andersen, R. (ed.) 1981, *New Dimensions in Second Language Acquisition Research*, Rowley; Mass., Newbury House.

Andersen, R. (ed.) 1983, *Pidginization and Creolization in Second Language Acquisition*, Rowley, Mass., Newbury House.

d'Anglejan, A. 1978, Language learning in and out of classrooms. In Richards (1978).

Anthony, M. 1963, Approach, method and technique, *English Language Teaching*, 17:63–7.

Asher, J. 1977, *Learning Another Language through Actions: The Complete Teacher's Guidebook*, Los Gatos, Calif., Sky Oaks Productions.

Aston, G. 1986, Trouble-shooting in interaction with learners: The more the merrier, *Applied Linguistics*, 7, 128–43.

Ausabel, D. 1971, Some psychological aspects of the structure of knowledge. In Johnson, P. (ed.), *Learning: Theory and Practice*, New York, Thomas Y. Crowell.

Bailey, K. 1983, Competitiveness and anxiety in adult second language learning: Looking at and through the diary studies. In Seliger and Long (1983).

Bailey, N., Madden, C. and Krashen, S. 1974, Is there a 'natural sequence' in adult second language learning?, *Language Learning*, 24:235–44.

Barasch, R. and James, V. (forthcoming), *Answers to Krashen*, Rowley, Mass., Newbury House.

Barnes, D. 1969, Language in the secondary classroom. In Barnes, D. (ed.) *Language, the Learner and the School*, Harmondsworth, Penguin.

Barnes, D. 1976, *From Communication to Curriculum*, Harmondsworth, Penguin.

Bellack, A., Kliebard, H., Hyman, R. and Smith, F. 1966, *The Language of the Classroom*, New York, Teachers College Press.

Belyayev, B. 1963, *Thy Psychology of Teaching Foreign Languages*, Oxford, Pergamon Press.

Bialystok, E. 1979, Explicit and implicit judgements of L2 grammaticality, *Language Learning*, 29:81–104.

Bialystok, E. 1981, Some evidence for the intergrity and interaction of two knowledge sources. In Andersen, R. (1981).

Bialystok, E. 1982, On the relationship between knowing and using linguistic forms, *Applied Linguistics*, 3:181–206.

Bialystok, E. 1983, Inferencing: Testing the 'hypothesis-testing' hypothesis. In Seliger and Long (1983).

Bialystok, E. 1988, Psycholinguistic dimensions of second language proficiency. In Rutherford, W. and Sharwood-Smith, M. (eds), *Grammar and Second Language Teaching*, Rowley, Mass., Newbury House.

Bialystock, E. and Sharwood-Smith, M. 1985, Interlanguage is not a state of mind: An evaluation of the construct for second-language acquisition, *Applied Linguistics*, 6, 101–17.

Bley-Vroman, R. 1983, The comparative fallacy in interlanguage studies: The case of systematicity, *Language Learning*, 33:1–17.

Bley-Vroman, R. 1988, The fundamental character of foreign language learning. In Rutherford, W. and Sharwood-Smith, M. (eds), *Grammar and Second Language Teaching*, Rowley, Mass., Newbury House.

Bloom, L. 1970, *Language Development: Form and Function in Merging Grammars*, Cambridge, Mass., MIT Press.

Bloomfield, L. 1942, *Outline Guide for the Practical Study of Foreign Languages*, Baltimore, Linguistic Society of America.

Bowers, R. 1980, The individual learner in the general class. In Altman, H. and James, C. (eds), *Foreign Language Teaching: Meeting Individual Needs*, Oxford, Pergamon.

Breen, M. 1985a, The social context for language learning – neglected situation? *Studies in Second Language Acquisition*, 7, 135–58.

Breen, M. 1985b, Authenticity in the language classroom, *Applied Linguistics*, 6, 60–70.

Brière, E. 1978, Variables affecting native Mexican children's learning Spanish as a second language, *Language Learning*, 28:159—74.

Brock, C. 1986, The effects of referential questions on ESL classroom discourse, *TESOL Quarterly*, 20:47—59.

Brooks, N. 1960, *Language and Language Learning*. New York, Harcourt Brace and World.

Brown, R. 1970, *Psycholinguistics*, New York, Free Press.

Brown, R. 1973, *A First Language: The Early Stages*, Cambridge, Mass., Harvard University Press.

Brumfit, C. 1979, Accuracy and fluency as polarities on foreign language teaching, *Bulletin CILA*, 29:89—99.

Brumfit, C. 1984, *Communicative Methodology in Language Teaching*, Cambridge, Cambridge University Press.

Bruton, A. and Samuda, V. 1980, Learner and teacher roles in the treatment of oral error in group work, *RELC Journal*, 11, 49—63.

Burt, M., Dulay, H. and Hernandez, E. 1973, *Bilingual Syntax Measure*, New York, Harcourt Brace Jovanovich.

Burt, M. and Kiparsky, C. 1974, *The Gooficon: A Repair Manual for English*, Rowley, Mass., Newbury House.

Callfee, G. and Freedman, S. 1980, Understanding and comprehending. Paper presented at the Center for the Study of Reading, Urbana, Illinois.

Canale, M. and Swain, M. 1980, Theoretical bases of communicative approaches to second language teaching and testing, *Applied Linguistics*, 1:1—47.

Cancino, H., Rosansky, E. and Schumann, J. 1974, Testing hypotheses about second language acquisition, *Working Papers on Bilingualism*, 3:8—96.

Cancino, H., Rosansky, E. and Schumann, J. 1978, The acquisition of English negatives and interrogatives by native Spanish speakers. In Hatch (1978a).

Carrell, P. 1983, Three components of background knowledge in reading comprehension, *Language Learning*, 33:183—207.

Carroll, J. 1963, Research on teaching foreign languages. In Gage, N. (ed.), *Handbook of Research on Teaching*, Chicago, Rand McNally.

Carroll, J. 1966, The contributions of psychological theory and educational research to the teaching of foreign languages. In Valdman (1966b).

Carroll, J. 1967, Foreign language proficiency levels attained by language majors near graduation from college, *Foreign Language Annals*, 1:131—51.

Catford, J. 1959, The teaching of English as a foreign language. In Quirk, R. et al., *The Teaching of English*, London, Secker and Warburg.

Cathcart, R. 1986, Situational differences and the sampling of young children's school language. In Day (1986).

Cathcart, R. and Olsen, J. 1976, Teachers' and students' preferences for correction of classroom conversation errors. In Fanselow, J. and Crymes, R. (eds), *On TESOL '76*, Washington, DC, TESOL.

Cavalcanti, M. 1987, Investigating FL reading performance through pause protocols. In Faerch and Kasper (1987).

Cazden, C., Cancino, H., Rosansky, E. and Schumann, J. 1975, *Second Language Acquisition Sequences in Children, Adolescents and Adults*, Final Report, US Department of Health, Education and Welfare.

Chastain K. 1969, The audiolingual habit theory versus cognitive code-learning theory: Some theoretical considerations, *International Review of Applied Linguistics*, 7:97—106.

Chastain, K. 1971, *The Development of Modern Language Skills: Theory to Practice*, Philadelphia, Center for Curriculum Development.

Chaudron, C. 1977, A descriptive model of discourse in the corrective treatment of learners' errors, *Language Learning*, 27:29–46.

Chaudron, C. 1983, Foreigner-talk in the classroom – An aid to learning? In Seliger and Long (1983).

Chaudron, C. 1985, Comprehension, comprehensibility and learning in the second language classroom, *Studies in Second Language Acquisition*, 7:216–32.

Chaudron, C. 1986a, Teachers' priorities in correcting learners' errors in French immersion classes. In Day (1986).

Chaudron, C. 1986b, The role of simplified input in classroom language. In Kasper (1986).

Chaudron, C. 1988, *Second Language Classrooms*, Cambridge, Cambridge University Press.

Chaudron, C. and Richards, J. 1986, The effect of discourse markers on the comprehension of lectures *Applied Linguistics*, 7:113–27.

Chihara, T. and Oller, J. 1978, Attitudes and attained proficiency in EFL: A sociolinguistic study of adult Japanese speakers, *Language Learning*, 28:55–68.

Chomsky, N. 1957, *Syntactic Structures*, The Hague, Mouton.

Chomsky, N. 1959, Review of *Verbal Behavior* by B.F. Skinner, *Language*, 35:26–58.

Chomsky, N. 1965, *Aspects of the Theory of Syntax* Cambridge, Mass., MIT Press.

Chomsky, N. 1966, Linguistic theory. In Mead, R. (ed.), *Northeast Conference on the Teaching of Foreign Languages*, Menasha, Wis., George Banta.

Chomsky, N. 1981, *Lectures on Government and Binding*, Dordrecht, Foris.

Chomsky, N. 1986, *Knowledge of Language: Its Nature, Origin and Use*, New York, Praeger.

Clahsen, H. 1984, The acquisition of German word order: A test case for cognitive approaches to L2 development. In Andersen R. (ed.), *Second Languages: A Crosslinguistic Perspective*, Rowley, Mass., Newbury House.

Clahsen, H. 1985, Profiling second language development: A procedure for assessing L2 proficiency. In Hyltenstam and Pienemann (1985).

Clahsen, H., Meisel, J. and Pienemann, M. 1983, *Deutsch als Zweitsprache, Der Spacherwerb ausländischer Arbeiter*, Tübingen, Gunter Narr.

Clark, J. 1969, The Pennsylvania Project and the 'Audiolingual vs Traditional' question, *Modern Language Journal*, 53:388–96.

Cohen, A. 1987, Using verbal reports in research on language learning. In Faerch and Kasper (1987).

Comrie, B. and Keenan, E. 1978, Noun phrase accessibility revisited, *Language*, 55:649–64.

Cook, V. 1969, The analogy between first and second language learning, *IRAL*. Reprinted in Lugton and Heinle (1971).

Cook, V. 1985, Universal grammar and second language learning, *Applied Linguistics*, 6:2–18.

Cook, V. 1988, *Chomsky's Universal Grammar: An Introduction*, Oxford, Basil Blackwell.

Corder, P. 1967, The significance of learners' errors. *International Review of Applied Linguistics*, 5:161–9.

Corder, P. 1973, *Introducing Applied Linguistics*, Harmondsworth, Penguin.

Corder, P. 1974, Error analysis and remedial teaching. Paper presented at the first overseas conference of the International Association of Teachers as a Foreign

Language, Budapest, Also in Corder (1981).

Corder, P. 1975, The language of second language learners: The broader issues, *Modern Language Journal*, 59:409–13.

Corder, P. 1976, The study of interlanguage. In *Proceedings of the Fourth International Congress of Applied Linguistics*, Münich, Hochschulverlag. Also in Corder (1981).

Corder, P. 1977, Language teaching and learning: A social encounter. In Brown, D., Yorio, C. and Crymes, R. (eds), *ON TESOL '77*, Washington, DC, TESOL.

Corder, P. 1978a, Language distance and the magnitude of the language learning task, *Studies in Second Language Acquisition*, 2/1.

Corder, P. 1978b, Language-learner language. In Richards (1978).

Corder, P. 1980, Second language acquisition research and the teaching of grammar, *BAAL Newsletter*, 10.

Corder, P. 1981, *Error Analysis and Interlanguage*, Oxford, Oxford University Press.

Coulthard, M. 1977, *An Introduction to Discourse Analysis*, London, Longman.

Crookes, G. 1986, Task classification: A cross-disciplinary review, *Technical Report No. 4*, Honolulu, Center for Second Language Classroom Research, University of Hawaii at Manoa.

Cross, T. 1977, Mothers' speech adjustments: the contribution of selected child listener variables. In Snow and Ferguson (1977).

Cummins, J. 1981, *Bilingualism and Minority-language Children*, Toronto, Ontario Institute for Studies in Education.

Dakin, J. 1973, *The Language Laboratory and Language Learning*, London, Longman.

Daniel, I. 1983, On first-year German foreign language learning: A comparison of language behaviour in response to two instructional methods. Unpublished Ph.D. dissertation, University of Southern California.

Davies, A., Criper, C. and Howatt, A. (eds) 1984, *Interlanguage*, Edinburgh, Edinburgh University Press.

Day, R. (ed.) 1986, *Talking to Learn: Conversation in Second Language Acquisition*, Rowley, Mass., Newbury House.

Delamont, S. 1976, *Interaction in the Classroom*, London, Methuen.

Dickerson, L. 1975, Interlanguage as a system of variable rules, *TESOL Quarterly*, 9:401–7.

Donaldson, W. 1971, Code-cognition approaches to language learning. In Lugton and Heinle (1971).

Doughty, C. and Pica, T. 1986, Information gap tasks: Do they facilitate second language acquisition?, *TESOL Quarterly*, 20:305–25.

Duff, P. 1986, Another look at interlanguage talk: Taking task to task. In Day (1986).

Dulay, H. and Burt, M. 1973, Should we teach children syntax?, *Language Learning*, 23:37–53.

Dulay, H. and Burt, M. 1974a, You can't learn without goofing. In Richards (1974).

Dulay, H. and Burt, M. 1974b, Natural sequences in child second language acquisition, *Language Learning*, 24:37–53.

Dulay, H. and Burt, M. 1975, Creative construction in second language learning. In Burt, M. and Dulay, H. (eds), *New Directions in Second Language Learning, Teaching and Bilingual Education*, Washington, DC, TESOL.

Eckman, F., Bell, L. and Nelson, D. 1988, On the generalization of relative clause instruction in the acquisition of English as a second language, *Applied Linguistics*, 9:1–20.

Edmondson, W. 1985, Discourse worlds in the classroom and in foreign language learning, *Studies in Second Language Acquisition*, 7:159–68.

Edmondson, W. 1986, Some ways in which the teacher brings errors into being. In Kasper (1986).

Ellis, R. 1981, The role of input in language acquisition; some implications for second language teaching, *Applied Linguistics*, 2:70–82.

Ellis, R. 1982, Discourse processes in classroom second language development. Unpublished Ph.D. thesis, University of London.

Ellis, R. 1984a, *Classroom Second Language Development*. Oxford, Pergamon.

Ellis, R. 1984b, Can syntax be taught? A study of the effects of formal instruction on the acquisition of WH questions by children, *Applied Linguistics*, 5:138–55.

Ellis, B. 1984c, The role of instruction in second language acquisition. In Singleton, D. and Little, D. (eds), *Language Learning in Formal and Informal Contexts*, Dublin, IRAAL.

Ellis, R. 1985a, *Understanding Second Language Acquisition*, Oxford, Oxford University Press.

Ellis, R. 1985b, The L1 = L2 hypothesis: A reconsideration, *System*, 13:9–24.

Ellis, R. 1985c, Teacher–pupil interaction in second language development. In Gass and Madden (1985).

Ellis, R. (1985d), Sources of variability in interlanguage, *Applied Linguistics*, 6:118–131.

Ellis, R. 1986, Developing interlanguage through fluency, *Focus*, 4:23–39.

Ellis, R. 1987a, Interlanguage variability in narrative discourse: Style shifting in the use of the past tense, *Studies in Second Language Acquisition*, 9:1–20.

Ellis, R. 1987b, Contextual variability in second language acquisition and the relevancy of language teaching. In Ellis (1987c).

Ellis, R. (ed.) 1987c, *Second Language Acquisition in Context*, Englewood Cliffs, NJ, Prentice-Hall.

Ellis, R. 1988a, Investigating language teaching: The case for an educational perspective, *System*, 16:1–11.

Ellis, R. 1988b, The role of practice in classroom language learning, *Teanga*, 8:1–25.

Ellis, R. 1989a, Sources of intra-learner variability in language use and their relationship to second language acquisition. In Gass, S., Madden, C., Preston, D. and Selinker, L. (eds), *Variation in Second Language Acquisition: Psycholinguistic Issues*, Clevedon, Avon, Multilingual Matters.

Ellis, R. 1989b, Are classroom and naturalistic acquisition the same?: A study of the classroom acquisition of German word order rules, *Studies in Second Language Acquisition*, 11:305–28.

Ellis, R. 1989c, Comprehension and the acquisition of grammatical competence. Paper given at the Conference on Comprehension and Language Learning, Ottawa, Canada.

Ellis, R. and Rathbone, M. 1987, *The Acquisition of German in a Classroom Context*, London, Ealing College of Higher Education.

Els, van T., Bongaerts, T., Extra, G., Os, van C. and Janssen-van-Dieten, A. 1984, *Applied Linguistics and the Learning and Teaching of Foreign Languages*, London, Edward Arnold.

Erickson, F. and Mohatt, G. 1982, Cultural organization of participation structures in two classrooms of Indian students. In Spindler, G. (ed.), *Doing the Ethnography of Schooling: Educational Ethnography in Action*, New York, CBS College Publishing.

Ervin-Tripp, S. 1974, Is second language learning like the first?, *TESOL Quarterly*, 8:111–27.

Ewbank, L. 1989, The acquisition of German negation by formal language learners. In Van Patten, B., Dvorak, T. and Less, J. (eds), *Foreign Language Learning: A Research Perspective*, Rowley, Mass., Newbury House.

Faerch, C. 1985, Meta talk in FL classroom discourse, *Studies in Second Language Acquisition*, 7:184−99.

Faerch, C., Haastrup, K. and Phillipson, R. 1984, *Learner Language and Language Learning*, Clevedon, Avon, Multilingual Matters.

Faerch, C. and Kasper, G. 1980, Processes in foreign language learning and communication, *Interlanguage Studies Bulletin*, 5:47−118.

Faerch, C. and Kasper, G. 1983, Procedural knowledge as a component of foreign language learners communicative competence. In Boete, H. and Herrlitz, W. (eds), *Kommunikation im Sprach-Unterricht*, Utrecht. Rijksuniversiteik.

Faerch, C. and Kasper, G. 1986, The role of comprehension in second-language learning, *Applied Linguistics*, 7:257−74.

Faerch, C. and Kasper, G. (eds), 1987, *Introspection in Second Language Research*, Clevedon, Avon, Multilingual Matters.

Fanselow, J. 1977, Beyond Rashomon − Conceptualising and describing the teaching act, *TESOL Quarterly*, 11:17−39.

Fathman, A. 1975, The relationship between age and second language productive ability, *Language Learning*, 25:245−53.

Fathman, A. 1976, Variables affecting the successful learning of English as a second language, *TESOL Quarterly*, 10:433−41.

Fathman, A. 1978, ESL and EFL learning: similar or dissimilar? In Blatchford, C. and Schacter, J. (eds), *On TESOL '78: EFL Policies, Programs, Practices*, Washington, DC, TESOL.

Felix, S. 1981, The effect of formal instruction on second language acquisition, *Language Learning*, 31:87−112.

Felix, S. and Simmet, A. 1981, Natural processes in classroom L2 learning. Revised version of a paper presented at the 3ème Colloque, Groupe de Recherche sur l'Acquisition des Languages, Paris.

Fillmore, W. 1976, The second time around: Cognitive and social strategies in second language acquisition. Unpublished Ph.D. thesis, Stanford University.

Fillmore, W. 1979, Individual differences in second language acquisition. In Fillmore, C., Kempler, D. and Wang, W. (eds), *Individual Differences in Language Ability and Language Behavior*, New York, Academic Press.

Fillmore, W. 1982, Instructional language as linguistic input: Second language learning in classrooms. In Wilkinson, L. (ed.), *Communicating in the Classroom*, New York, Academic Press.

Fillmore, W. 1985, When does teacher talk work as input? In Gass and Madden (1985).

Fisiak, J. (ed.) 1981, *Contrastive Linguistics and the Language Teacher*, Oxford, Pergamon.

Fishman, J. 1964, Language maintenance and language shift as fields of inquiry, *Linguistics*, 9:32−70.

Flanders, N. 1970, *Analyzing Teacher Behavior*, Reading, Mass., Addison-Wesley.

French, F. 1949, *Common Errors in English*, London, Oxford University Press.

Freudenstein, R. 1977, Interaction in the foreign language classroom. In Burt, M., Dulay, H. and Finocchiaro, M. (eds), *Viewpoints on English as a Second Language*, New York, Regents.

Fries, C. 1948, As we see it, *Language Learning*, 1:12−16.

Gaies, S. 1977, The nature of linguistic input in formal second language learning:

linguistic and communicative strategies. In Brown, H., Yorio, C. and Crymes, R. (eds), *On TESOL '77*, Washington, DC TESOL.

Gaies, S. 1983a, The investigation of language classroom processes, *TESOL Quarterly*, 17:205−18.

Gaies, S. 1983b, Learner feedback: An exploratory study of its role in the second language classroom. In Seliger and Long (1983).

Gass, S. 1979, Language transfer and universal grammatical relations, *Language Learning*, 27:327−44.

Gass, S. 1982, From theory to practice. In Rutherford, W. and Hines, M. (eds), *On TESOL '81*, Washington, DC, TESOL.

Gass, S. and Selinker, L. (eds), 1983, *Language Transfer in Language Learning*, Rowley, Mass., Newbury House.

Gass, S. and Madden, C. (eds) 1985, *Input in Second Language Acquisition*, Rowley, Mass., Newbury House.

Gass, S. and Varonis, E. 1985, Task variation and nonnative/nonnative negotiation of meaning. In Gass and Madden (1985).

George, H. 1972, *Common Errors in Language Learning: Insights from English*, Rowley, Mass., Newbury House.

Givon, R. 1979, *On Understanding Grammar*, New York, Academic Press.

Glahn, E. and Holmen, A. (eds), 1985, *Learner Discourse, Anglica et Americana*, Copenhagen, University of Copenhagen.

Gleitman, L., Newport, E. and Gleitman, H. 1984, The current state of the motherese hypothesis, *Journal of Child Language*, 11:43−79.

Gower, R. and Walters, S. 1983, *Teaching Practice Handbook*, London, Heinemann Educational.

Gregg, K. 1984, Krashen's Monitor and Occam's Razor, *Applied Linguistics*, 5:79−100.

Gregg, K. (forthcoming). The variable competence model of second language acquisition, and why it isn't, *Applied Linguistics*.

Gremmo, M., Holec, H., Riley, P. 1977, Interactional structure: the role of role, *Mélanges Pédagogiques*, University of Nancy, CRAPEL.

Gremmo, M., Holec, H. and Riley, P. 1978, Taking the initiative: some pedagogical applications of discourse analysis, *Melanges Pédagogiques*, CRAPEL.

Grittner, F. 1968, Letter to the Editor, *Newsletter of the National Association of Laboratory Directors*, 3:7.

Grotjahn, R. 1987, On the methodological basis of introspective methods. In Faerch and Kasper (1987).

Hakansson, G. 1986, Quantitative studies of teacher talk. In Kasper (1986).

Hakuta, K. 1976, A case study of a Japanese child learning English as a second language, *Language Learning*, 26, 321−51.

Hale, T. and Budar, E. 1970, Are TESOL classes the only answer? *Modern Language Journal*, 54:487−92.

Hamayan, E. and Tucker, R. 1980, Language input in the bilingual classroom and its relationship to second language achievement, *TESOL Quarterly*, 14:453−68.

Harley, B. 1987, Functional grammar in French immersion: a classroom experiment. Paper given at 1987 AILA Conference in Sydney, Australia.

Harmer, J. 1983, The Practice of English Language Teaching, London, Longman.

Hatch, E. 1974, Second language learning − Universals, *Working Papers on Bilingualism*, 3:1−18.

Hatch, E. (ed.), 1978a, *Second Language Acquisition*, Rowley, Mass., Newbury House.

Hatch, E. 1978b, Discourse analysis and second language acquisition. In Hatch (1978a)

Hatch, E. 1978c, Discourse analysis, speech acts and second language acquisition. In Ritchie, W. (ed.), *Second Language Acquisition Research*, New York, Academic Press.

Hatch, E. 1978d, Acquisition of syntax in a second language. In Richards, J. (ed.), *Understanding Second and Foreign Language Learning*, Rowley, Mass., Newbury House.

Hatch, E. 1983a, *Psycholinguistics: A Second Language Perspective*, Rowley, Mass., Newbury House.

Hatch, E. 1983b, Simplified input and second language acquisition. In Andersen R. (1983).

Hatch, E., Shapira, R. and Gough, J. 1978, 'Foreigner-talk' discourse, *ITL Review of Applied Linguistics*, 39/40, 39−59.

Hatch, E. and Wagner-Gough, J. 1976, Explaining sequence and variation in second language acquisition, *Language Learning*, Special Issue No. 4:39−57.

Hawkins, B. 1985, Is an 'appropriate response' always so appropriate? In Gass and Madden (1985).

Hendrickson, J. 1978, Error correction in foreign language teaching: Recent research, theory and practice, *Modern Language Journal*, 67:41−5.

Henry, A. 1986, Linguistic theory and second language teaching. Paper given at CILT Workshop on Acquiring Language and Learning Languages, Cumberland Lodge, Windsor Great Park.

Henzl, V. 1973, Linguistic register of foreign language instruction, *Language Learning*, 23, 207−22.

Henzl, V. 1979, Foreign talk in the classroom. *International Review of Applied Linguistics*, 17, 159−67.

Holley, F. and King, J. 1975, Imitation and correction in foreign language learning. In Schumann, J. and Stenson, N. (eds), *New Frontiers in Second Language Learning*, Rowley, Mass., Newbury House.

Holmen, A. 1985a, Analysis of some discourse areas in the PIF data and in classroom interaction. In Glahn and Holmen (1985).

Holmen, A. 1985b, Distribution of roles in learner−native speaker interaction. In Glahn and Holmen (1985).

Holmes, J. 1978, Sociolinguistic competence in the classroom. In Richards (1978).

House, J. 1986, Learning to talk: talking to learn. An investigation of learner performance in two types of discourse. In Kasper (1986).

Howatt, A. 1984, *A History of English Language Teaching*. Oxford, Oxford University Press.

Huang, J. and Hatch, E. 1978, A Chinese child's acquisition of English. In Hatch (1978a).

Huebner, T. 1979, Order-of-acquisition vs. dynamic paradigm: A comparison of method in interlanguage research, *TESOL Quarterly*, 13:21−8.

Huebner, T. 1983, *Longitudinal Analysis of the Acquisition of English* Ann Arbor, Mich. Karoma Publishers.

Hughes, A. 1983, Second language learning and communicative language teaching. In Johnson, K. and Porter, D. (eds), *Perspectives in Communicative Language Teaching*, New York, Academic Press.

Hughes, A. and Lascaratou, C. 1982, Competing criteria for error gravity, *ELT*

Journal, 36, 175—82.

Hulstijn, J. 1987, Onset and development of grammatical features: Two approaches to acquisition orders, Paper given at Interlanguage Conference, Trobe University, Melbourne.

Hulstijn, J. 1988, Implicit and incidental second language learning: Experiments in processing of natural and partly artificial input. Mimeograph to be published in Dechert, H. (ed.), *Interlingual Processing*, Tübingen, Gunter Narr.

Hulstijn, J. and Hulstijn, W. 1984, Grammatical errors as a function of processing constraints and explicit knowledge, *Language Learning*, 34:23—43.

Hyltenstam, K. and Pienemann, M. (eds) 1985, *Modelling and Assessing Second Language Acquisition*, Clevedon, Avon, Multilingual Matters.

Jakobovits, L. 1968, Implications of recent psycholinguistic developments for the teaching of a second language, *Language Learning*, 18:89—109.

Jakobovits, L. 1970, *Foreign Language Learning: A Psycholinguistic Analysis of the Issue*, Rowley, Mass., Newbury House.

James, C. 1974, Linguistic measures for error gravity, *AVLA Journal*, 12:3—9.

Jansen, L. 1987, The development of word order in formal German second language acquisition. Unpublished paper, Australian National University.

Johnson, K. 1988, Mistake correction, *ELT Journal*, 2:89—96.

Johnston, M. 1987a, Second language acquisition research: A classroom perspective. In Johnston and Pienemann (1987).

Johnston, M. 1987b, Second language acquisition research in the Adult Migrant Education Program. In Johnston and Pienemann, (1987).

Johnston, M. and Pienemann, M. 1987, *Second Language Acquisition: A Classroom Perspective*, NSW Adult Migrant Education Service.

Kadia, K. 1988, The effect of formal instruction on monitored and spontaneous naturalistic interlanguage performance, *TESOL Quarterly*, 22:509—15.

Karmiloff-Smith, A. 1986, Stage/structure versus phase/process in modelling linguistic and cognitive development. In Levin, J. (ed.), *Stage and Structure: Reopening the Debate*, Norwood, Ablex.

Kasper, G. 1985, Repair in foreign language teaching, *Studies in Second Language Acquisition*, 7:200—15.

Kasper, G. 1986, (ed.), *Learning, Teaching and Communication in the Foreign Language Classroom*, Aarhus, Aarhus University Press.

Kelch, K. 1985, Modified input as an aid to comprehension, *Studies in Second Language Acquisition*, 7:81—90.

Kellerman, E. 1984, The empirical evidence for the influence of the L1 in interlanguage. In Davies, A, Criper, C. and Howatt, T. (eds), *Interlanguage*, Edinburgh, Edinburgh University Press.

Kellerman, E. and Sharwood-Smith, M. (eds), 1986, *Crosslinguistic Influence on Second Language Acquisition*, Oxford, Pergamon.

Kennedy, G. 1973, Conditions for language learning. In Oller and Richards (1973).

Kleifgen, J. 1985, Skilled variation in a kindergarten teacher's use of foreigner talk. In Gass and Madden (1985).

Klein, W. 1986, *Second Language Acquisition*, Cambridge, Cambridge University Press.

Kramsch, C. 1985, Classroom interaction and discourse options, *Studies in Second Language Acquisition*, 7:169—83.

Krashen, S. 1973, Lateralization, language learning and the critical period, *Language Learning*, 23:63—74.

Krashen, S. 1977, The Monitor Model for adult second language performance. In Burt, M., Dulay, H. and Finocchiaro, M. (eds), *Viewpoints on English as a Second Language*, New York, Regents.

Krashen, S. 1980, The theoretical and practical relevance of simple codes in second language acquisition. In Scarcella and Krashen (1980).

Krashen, S. 1981, *Second Language Acquisition and Second Language Learning*, Oxford, Pergamon.

Krashen, S. 1982, *Principles and Practice in Second Language Acquisition*, Oxford, Pergamon.

Krashen, S. 1984, *Writing: Research, Theory and Application*, Oxford, Pergamon.

Krashen, S. 1985, *The Input Hypothesis*, London, Longman.

Krashen, S., Jones, C., Zelinksi, C. and Usprich, C. 1978, How important is instruction?, *ELT Journal*, 32:257−61.

Krashen, S. and Pon, P. 1975, An error analysis of an advanced ESL learner: The importance of the Monitor, *Working Papers on Bilingualism*, 7:125−9.

Krashen, S. and Scarcella, R. 1978, On routines and patterns in language acquisition and performance, *Language Learning*, 28:283−300.

Krashen, S. and Seliger, H. 1976, The role of formal and informal linguistic environments in adult second language learning *International Journal of Psycholinguistics*, 3:15−21.

Krashen, S., Seliger, H. and Hartnett, D. 1974, Two studies in adult second language learning, *Kritikon Litterarum*, 3:220−8.

Krashen, S., Sferlazza, V., Feldman, L. and Fathman, A. 1976, Adult performance on the SLOPE test: More evidence for a natural sequence in adult second language acquisition, *Language Learning*, 26:145−51.

Krashen, S. and Terrell, T. 1984, *The Natural Method: Language Acquisition in the Classroom*, Oxford, Pergamon.

Labov, W. 1969, The study of language in its social context, *Studium Generale*, 23:3−87.

Lado, R. 1957, *Linguistics across Cultures: Applied Linguistics for Language Teachers*, Ann Arbor, University of Michigan.

Lado, R. 1964, *Language Teaching: A Scientific Approach*. New York, McGraw Hill.

Larsen-Freeman, D. 1976a, The acquisition of grammatical morphemes by adult learners of English as a second language, Unpublished Ph.D. thesis, University of Michigan.

Larsen-Freeman, D. 1976b, An explanation for the morpheme accuracy order of learners of English as a second language, *Language Learning*, 26/1, 125−35.

Larsen-Freeman, D. (ed.) 1980, *Discourse Analysis in Second Language Acquisition Research*, Rowley, Mass., Newbury House.

Lenneberg, E. 1967, *Biological Foundations of Language*, New York, Wiley.

Lester, M. (ed.) 1971, Readings in Applied Transformational Grammar, New York, Holt, Rinehart and Winston.

Lightbown, P. 1983, Exploring relationships between developmental and instructional sequences in L2 acquisition. In Seliger and Long (1983).

Lightbown, P. 1984, The relationship between theory and method in second language acquisition research. In Davies et al.(1984).

Lightbown, P. 1985a, Great expectations: second-language acquisition research and classroom teaching, *Applied Linguistics*, 6:173−89.

Lightbown, P. 1985b, Input and acquisition for second language learners in and out of classrooms, *Applied Linguistics*, 6:263–73.

Lightbown, P. 1985c, Can language acquisition be altered by instruction? In Hyltenstam and Pienemann (1985).

Lightbown, P. 1987, Classroom language as input to second language acquisition. In Pfaff, C. (ed.), *First and Second Language Acquisition Processes*, Rowley, Mass., Newbury House.

Lightbown, P., Spada, N. and Wallace, R. 1980, Some effects of instruction on child and adolescent ESL learners. In Scarcella and Krashen (1980).

Long, M. 1977, Teacher feedback on learner error: Mapping cognitions. In Brown, H., Yorio, C. and Crymes, R. (eds), *On TESOL '77*, Washington, DC, TESOL.

Long, M. 1980, Inside the 'black box': methodological issues in classroom research on language learning, *Language Learning*, 30:1–42. Also in Seliger and Long (1983).

Long, M. 1981, Input, interaction and second language acquisition. In Winitz, H. (ed.), *Native Language and Foreign Language Acquisition*, Annals of the New York Academy of Sciences, 379.

Long, M. 1983a, Native speaker/non-native speaker conversation in the second language classroom. In Clarke, M. and Handscombe, J. (eds), *On TESOL '82: Pacific Perspectives on Language Learning and Teaching*, Washington, DC, TESOL.

Long, M. 1983b, Does second language instruction make a difference? A review of the research, *TESOL Quarterly*, 17:359–82.

Long, M. 1983c, Native speaker/non-native speaker conversation and the negotiation of meaning, *Applied Linguistics*, 4:126–41.

Long, M. 1985a, Input and second language acquisition theory. In Gass and Madden (1985).

Long, M. 1985b, A role for instruction in second language acquisition: task-based language training. In Hyltenstam and Pienemann (1985).

Long, M. 1988a, Instructed interlanguage development. In Beebe, L. (ed.), *Issues in Second Language Acquisition: Multiple Perspectives*, Rowley, Mass., Newbury House.

Long, M. 1988b, Focus on form: A design feature in language teaching methodology. Paper presented at the Conference on Empirical Research on Second Language Learning in Institutional Settings, Bellagio, Italy.

Long, M. 1988c, Maturational constraints on language development. Mimeograph, University of Hawaii.

Long, M., Brock, C., Crookes, G., Deicke, C., Potter, L. and Zhang, S. 1984, The effect of teachers' questioning patterns and wait-time on pupil participation in public high school in Hawaii for students of limited English proficiency, *Technical Report No. 1*, Honolulu, Center for Second Language Classroom Research, University of Hawaii at Manoa.

Long, M. and Larsen-Freeman, D. (forthcoming), *Introduction to Second Language Acquisition Research*, London, Longman.

Long, M. and Porter, R. 1985, Group work, interlanguage talk and second language acquisition, *TESOL Quarterly*, 19:207–28.

Long, M. and Sato, C. 1983, Classroom foreigner talk discourse: Forms and functions of teachers' questions. In Seliger and Long (1983).

Long, M. and Sato, C. 1984, Methodological issues in interlanguage studies: An interactionist perspective. In Davies et al. (1984).

Lörscher, W. 1986, Conversational structures in the foreign language classroom. In Kasper (1986).

Lugton, R. and Heinle, C. (eds) 1971, *Toward a Cognitive Approach to Second-Language*

Acquisition, Philadelphia, Center for Curriculum Development.

Lynch, A. 1988, Speaking up or talking down: foreign learners' reactions to teacher talk, *ELT Journal*, 42:109–16.

McHoul, A. 1978, The organization of turns at formal talk in the classroom, *Language and Society*, 7:183–213.

Mackey, W. 1965, *Language Teaching Analysis*, London, Longman.

McLaughlin, B. 1978a, *Second Language Acquisition in Childhood*, Hillsdale, NJ, Lawrence Erlbaum.

McLaughlin, B. 1978b, The Monitor Model: some methodological considerations, *Language Learning*, 23:309–32.

McLaughlin, B. 1985, *Second Language Acquisition in Childhood, vol. 2: School-Age Children*, 2nd edn, Hillsdale, NJ, Lawrence Erlbaum.

McLaughlin, B. 1987, *Theories of Second Language Acquisition*, London, Edward Arnold.

Macnamara, J. 1973, The cognitive strategies of language learning. In Oller and Richards (1973).

McNeill, D. 1965, Some thoughts on first and second language acquisition. Mimeograph, Center for Cognitive Studies, Harvard University.

McNeill, D. 1966, Developmental psycholinguistics. In Smith, F. and Miller, G. (eds), *The Genesis of Language: A Psycholinguistic Approach*, Cambridge, Mass., MIT Press.

McNeill, D. 1970, *The Acquisition of Language*, New York, Harper and Row.

McTear, M. 1975, Structure and categories of foreign language teaching sequences. In Allwright, R. (ed.), *Working Papers: Language Teaching Classroom Research*, University of Essex, Department of Language and Linguistics.

Makino, T. 1980, Acquisition order of English morphemes by Japanese secondary school students, *Journal of Hokkaido University of Education*, Section IV (Humanities), 30/2; 101–48.

Marton, W. 1981, Contrastive analysis in the classroom. In Fisiak (1981).

Mason, C. 1971, The relevance of intensive training in English as a foreign language for university students, *Language Learning*, 21:197–204.

Mazurkewich, I. 1985, Syntactic markedness and language acquisition, *Studies in Second Language Acquisition*, 7:15–36.

Mehan, H. 1974, Accomplishing classroom lessons, In Cicourel, A. et al., *Language Use and School Performance*, New York, Academic Press.

Mehan, H. 1979, *Learning Lessons: Social Organization in the Classroom*, Cambridge, Mass., Harvard University Press.

Meisel, J. 1983, Strategies of second language acquisition: More than one kind of simplification. In Andersen, R. (ed.), *Pidginization and Creolization as Language Acquisition*, Rowley, Mass., Newbury House.

Meisel, J., Clahsen, H. and Pienemann, M. 1981, On determining developmental stages in natural second language acquisition, *Studies in Second Language Acquisition*, 3:109–35.

Mitchell, R. 1985, Process research in second-language classrooms, *Language Teaching*, 18:330–51.

Mitchell, R. 1988a, Evaluation of foreign language teaching projects and programmes. Paper given at Conference on Empirical Research into Foreign Language Teaching Methods, Bellagio, Italy.

Mitchell, R. 1988b, *Communicative Language Teaching in Practice*, London, CILT.

Mitchell, R., Parkinson, B. and Johnstone, R. 1981, *The Foreign Language Classroom:*

An Observational Study, Stirling Education Monographs, No. 9, University of Stirling.

Modern Language Materials Development Center 1961, *Teacher's Manual*, New York, Modern Language Materials Development Center.

Morton, F. 1960, The language laboratory as a teaching machine. In Oinas, F. (ed.), *Language Teaching Today*, *International Journal of American Linguistics*, 26, 1.

Morton, F. 1964, Audio-lingual language programming project. Unpublished report, Contract No. OE-3-14-012, US Office of Education, Language Development Branch.

Moscowitz, G. 1970, *The Foreign Language Teacher Interacts*, Minneapolis; Association for Productive Teaching.

Mowrer, O. 1960, *Learning Theory and Behavior*, New York, Wiley.

Naiman, N. 1974, The use of elicited imitation in second language acquisition research, *Working Papers on Bilingualism*, 2:137–53.

Newmark, L. 1963, Grammatical theory and the teaching of English as a foreign language. In Harris, D. (ed.), *The 1963 Conference Papers of the English Language Section of the National Association for Foreign Affairs*. Also in Lester (1971).

Newmark, L. 1966, How not to interfere in language learning, *International Journal of American Linguistics*, 32:77–83. Also in Lester (1971).

Newmark, L. and Reibel, D. 1968, Necessity and sufficiency in language learning, *International Review of Applied Linguistics in Language Teaching*, 6:145–64. Also in Lester (1971).

Nicholas, H. 1985, Learner variations and the teachability hypothesis. In Hyltenstam and Pienemann (1985).

Nickel, G. 1973, Aspects of error analysis and grading. In Svartvik, J. (ed.), *Errata: Papers in Error Analysis*, Lund, Gleerup.

Norton, R. 1975, Measurement of ambiguity tolerance, *Journal of Personality Assessment*, 39:607–18.

Nunan, D. 1987, Communicative language teaching: Making it work, *English Language Teaching Journal*, 41:136–45.

Nystrom, N. 1983, Teacher–student interaction in bilingual classrooms: Four approaches to error feedback. In Seliger and Long (1983).

Oller, J. & Richards, J. 1983, (eds), *Focus on the Learner*, Rowley, Mass. Newbury House.

Olson, D. 1977, From utterance to text: The bias of language in speech and writing, Harvard Educational Review, 47:257–281.

O'Malley, J., Chamot, A. and Walker, C. 1987, Some applications of cognitive theory to second language acquisition, *Studies in Second Language Acquisition*, 9:287–306.

Osgood, C. 1953, *Method and Theory in Experimental Psychology*, New York, Oxford University Press.

Palmer, H. 1921, *The Principles of Language Study*, London, Harrap.

Pavesi, M. 1984, The acquisition of relative clauses in a formal and in an informal setting: Further evidence in support of the markedness hypothesis. In Singleton, D. and Little, D. (eds), *Language Learning in Formal and Informal Contexts*, Dublin, IRAAL.

Pavesi, M. 1986, Markedness, discourse modes and relative clause formation in a formal and informal context, *Studies in Second Language Acquisition*, 8:38–55.

Pawley, A. and Syder, F. 1983, Two puzzles for linguistic theory; nativelike selection and nativelike fluency. In Richards, J. and Schmidt, R. (eds), *Language and Communication*, London, Longman.

Penfield, W. and Roberts, L. 1959, *Speech and Brain Mechanisms*, New York, Atheneum Press.

Perkins, K. and Larsen-Freeman, D. 1975, The effect of formal language instruction on the order of morpheme acquisition, *Language Learning*, 25:237–43.

Philips, S. 1972, Participant structures and communicative competence, Warm Springs children in community and classroom. In Cazden, C., John, V. and Hymes, D. (eds), *Functions of Language in the Classroom*, New York, Teachers College Press.

Pica, T. 1983, Adult acquisition of English as a second language under different conditions of exposure, *Language Learning*, 33:465–97.

Pica, T. 1985a, Instruction on second-language acquisition, *Applied Linguistics*, 6:214–22.

Pica, T. 1985b, Linguistic simplicity and learnability: Implications for syllabus design. In Hyltenstam and Pienemann (1985).

Pica, T. 1988, Interlanguage adjustments as an outcome of NS–NNS negotiated interaction, *Language Learning*, 38, 45–73.

Pica, T. and Doughty, C. 1985a, The role of group work in classroom second language acquisition, *Studies in Second Language Acquisition*, 7:233–49.

Pica, T. and Doughty, C. 1985b, Input and interaction in the communicative classroom: a comparison of teacher-fronted and group activities. In Gass and Madden (1985).

Pica, T., Holliday, L., Lewis, N. and Morganthaler, L. 1989, Comprehensible output as an outcome of linguistic demands on the learner, *Studies in Second Language Acquisition*, 11:63–90.

Pica, T. and Long, M. 1986, The linguistic and conversational performance of experienced and inexperienced teachers. In Day (1986).

Pica, T., Young, R. and Doughty, C. 1987, The impact of interaction on comprehension, *TESOL Quarterly*, 21:737–58.

Pickett, G. 1978, *The Foreign Language Learning Process*, London, British Council.

Pienemann, M. 1984, Psychological constraints on the teachability of languages, *Studies in Second Language Acquisition*, 6:186–214.

Pienemann, M. 1985, Learnability and syllabus construction. In Hyltenstam and Pienemann (1985).

Pienemann, M. 1986, Is language teachable? Psycholinguistic experiments and hypotheses, *Australian Working Papers in Language Development*, 1/3.

Pienemann, M. 1987, Determining the influence of instruction on L2 speech processing. Unpublished paper, University of Sydney.

Pienemann, M. and Johnston, M. 1987, Factors affecting the development of language proficiency. In Nunan, D. (ed.) *Applying Second Language Acquisition Research*, National Curriculum Resource Centre, Adult Migrant Education Program, Australia.

Pienemann, M., Johnston, M. and Brindley, G. 1988, Constructing an acquisition-based procedure for second language assessment, *Studies in Second Language Acquisition*, 10, 2:217–44.

Pimsleur, P. 1960, Report of the conference on psychological experiments related to second language learning. Mimeograph report of conference held in Los Angeles.

Politzer, R. 1961, *Teaching French: An Introduction to Applied Linguistics*, Boston, Ginn.

Politzer, R. 1965, *Foreign Language Learning: A Linguistic Introduction*, Englewood Cliffs, NJ, Prentice-Hall.

Politzer, R. 1970, Some reflections on 'good' and 'bad' language teaching behaviors, *Language Learning*, 20:31−43.

Politzer, R., Ramirez, A. and Lewis, S. 1981, Teaching standard English in the third grade: Classroom functions of language, *Language Learning*, 31:171−93.

Popper, K. 1976, *Unended Quest*, London, Fontana-Collins.

Porter, P. 1986, How learners talk to each other: Input and interaction in task-centred discussions. In Day (1986).

Posner, M. and Synder, C. 1975, Attention and cognitive control. In Solso, R. (ed.), *Information Processing and Cognition: The Loyola Symposium*, Hillsdale, NJ, Lawrence Erlbaum.

Prator, C. 1969, Adding a second language, *TESOL Quarterly*, 3/2.

Ramirez, A. and Stromquist, N. 1979, ESL methodology and student language learning in bilingual elementary schools, *TESOL Quarterly*, 13:145−58.

Ravem, R. 1968, Language acquisition in a second language environment, *International Review of Applied Linguistics*, 6:175−85.

Reiss, M. 1983, Helping the unsuccessful language learner, *Canadian Modern Language Review*, 39:257−66.

Reynolds, P. 1971, *A Primer in Theory Construction*, Indianapolis, Bobbs-Merrill.

Richards, J. (ed.) 1974, *Error Analysis*, London, Longman.

Richards, J. (ed.) 1978, *Understanding Second and Foreign Language Learning*, Rowley, Mass., Newbury House.

Richards, J. and Rogers, T. 1986, *Approaches and Methods in Language Teaching: A Description and Analysis*, Cambridge, Cambridge University Press.

Riley, P. 1977, Discourse networks in classroom interaction: some problems in communicative language teaching. *Mélangues Pédagogiques*, University of Nancy, CRAPEL.

Riley, P. 1985, *Discourse and Learning*, London, Longman.

Rivers, W. 1964, *The Psychologist and the Foreign Language Teacher*, Chicago, University of Chicago, Press.

Rivers, W. 1968 *Teaching Foreign Language Skills*, Chicago, University Press of Chicago Press.

Rosansky, E. 1976, Methods and morphemes in second language acquisition research, *Language Learning*, 26:409−25.

Rosing-Schow, D. and Haastrup, F. 1982, The use of communication strategies in classroom and spontaneous discourse. Unpublished MS, Department of English, University of Copenhagen.

Rulon, K. and Creary, J. 1986, Negotiation of content: teacher-fronted and small-group interaction. In Day (1986).

Rutherford, W. 1987, *Second Language Grammar: Learning and Teaching*, London, Longman.

Rutherford, W. and Sharwood-Smith, M. 1985, Consciousness-raising and universal grammar, *Applied Linguistics*, 6:274−81.

Rutherford, W. and Sharwood Smith, M. (eds) 1988, *Grammar and Second Language Teaching: A Book of Readings*, Rowley, Mass. Newbury House.

Sacks, H., Schegloff, E. and Jefferson, G. 1974, A simplest systematics for the organization of turn taking in conversation, *Language*, 50:696−735.

Sajavaara, K. 1978, The Monitor Model and monitoring in second language speech communication. In Gingras, R. (ed.), *Second Language Acquisition and Foreign Language Learning*, Washington, DC, Center for Applied Linguistics.

Sajavaara, K. 1981, The nature of first language transfer: English as L2 in a foreign language setting. Paper presented at the first European–North American Workshop in Second Language Acquisition Research, Lake Arrowhead, Calif.

Sato, C. 1981, Ethnic styles in classroom discourse. In Hines, M. and Rutherford, W. (eds), *On TESOL '81*, Washington, DC, TESOL.

Sato, C. 1986, Conversation and interlanguage development: Rethinking the connection. In Day (1986).

Scarcella, R. and Higa, C. 1981, Input, negotiation and age differences in second language acquisition, *Language Learning*, 31:409–37.

Scarcella, R. and Krashen, S. (eds) 1980, *Research in Second Language Acquisition*, Rowley, Mass., Newbury House.

Schachter, J. 1974, An error in error analysis, *Language Learning*, 24:205–14.

Schachter, J. 1986, In search of systematicity in interlanguage production, *Studies in Second Language Acquisition*, 8:119–34.

Schegloff, E., Jefferson, G. and Sacks, H. 1977, The preference for self-correction in the organization of repair in conversation, *Language*, 53:361–82.

Scherer, A. and Wertheimer, M. 1964, *A Psycholinguistic Experiment in Foreign Language Teaching*. New York, McGraw Hill.

Schinke-Llano, L. 1983, Foreigner-talk in the content classroom. In Seliger and Long (1983).

Schmidt, R. 1983, Interaction, acculturation and the acquisition of communicative competence. In Wolfson, N. and Judd, E. (eds), *Sociolinguistics and Second Language Acquisition*, Rowley, Mass., Newbury House.

Schmidt, R. and Frota, S. 1986, Developing basic conversational ability in a second language: A case study of an adult learner of Portuguese. In Day (1986).

Schneider, W. and Shiffrin, R. 1977, Controlled and automatic human information processing in detection, search and attention, *Psychological Review*, 84:1–66.

Schumann, J. 1978, *The Pidginization Process: A Model for Second Language Acquisition*, Rowley, Mass., Newbury House.

Scollon, R. 1976, *Conversations with a One Year Old*, Honolulu, University of Hawaii.

Seliger, H. 1977, Does practice make perfect? A study of interaction patterns and L2 competence. *Language Learning*, 27:263–75.

Seliger, H. 1978, Implications of a multiple critical periods hypothesis for second language learning. In Ritchie, W. (ed.), *Second Language Acquisition Research*, New York, Academic Press.

Seliger, H. 1979, On the nature and function of language rules in language teaching, *TESOL Quarterly*, 13, 359–69.

Seliger, H. and Long, M. (eds) 1983, *Classroom Oriented Research in Second Language Acquisition*, Rowley, Mass., Newbury House.

Selinker, L. 1972, Interlanguage, *International Review of Applied Linguistics*, 10:209–30.

Selinker, L. and Lamendella, J. 1978, Two perspectives on fossilization in interlanguage, *Interlanguage Studies Bulletin*, 3:143–91.

Sharwood-Smith, M. 1981, Consciousness-raising and the second language learner, *Applied Linguistics*, 2:159–69.

Shiffrin, R. and Schneider, W. 1977, Controlled and automatic information processing, II: Perceptual learning, automatic attending and a general theory, *Psychological Review*, 84:127–90.

Simon, A. and Boyer, E. (eds) 1967, *Mirrors for Behavior*, Philadelphia, Researcher for Better Schools, 71.

Sinclair, J. and Brazil, D. 1982, *Teacher Talk*, Oxford, Oxford University Press.

Sinclair, J. and Coulthard, M. 1975, *Towards an Analysis of Discourse*, Oxford, Oxford University Press.

Skinner, B. 1957, *Verbal Behavior*, New York, Appleton Century Crofts.

Slimani, A. 1987, The teaching–learning relationship: Learning opportunities and learning outcomes, and Algerian case study. Unpublished Ph.D. thesis, University of Lancaster.

Slobin, D. 1973, Cognitive prerequisites for the development of grammar. In Ferguson, C. and Slobin, D. (eds), *Studies of Child Language Development*, New York, Holt, Rinehart and Winston.

Smith, P. (Jr.) 1970, *A Comparison of the Cognitive and Audiolingual Approaches to Foreign Language Instruction: The Pennsylvania Foreign Language Project*. Philadelphia, Center for Curriculum Development.

Smith, P. (Jr.) 1971, Toward a cognitive approach. In Lugton and Heinle (1971).

Snow, C. and Ferguson, C. (eds) 1977, *Talking to Children*, Cambridge, Cambridge University Press.

Snow, C. and Hoefnagel-Höhle, M. 1978 Age differences in second language acquisition. In Hatch (1978a).

Snow, C. and Hoefnagel-Höhle, M. 1982, School age second language learners' access to simplified linguistic input, *Language Learning*, 32:411–30.

Spada, N. 1986, The interaction between type of contact and type of instruction: Some effects on the L2 proficiency of adult learners, *Studies in Second Language Acquisition*, 8:181–200.

Spada, N. 1987, Relationships between instructional differences and learning outcomes: A process–product study of communicative language teaching. *Applied Linguistics*, 8:137–55.

Spolsky, B. 1988, Bridging the gap: A general theory of second language learning, *TESOL Quarterly*, 22:377–96.

Stenson, N. 1975, Induced errors. In Schumann, J. and Stenson, N. (eds), *New Frontiers in Second Language Learning*, Rowley, Mass., Newbury House.

Stern, H. 1981, Communicative language teaching and learning: toward a synthesis. In Alatis, J. and Altman, H. and Alatis, P. (eds) 1981, *The Second Language Classroom*, New York, Oxford University Press.

Stern, H. 1983, *Fundamental Concepts of Language Teaching*. Oxford, Oxford University Press.

Stevick, E. 1976, *Memory, Meaning and Method*, Rowley, Mass., Newbury House.

Stevick, E. 1980, *Teaching Languages: A Way and Ways*, Rowley, Mass., Newbury House.

Stockwell, R. and Bowen, J. 1965, *The Sounds of English and Spanish*, Chicago, University of Chicago, Press.

Stockwell, R., Bowen, J. and Martin, J. 1965, *The Grammatical Structures of English and Spanish*, Chicago, University of Chicago Press.

Stubbs, M. 1976, *Language, Schools and Classrooms*, London, Methuen.

Swain, M. 1985, Communicative competence: some roles of comprehensible input and comprehensible output in its development. In Gass and Madden (1985).

Swain, M., Allen, P., Harley, B. and Cummins, J. 1989, The Development of Bilingual Proficiency Project, Ontario Institute of Educational Studies, University of Toronto.

Swain, M. and Lapkin, S. 1982, *Evaluating Bilingual Education: A Canadian Case Study*, Clevedon, Avon, Multilingual Matters.

Tarone, E. 1983, On the variability of interlanguage systems, *Applied Linguistics*, 4:143–63.

Tarone, E. 1988, *Variation in Interlanguage*, London, Edward Arnold.

Tarone, E., Cohen, A. and Dumas, G. 1976, A closer look at some interlanguage terminology: A framework for communication strategies, *Working Papers on Bilingualism*, 9:76–90.

Taylor, D. 1988, The meaning and use of the term 'competence' in linguistics and applied linguistics, *Applied Linguistics*, 9:148–68.

Terrell, T., Gomez, E. and Mariscal, J. 1980, Can acquisition take place in the classroom? In Scarcella and Krashen (1980).

Tong-Fredericks, C. 1984, Types of oral communication activities and the language they generate: A comparison, *System*, 12:133–46.

Turner, D. 1979, The effect of instruction on second language learning and second language acquisition. In Andersen, R. (ed.), *The Acquisition and Use of Spanish as First and Second Languages*, Washington, DC, TESOL.

Upshur, J. 1968, Four experiments on the relation between foreign language teaching and learning, *Language Learning*, 18:111–24.

Valdman, A. 1966a, Introduction. In Valdman (1966b).

Valdman, A. (ed.), 1966b, *Trends in Language Teaching*, New York, McGraw Hill.

Valdman, A. 1978, On the relevance of the pidginization–creolization model for second language learning, *Studies in Second Language Acquisition*, 1:55–77.

Van Lier, L. 1982, Analysing interaction in second language classrooms. Ph.D. dissertation, University of Lancaster, Lancaster, England.

Van Lier, L. 1988, *The Classroom and the Learner*, London, Longman.

Varonis, E. and Gass, S. 1985, Non-native/non-native conversations: A model for the negotiation of meaning, *Applied Linguistics*, 6:71–90.

de Villiers, J. and de Villiers, P. 1973, A cross-sectional study of the acquisition of grammatical morphemes in child speech, *Journal of Psycholinguistic Research*, 2:267–78.

Wagner-Gough, J. 1975, *Comparative Studies in Second Language Learning*, CAL-ERIC/CLL Series on Language and Linguistics, 26.

Walker, R. and Adelman, C. 1972, *Towards a Sociography of the Classroom*. Mimeo, Report to Social Science Research Council.

Wardhaugh, R. 1970, The contrastive analysis hypothesis, *TESOL Quarterly*, 4:123–30.

Wardhaugh, R. 1971, Teaching English to speakers of other languages: The state of the art. In Lugton and Heinle (1971).

Watson, J. 1924, *Behaviorism*, New York, Norton.

Weinert, R. 1987, Processes in classroom second language development: The acquisition of negation in German. In Ellis (1987c).

Weinstein, C. and Mayer, R. 1986, The teaching of learning strategies. In Wittrock, M. (ed.), *Handbook of Research on Teaching* (3rd edn), New York, Macmillan.

Wells, G. 1985, *Language Development in the Pre-School Years*, Cambridge, Cambridge University Press.

Wesche, M. 1981, Language aptitude measures in streaming, matching students with methods and diagnosis of learning problems. In Diller, K. (ed.), *Individual Differences and Universals in Language Learning Aptitude*, Rowley, Mass., Newbury House.

Wesche, M. and Ready, D. 1985, Foreigner talk in the university classroom. In Gass and Madden (1985).

Weslander, D. and Stephany G. 1983, Evaluation of an English as a second language program for southeast Asian students, *TESOL Quarterly*, 17:473–80.

Westmoreland, R. 1983, L2 German acquisition by instructed adults. Unpublished, University of Hawaii at Manoa.

White, L. 1985, Is there a logical problem of second language acquisition, *TESL Canada*, 2:29–41.

White, L. 1987, Against comprehensible input: The Input Hypothesis and the development of second-language competence, *Applied Linguistics*, 8:95–110.

Widdowson, H. 1975, The significance of simplification, *Studies in Second Language Acquisition*, 1:11–20.

Widdowson, H. 1978, *Teaching Language as Communication*, Oxford, Oxford University Press.

Wilkins, D. 1974, *Second-language Learning and Teaching*, London, Edward Arnold.

Wilkins, D. 1976, *Notional Syllabuses*, Oxford, Oxford University Press.

Willing, K. 1987, *Learning Styles in Adult Migrant Education*. National Curriculum Resource Centre, Adelaide, Australia.

Winitz, H. 1978, A reconsideration of comprehension and production in language training, *Allied Health and Behavioral Sciences*, 1:272–315.

Wode, H. 1976, Developmental sequences in naturalistic L2 acquisition, *Working Papers on Bilingualism*, 11:1–13.

Wolff, D. 1987, Some assumptions about second language text comprehension, *Studies in Second Language Acquisition*, 9:307–26.

Zobl, H. 1983, Markedness and the projection problem, *Language Learning*, 33:293–313.

Zobl, H. 1985, Grammars in search of input and intake. In Gass and Madden (1985).

Index